HENRY PAOLUCCI

PUBLIC IMAGE, PRIVATE INTEREST:

Kissinger's Foreign Policy Strategies in Vietnam

PREFACE BY ANNE PAOLUCCI

Who is Kissinger? was first published by Griffon House Publications for the Walter Bagehot Research Council in 1972, second edition 1980.

Kissinger's War: 1957-1975 was first published by Griffon House Publications for the Walter Bagehot Research Council in 1980.

Part Three of this volume consists of various numbers of the monthly newsletter *State of the Nation* published between 1969 and 1980 by the Walter Bagehot Research Council.

Library of Congress Cataloging-in-Publication Date

Paolucci, Henry.
   Public image, private interest: Kissinger's foreign policy strategies in Vietnam / Henry Paolucci; preface by Anne Paolucci.
   Compilation of two previously published works with the addition of various numbers of the monthly newsletter State of the nation, published between 1969 and 1980 by the Bagehot Council.
   First work, Who is Kissinger?, originally published: New York: Griffon Publications, 1972. Second work, Kissinger's war, 1957-1975, originally published: Whitestone, N.Y.: Published for the Walter Bagehot Research Council by Griffon House Publications, c.1980.
   ISBN 0-918680-97-2
   1. Kissinger, Henry, 1923- 2. United States—Foreign relations—1961-1963. 3. United States—Foreign relations—1963-1969. 4. United States—Foreign Relations—1969-1974. 5. Vietnamese Conflict, 1961-1975—Diplomatic history. 6. Vietnamese Conflict, 1961-1975—Peace. 7. Statesmen—United States—Biography. I. Paolucci, Henry, Who is Kissinger? II. Paolucci, Henry, Kissinger's War, 1957-1975. III. Title.

E840.8.K58 P35 2002
973.924'092—dc21

                                        2001054339

Published for
THE BAGEHOT COUNCIL
by
GRIFFON HOUSE PUBLICATIONS
P.O. BOX 468
SMYRNA, DELAWARE 19977

CONTENTS

Preface (Anne Paolucci)   5

About The Walter Bagehot Research Council
    On National Sovereignty (Henry Paolucci, 1980)   7

PART ONE (13-56)
WHO IS KISSINGER?

Publisher's Foreword to the 1980 Edition   17

Author's Preface to the First Edition (1972)   19

1. "NIXON'S MOST ASTUTE APPOINTMENT"   22
   - Critic of the Eisenhower-Dulles Strategy   23
   - The Limited-War Strategy   25
   - Beyond the Nation State   27
   - The Kissinger Riddle   28
2. NIXON'S SUPREME STRATEGIST   31
3. OUR CAPTIVE PRESIDENT: THE ASCENDANCY OF A
   SUPRANATIONALIST PROFESSOR   37
4. THE LAST WAR   43
5. KISSINGER, POOR RICHARD, AND *NATIONAL REVIEW*   48
6. CONCLUSION   54

PART TWO (57-164)
KISSINGER'S WAR: 1957-1975

Note to the 1980 Edition   58

7. INTRODUCTION: THE KISSINGER LEGACY   59
   - The War in Theory: Kissinger's Apprenticeship   60
   - Back Door to Nixon   66
   - The Buckley "Passport"   69
   - The Clark Clifford Connection   71
   - Nixon's Inaugural: The Pledge to Negotiate   75
   - What Price Kissinger?   78
8. THE DETENTE POWER-VACUUM   82
   - Kissinger's "Detente or Bust" Policy   83
   - C. B. Marshall on the Logic of Detente   85
9. OUR VIETNAM DEFEAT: WHY THE SIX-YEAR DELAY?   91
   - Kissinger's Limited-War Doctrine   93
10. THE CRIME OF NO-WIN BELLIGERENCY   95
    - Angola and Watergate   96
    - The Soft Core   99
    - Kissinger's Protracted Deception   100
11. AN EXEMPLARY DEBATE ON ANGOLA:
    TUNNEY, STEVENSON, GOLDWATER, AND HELMS   104
    - Senator Byrd on the Role of Congress   106

Tunney Cites Taft 108
The Stevenson-Goldwater Resolution 108
Garn and Domenici 110
Helms' Rejection of Negotiated Settlements 111
12. THE "SECRET" KREMLIN SPEECH 114
A "Nixon" Profile for the Kremlin Leaders 115
The Carrot and the Stick 119
Euphoria in Warsaw 120
13. KISSINGER'S WAR: A REVISIONIST PERSPECTIVE 124
Theory in Action: The Moscow Summit of 1972 126
The Incredible Credibility Doctrine 129
False Counselors, Benighted Presidents 131
14. CARTER AND MOYNIHAN VS. KISSINGER:
FREEDOM OR PEACE? 133
George Will: The Detente Drunk Has Ended 133
"How Much Does Freedom Matter?" 135
Johnson's Fall, Nixon's Rise 139
Kissinger or Moynihan? 141
15. FROM KANT TO KISSINGER AND BRZEZINSKI 142
Kant's Imperative for Peace 142
Carl Friedrich's Marxist Transformation 144
From Friedrich to Rostow 145
Kissinger and Kant at the U.N. 147
Brzezinski and Gardner 149
The Peace and Freedom of Peers 152
16. CONCLUSION: THE FIXED FIGHT 156

PART THREE (165-204)
MORE ON KISSINGER

17. VIETNAM: MASK OF PEACE 167
18. THE ATROCITIES OF MARCH 1968 172
19. CAMOUFLAGED SURRENDER IN VIETNAM:
NIXON MUST DISMISS KISSINGER OR KISSINGER MUST
VOLUNTARILY RESIGN 177
20. A RED-CHINA PUPPET SHOW: NIXON KOWTOWS,
KISSINGER PULLS THE STRINGS 181
21. "HOWEVER VAGUE, HOWEVER ELUSIVE,
HOWEVER INDIRECT": KISSINGER'S PLEA FOR A
FACE-SAVING FORMULA 185
22. NATIONAL REVIEWS'S WHITE HOUSE CONTACT:
THE KISSINGER-BUCKLEY ODYSSEY 189
23. WILL AMERICA SURRENDER? 198

APPENDIX (FROM THE CONGRESSIONAL RECORD, AUGUST 4, 1971) 205

ABOUT . . . WHO IS KISSINGER?" 211

HENRY PAOLUCCI 212

PREFACE

This volume brings together Henry Paolucci's *Who Is Kissinger?* (1972, 1980) and *Kissinger's War: 1957-1975* (1980). A third section includes several *State of the Nation* newsletters (published between 1969 and 1980) in which Kissinger's policies are the focal point of discussion.

In the present format and at a distance of three decades, Professor Paolucci's keen assessment of Kissinger's policies in Southeast Asia, especially Kissinger's "orchestration" of the peace in Vietnam, remains as sharp and convincing as it was at the time it was first articulated. There were few then who were prepared to acknowledge publicly his carefully documented account of Kissinger's devious, self-serving actions and ambiguous statements. Even the leading conservatives were at a loss as to how to deal with such a man, especially when one of their own took credit for bringing Nixon and Kissinger together.

Paolucci approached his subject from a solid historical base, which gave his writings what some readers have described as a "prophetic" quality. His critique of Kissinger has in fact withstood the passage of time, as recent new studies show.*

That critique has also survived the glib liberal advocacy for "world peace" and for an end to the nation-state system. Paolucci warned against empty abstract notions about democracy, freedom, peace–the wonderful things no one dares contest but which in fact cannot be realized except through hard and long adjustments and often disappointing efforts at negotiations, as well as confrontations and constant police activity on a worldwide basis. He saw the self-serving Hollywood/press definitions of the good life as self-indulgence of the most simplistic kind. The grim reality we face as the most powerful nation in the world–whose foreign policy is, at its best, erratic and unfocused, at its worst, naive and contradictory– has been dramatically brought home to us in the recent terrorist attacks on New York and Washington. Until now, most of us were confident enough in our way of life to let our leaders work out and implement, without too many questions, American foreign policy. But the daring surprise attacks on the World Trade Center and the Pentagon made clear that, when threatened, the majority of Americans will not accept "peace at any price" but will respond decisively, as one, when our American nation and our American way of life are threatened.

For Professor Paolucci, the long lesson of history was a prerequisite for an accurate reading of current world affairs. He would often remind his readers and colleagues that freedom could not be *given* but had to be *won,* and that it was the result of the arduous transition from a people governed by force to a society governed by consent of the governed. He never shied away from the difficult questions and hard conclusions a nation like ours faces in dealing with other nations in the world and was firm in his insistence that we should recognize and act on the realistic premise of "stages of diplomatic recognition," especially in our middle east policy.

History still proves him right.

Anne Paolucci
November, 2001

* A new generation of critics, historians and reviewers have begun to examine, in a new way and at a distance of thirty years, Kissinger's policies. Their conclusions, in many cases, support Professor Paolucci's analysis. See, especially: Larry Berman, *No Peace, No Honor: Nixon, Kissinger, and Betrayal in Vietnam* (2001) and Christopher Hitchens, *The Trial of Henry Kissinger* (2001). Kissinger himself continues, unabashed, to give advice as to how America should formulate its foreign policy in the next decades (see: *Does America Need a Foreign Policy? Toward a Diplomacy for the 21st Century*). We desperately need a consistent and realistic foreign policy, but one based on American priorities not on Kissinger's biased and confused formula for world peace at all costs.

[With the launching of State of the Nation, *in 1969, Professor Paolucci, together with a few colleagues, decided to form The Walter Bagehot Research Council on National Sovereignty, a nonprofit educational foundation, to serve as the parent organization not only for the monthly newsletter but also for books and other publications. Over the years, the Bagehot Council has also sponsored annual meetings at the American Political Science Association (APSA). The Council was restructured after Professor Paolucci's death, in January, 1999, to include a broader publications program and "The Bagehot Council/Henry Paolucci Publishers' Book Award," an annual prize of $2,000 for the best volume published in the preceding year on American domestic or foreign policy, constitutional law, jurisprudence, American history, and the Presidency. (Nominations are by publishers only.) The first award was presented to Professor Thomas West on October 5, 2000, at a reception at the City Club in Washington DC.]*

ABOUT . . .
THE WALTER BAGEHOT RESEARCH COUNCIL
ON NATIONAL SOVEREIGNTY

Who is Walter Bagehot?

Although he "has been conceded genius often and willingly enough," Jacques Barzun has written, "yet he remains a shadowy figure in that part of the public mind where reputations are considered settled." For the uncertainty of his fame—Barzun suggests lightly—Bagehot is himself, of course, in part responsible; for it appears that he made "two capital mistakes: one, the mistake of bearing a name puzzling to pronounce; the other, the mistake of dying at 51, before the variety and superiority of his mind could force themselves on public opinion by the necessary repetition of tenets and attitudes."

Reference books unpuzzle his name and identify him typically as follows: "Bagehot, Walter (baj´ut), 1826-77, a banker and shipowner, joint-editor with R. H. Hutton of the *National Review* after 1855, and editor of the *Economist* from 1860 to 1877, during which time its high reputation as a financial journal was established. The work that established his own reputation as an economist was his noted study of the English banking system, *Lombard Street* (1873). His classic *English Constitution* (1864, 1867) distinguished between the effective institutions of government and those, like the House of Lords, that had entered decay. Other books by him include *Literary Studies* (1879), and

Economic Studies (1880). In *Physics and Politics* (1867, 1875) he made a pioneer analysis of the interrelations of natural and social sciences."

Bagehot was an enrolled member of the British Liberal Party. But, as Professor Hans Kohn stresses in *The Idea of Nationalism,* he was in fact "much nearer to the Liberal conservative than to the Liberal reformer. He welcomed reform, but only as far as it helped to produce greater stability. The preservation of society appeared to him as society's first duty." Significantly, Bagehot's *Collected Works* are now being re-edited for publication by Norman St. John-Stevas, who was political correspondent for the *Economist* till he entered Parliament in 1964 as Conservative Member for Chelmsford.

The work in which Bagehot most concisely summed up his thought on the meaning of sovereign nationhood is his *Physics and Politics.* There he confronts the same hard facts of the rapidly developing industrial society of the West that his contemporary Karl Marx confronted. But whereas Marx brought to the study of those facts a spirit of alien hostility, bent on subversion and revolutionary destruction of the nations in which he happened to live, Bagehot's concern, as a Westerner and Englishman, was invariably to perfect the national union of his own people, and to strengthen the nation-state system of which England is a responsible member.

Bagehot repeatedly cautions Englishmen not to take their free government, based on the deferential stability of patriotic feeling, for granted. England's Parliamentary form of "government by discussion" presupposed, he reminded them, two earlier necessary stages of political development. There had first to be, he said, the essentially *forced* unity of the coercive state, the unity secured for modern England by the Norman conquest of 1066. The second stage was that of *felt* unity, which transforms a merely coercive state into a nation-state. That came slowly for England. Only after centuries of social contention, of fierce competition and forced cooperation, of mixing blood on battlefields as well as in beds, was it possible for Saxons and Normans to think of themselves as constituting one nation. It is their felt unity that Shakespeare's Henry V celebrates at Agincourt with the cry:

> *We few, we happy few, we band of brothers;*
> *For he to-day that sheds his blood with me*
> *Shall be my brother; be he ne'er so vile*
> *This day shall gentle his condition:*
> *And gentlemen in England, now a-bed*
> *Shall think themselves accursed they were not here,*
> *And hold their manhoods cheap. . . .*

Only when forced unity has become deeply felt, to the point of being ingrained as national character, is it possible, according to Bagehot, to attain the final phase of political progress, which is government by discussion.

The ideal of nationhood is thus to form an ever more perfect union of free citizens; a union thoroughly secure in its national premise, and therefore competent to occupy a "separate and equal station" among the powers of the earth, in a system of mutual respect for the independence of all member nations in their severality.

Bagehot's concept of social progress culminating in the perfection of nationhood at home and the nation-state system of mutual recognition of sovereignty abroad contrasts sharply with the Marxist concept of progress through class warfare, leading finally to the domination of a denationalized world community by a cadre of rootless revolutionaries. Bagehot was keenly aware of the Marxist ideology. The leading noncommunist antinationalists of the West–the Arthur Bentleys and Harold Laskis, the Walt Rostows and David Trumans whose ideas have come to dominate the teaching of political science in our major universities–were still a long way off. Yet Bagehot seems to have anticipated their rejection of national values, perhaps as part of the inevitable dialectic that brings nations to the stage of government by discussion.

But it was America's experience in the forge of nationhood that most directly excited Bagehot to undertake his defense of the ideal. He in fact applied himself to a concise formulation of that defense only after long study of the American Civil War and its aftermath, when our Presidential form of government by discussion passed through its most agonizing trial.

In articles that appeared almost weekly in the *National Review* and *Economist* from 1860 until his death in 1877, Bagehot has left us an impressive record of those tragic years of war and so-called reconstruction; and in all his major political writings, but especially in the second edition of his *English Constitution,* the hard constitutional lessons of those years (Bagehot focuses on the challenge of impeachment) are repeatedly projected ahead for us in anticipation of greater trials of nationhood yet to be faced.

The American trial of nationhood today is, of course, far different from that of the Civil War. The Nixon impeachment controversy is really but a symptom of the profounder trial. Despite the fact that "we the people of the United States" are pledged constitutionally to perfect our nation as a sovereign nation-state, America's reigning intelligentsia, in the highest decision-making councils of government as well as in the major universities and tax-exempt educational foundations, is at present carrying on a relentless war against the very concepts of sovereignty and nationhood. Professor Rostow, for instance, who was Henry Kissinger's predecessor as presidential advisor for national security affairs, argued emphatically in his *Stages of Economic Growth* (1960) that "war, ultimately, arises from the existence and acceptance of the concept of national sovereignty"; and he echoed the bias of many academic colleagues when he alleged, in his *United States in the World Arena* (1961), that "it is a legitimate American national objective to see removed from all nations–including the United States–the right to use substantial military force to pursue their own interests. Since this residual right is the root of national sovereignty and the basis for the existence of an international arena of power, it is, therefore, an American interest to see an end to nationhood as it has been historically defined."

In England, Harold Laski, Bertrand Russell, and Arnold Toynbee have urged the same sort of polemic against nationhood. Laski had argued back in 1941 that "it would be a lasting benefit to political science if the whole concept of sovereignty were surrendered"; but fortunately for England the exercise of its sovereignty in that dark hour was entrusted to other hands. More recently, Arnold Toynbee has written of the "Reluctant Death of Sovereignty" (*The Center Magazine* of the Fund for the Republic), insisting that, "if the human race is to survive, it will have to abandon the idea of national sovereignty." Directing his remarks with particular severity against the assumption of the prerogatives of sovereign nationhood by the Jewish people in the Middle East, Toynbee drew this emphatic response from Abba Eban (*The Voice of Israel*): "The eclipse of nationalism by some supranational federalism has been predicted so often that it is one of the platitudes of twentieth century writing. But, in fact, this century is the triumphant epoch of the nation state, and the burial ground of broader associations and groupings."

But it is in the United States, unhappily, that the polemic against sovereign nationhood has had its broadest academic success. We have cited Walt Rostow's extraordinary claim of "legitimacy" for his interest in seeing an "end to nationhood as it has been historically defined"–by which he must mean, of course, a thoroughly *unconstitutional* legitimacy since, upon the sacrifice of our nationhood, our Constitution would manifestly constitute nothing. With comparable candor, presidential advisor Louis W. Koenig in his influential textbook *The Chief Executive* (1968) calls for a constitutional amendment to facilitate presidential liquidation of our sovereign union, arguing that, "if in future decades the United States is to enter into international arrangements to solidify the world community and strengthen its powers at the sacrifice of national sovereignty, the practicality of the treaty power will become crucial."

How pervasive is this view in the American academy? In his *Masters of Political Thought* (1968), L. W. Lancaster notes that among the rank and file of "political scientists and publicists" in the U.S. "there is no doubt general agreement with Arthur Bentley's dicta that the 'idea of the state' was only an 'intellectual amusement' of the past, and that 'sovereignty,' once out of the pages of the law book, is a 'threadbare joke.'"

Such extraordinary views have by no means remained academic. Walt Rostow implemented them in his State Department and White House service. And Henry Kissinger has brought to their implementation now, all the cunning and secrecy of inscrutable *realpolitik*. In his *Troubled Partnership* (1965), Kissinger very clearly mapped his foreign policy course: "Institutions based on present concepts of national sovereignty are not enough . . .; many intermediate stages must be traversed before [our goal] can be reached. It is not too early, however, to prepare ourselves now for this step beyond the nation state."

Even as our nation prepares to celebrate the 200th anniversary of its sovereign independence, rare is the voice raised in effective protest against this anti-nationalist attitude so one-sidedly advanced in our academy and councils of government. William Ernest Hocking, Alford Professor Emeritus of Philosophy of Harvard, raised such a voice in 1959. In his *Strength of Men and Nations* he wrote with admirable frankness:

"The USA is not immune to the danger of dissipating its national being. Its hospitality, a matter of just traditional pride, expresses also a justified self-confidence: we can be almost endlessly hospitable and remain ourselves—almost. But we must *know ourselves* as a specific nation, and refuse to be driven by national fragments, nostalgic for former national premises, toward a fallacious ideal of the world state devoid of nationhood. Any national premise holds the vulnerable position of a vital organ incapable of legal formulation, hence subject to being sublimated away, through an ostensible flattery inviting it to the angelic existence of pure abstract brotherhood, by way of emasculation. It will be sufficient to recognize this problem for what it is, and allow firmness in holding to our national identity to dissuade those entrants whose happiness depends on canceling our specific character."

In the *Exercise of Sovereignty* (1965), Professor C.B. Marshall, one-time principal advisor to Dean Acheson under President Truman, affirms in a similar vein: "The perils and perplexities in the world about us rise not so much from an excess of the constituent qualities of sovereignty in the entities passing as nation-states, as from an entirely opposite circumstance. A great many of them have not achieved those qualities. Realizing them may be beyond the ultimate capabilities of some. . . . I would wish my own society to prize, to hold on to, and go on cultivating every one of the attributes of sovereignty. It would forfeit any one of them at its peril."

Hocking and Marshall—and I should add also the name of William Y. Elliott of Harvard—write in the spirit of Walter Bagehot.

PART ONE

WHO IS KISSINGER?

Is President Nixon's top advisor a cunning architect of our national suicide? Or is he just an ambitious betrayer of his internationalist friends at Harvard and MIT?

If America is finally overwhelmed by its professed enemies, there can be little doubt about the verdict of future historians.

Whether they write court histories in Russian or Chinese, Hebrew or Arabic, they will all have to register it as a fact that Kissinger was the man who, by himself, has made it possible for President Nixon to seek re-election by selling this nation down the river. The leading organizers of the American Conservative movement—the Goldwater Republicans and editors of *National Review*—miscalculated on Nixon, but much more on his national security adviser.

From front cover of the original edition of
Who is Kissinger? (1972)

"History is strewn with the wrecks of nations which have gained a little progressiveness at the cost of a great deal of manliness, and have thus prepared themselves for destruction as soon as the movement of the world gave it a chance."

Walter Bagehot
Physics and Politics (1867)

PUBLISHER'S FOREWORD TO THE 1980 EDITION

Who is Kissinger? was first published in 1971. The original edition and subsequent reprintings in 1972 and 1973 quickly sold out. Here it is reissued with Dr. Paolucci's brilliant essay on "The 'Top Secret' Strategic Arms-Limitation Talks and Our National Sovereignty"—reprinted as it appeared in *The Congressional Record,* August 4, 1971, with introductory comments by Representative Samuel S. Stratton of New York and Ben P. Blackburn of Georgia. (A shorter version was published on the "Op-Ed" page of the *New York Times,* October 8, 1971, under the title "Sovereignty and Salt.")

The rest of the book has not, however, undergone any retrospective editing, since its scholarly as well as its journalistic importance lies in the extraordinarily prophetic *timeliness* of its running commentary on contemporary events. Its six chapters, covering the first three of Henry Kissinger's "White House Years," had previously appeared in the Milan-Rome magazine *Il Borghese, State of the Nation,* or *American Mercury.* The earliest, dated February 1969, reviewed Kissinger's writings to support a prediction that, as President Nixon's chief "pilot," the ex-Harvard professor would almost certainly set the ship of state on a course of no-win belligerency designed to wear out the American spirit for the sake of peace without risking the sort of right-wing backlash the Kennedy advisors had risked. The essay elicited several letters from William F. Buckley, editor of *National Review,* who had not only endorsed Kissinger's appointment but—as he himself later revealed—had also personally paved the way for it. In those letters, Buckley said among other things: "You have greatly troubled my conscience. . . . But I am at this moment especially convinced that Henry Kissinger is a great patriot. . . . Either that or he is the greatest hypocrite in the history of the world, and I don't think that."

A decade has elapsed since those words were written and Buckley has apparently not changed his mind. Still, in a recent column on Kissinger's *White House Years,* he has managed to temper his praise of that "trenchant and grand" volume with these final sentences: "My own judgment, frequently reiterated, is that the Nixon-Kissinger approach to foreign policy broke the American spirit, but policies to one side, his is the most engrossing political narrative I have ever read." The point to stress, however, is this: having broken the American spirit in office, Kissinger, out of office, is again cavorting like a hawk—"playing tough," as Barbara Tuchman has aptly put it—to earn for himself the "third spot" on a Republican presidential ticket.

All America saw Kissinger's brazen bid for power at the Republican National Convention held in Detroit in July 1980. The historical perspective provided by the chapters of this book is one we can hardly afford to ignore if we are to assess correctly the impact of Henry Kissinger on our time. His play-tough Disraelian approach to policy, which gave America its first governmental interregnum as preparation for disastrous defeat in Vietnam, has been something for which our political process has never been adequately prepared. Our Presidential "government by discussion" must be on its guard against a recurrence of it in the future. Read in retrospect, the startlingly accurate anticipation of "things to come" republished here can be of inestimable value.

August, 1980

AUTHOR'S PREFACE TO THE FIRST EDITION (1972)

General Curtis LeMay was ridiculed by *Time* magazine back in December 1968 for confusing Henry A. Kissinger with Arthur M. Schlesinger. When his error was pointed out to him, the general replied with something to the effect that there wasn't really a dime's worth of difference between the two, and that, by appointing Kissinger to the office of chief presidential advisor for national security affairs, President-elect Nixon was, in effect, ceding control of American foreign policy back into the hands of the Kennedy people.

The editors of *National Review,* on the contrary, insisted that there was a world of difference between Kissinger and Schlesinger. Both of them were prize professors at Harvard, and they shared the same company of academic friends; but there, according to a *National Review* editorial, the correspondences stopped. Schlesinger—not Kissinger—was the New Deal-New Frontier Democrat, avowed Fabian Socialist, appeaser of communist might, and advocate of U.S.–Soviet convergence on a common supranationalist goal of world peace to be enforced by world government.

In sum, Schlesinger was exactly the sort of liberal that James Burnham had written about in his brilliant *Suicide of the West,* whereas Kissinger, despite his Harvard and Rockefeller connections, was apparently of an altogether different breed.

Burnham's book, it will be recalled, originally appeared in the mid-1960s, when it was still possible to argue that, if America were to suffer the agonies of suicidal death, it could only happen with a Democratic liberal in the White House and with the usual cabala of Eastern Establishment Democrats at the national bedside trying with sweet talk to reconcile us to our national dissolution. The prevailing conservative notion then was that if ever a Republican supported by *National Review* got into the White House, everything would change for the better—particularly if that Republican would let himself be counselled by men of tried intelligence who enjoyed the prior approval of the Buckleys, Burnhams, and Goldwaters. The danger of national suicide would soon fade. America thereafter would willingly face up to its sovereign responsibilities. It would surely not desert its long-time, anti-communist allies in Asia, or give up the Mediterranean, or push West Germany into the Soviet embrace, or disarm itself unilaterally of its deterrent nuclear force, or plunge its economy into the bottomless pit of deficit spending to finance "creative disorder" in its city streets and schools as well as its prisons.

How pathetically mistaken that conservative notion was! Bad as things were under the Democrats, they have gone from bad to worse under the Nixon Administration. When the Goldwater Republicans and editors of *National Review* formed their unprincipled coalition with Rockefeller Republicans to elect Nixon in 1968, they might not have known it consciously, but they were unmistakably acting on a suicidal urge. Even when they introduced Henry Kissinger to candidate Nixon, they might still have mistaken their suicidal urge for an urge to save America through compromise; but their intentions then have long ceased to be relevant.

The record of the Kissinger-Nixon years is now plain enough for all to read. Abroad, the world communist leaders have piled one spectacular victory upon another, while our former allies are abandoned to a destiny which leaves them ashen-eyed. At home, the Democratic liberal internationalists, relieved of direct responsibility for American policy, are literally jumping for joy over the "miracle" that their Harvard colleague has single-handedly wrought for them, while the old conservatives labor in vain to conceal their obvious nakedness from the sight of their fellow Americans.

If Mr. Burnham ever puts out a new edition of his classic study of the suicidal mania of Western intellectuals, he will surely have to append a final section on the American conservative contribution to that mania. And a fitting caption for such a chapter might well be drawn from one of the chapters that follow: "Henry Kissinger, Poor Richard, and *National Review*."

The first essay in this part of the present volume was started shortly after Nixon announced Kissinger's appointment to succeed Walt Rostow as chief presidential advisor for national security affairs, and immediately after *National Review* published its glowing endorsement of the Harvard professor. The title, "Nixon's Most Astute Appointment," was meant to relate the piece to *Time* magazine's first cover-story on Kissinger, which appeared in early February 1969. There, the *Time* reporter mocked the intelligence of the Buckley conservatives for not recognizing a clever enemy in Henry Kissinger. Aware of *National Review*'s respectful regard for good grammar and large dictionaries, the *Time* writer had nevertheless accused its editors of being superficial readers whose level of comprehension was so poor that, in Kissinger's case, they had mistaken a liberal dove for a conservative hawk. "A superficial reading of some of Kissinger's works makes him seem like a hawk," the cover-story had charged, "but intelligent doves regard him as Richard Nixon's most astute appointment."

My hope in writing that piece had been that it would help the editors of *National Review,* if not the Goldwater Republicans generally, to see through the Straussian ambiguities of Kissinger's long-range designs for America. But in fact it had the opposite effect. There was a troubled instant of doubt, but that immediately gave way to a re-affirmation of the original confident endorsement. Indeed, one *National Review* editor spelled it out for me quite plainly, saying: "You have greatly troubled my conscience. . . . But I am at this moment especially convinced that Henry Kissinger is a great patriot, and that you will one day come to agree. . . . Either that or he is the greatest hypocrite in the history of the world, and I cannot think so."

The subsequent pieces presented in chronological sequence here were all originally Published in a European conservative journal, *Il Borghese,* or in my own monthly newsletter *State of the Nation,* or in both. Several of them examine the impact of Henry Kissinger's designs on the major foreign policy declarations of the Nixon Administration. Only the last takes into account the revelation made to me early in 1971 that Kissinger had been introduced to Nixon for the first time under the auspices of *National Review* and that, as a consequence, Nixon could thereafter regard the counsels of Kissinger as coming to him with at least the blessings of its distinguished conservative editors, if not with their prior advice and consent.

The time has come to set the record straight. The sad truth is that Kissinger need not have triumphed so easily as he obviously has over the American conservative intelligentsia. Even now, though the chances are slight, there is still time to make amends. But there must be a public act of political contrition. It will not do for the old conservative leadership to sit back and simply let things happen in 1972. Its much publicized "suspended support" of Mr. Nixon must not be used to veil an abject desertion of grave political responsibilities. For that would be a supreme betrayal of our American nationhood at a time of clear and present danger.

Half-hearted disapproval amounts to acquiescence. And acquiescence of any sort at this time would be on a par with the cynicism of that pathetic cry of the decadent French aristocrats on the eve of the revolution that swept them out of existence: *"Aprés nous le déluge."*

1. NIXON'S "MOST ASTUTE APPOINTMENT"

Harvard's Kissinger is an expert planner. But what has he planned for our national security? Are we to remain secure in the traditional sense, or through a deliberate phasing-out of our political sovereignty?

Henry A. Kissinger (not to be "mixed up . . . with Arthur Schlesinger" [*Time*, Feb. 14, 1961]) has written three major books on American Foreign policy. They are: *Nuclear Weapons and Foreign Policy* (1957), *The Necessity For Choice* (1961), and *The Troubled Partnership* (1965). He has edited a book of readings on *Problems of National Strategy* (1965), epitomizing the views of many leading scholars and public officials on our military and diplomatic preparedness. There are also magazine pieces, particularly in *Foreign Affairs,* not yet republished in book form. From these works it is possible to learn what Professor Kissinger thinks is the principle that must guide our government in the exercise of its sovereign powers. And his thoughts on that subject ought to be of vital concern to us; for he can now influence the day-to-day decision-making of a Chief Executive who must bear at this time not only the awesome responsibilities of his Presidential oath, but also the burden of placating his chief critics, with a view to strengthening his chances for re-election in 1972.

Kissinger serves Nixon in the capacity that Walt W. Rostow served his predecessor. And he has come to Nixon's side, as Rostow first came to Kennedy's, not as an old-time confidant, but on the strength of academic expertise manifested in the same intellectual environment: the vast educational ellipse that sweeps ideologically around the richly endowed foci of Harvard and MIT.

When the appointment was first announced, the *New York Times* reported that it was "hailed almost unanimously by political scientists and law professors, many of them liberal Democrats and former members of the Kennedy Administration." The consensus among them seemed to be that, in Kissinger, the Nixon Administration had gained "a force for reason, balance and discretion in foreign affairs and arms control." *National Review* also approved the appointment, however; and its judgment, based apparently on the scholar's manifest competence as a political analyst, served to quiet the fears of some conservatives who had read with dismay Professor Schlesinger's praise of the designation as "very very encouraging," coupled with the boast that Kissinger "had asked my advice a few weeks ago and I urged him to accept."

Kissinger has been in office for several months. The internationalist intelligentsia has not yet singled him out for criticism, and conservative supporters of Nixon's candidacy have also, on the whole, kept a respectful silence. Why is that? Is it because, at long last, the talent scouts of the "public sector" have come up with an expert who can please everybody? Obviously it isn't easy to pigeonhole the new presidential advisor for national security affairs. "A superficial reading of some of his works makes him seem like a hawk," the *Time* cover story acknowledged; and then, perhaps with *Time*-ish respect for the capacities and sensibilities of its own readers, it added almost irrelevantly: "but intelligent doves regard him as Richard Nixon's most astute appointment."

The intelligent doves, we take it, are not superficial readers. But what about the editors and readers of *National Review* who preferred Reagan to Nixon for the Presidency in 1968? Do they read Kissinger as carefully as the members of the Council on Foreign Relations, the Harvard Center for International Affairs, the Ford Foundation, and the Carnegie Corporation read him?

The point is this: Are we to live with a mystery? Is there no way of discovering, before the storms or the hi-jackers hit us, what sort of directional pressure Kissinger is prepared to exert on the ship's captain? Is he, in his ideological orientation, another Rostow, or a Morgenthau, or a McGeorge Bundy? Does he or does he not share with the Schlesingers, Niebuhrs, and Fulbrights the conviction that our ultimate foreign policy objective must be to put an end to our nationhood and induce our allies and enemies to do the same?

The question is not one we can comfortably pose in the ordinary social discourse of these troubled times. Unless it is precisely phrased, it is apt to sound more like an accusation than an inquiry into matters of fact. But surely it must make a vast difference to us as a nation whether, in our dealings with foreign states–with the Soviet Union, our NATO allies, and the emerging nations–our object is to secure, or surrender, or "share" our political sovereignty.

We owe it to our posterity, therefore, if not to ourselves, to try to exact an answer to our question from the tightly woven arguments of Kissinger's major writings.

Critic of The Eisenhower-Dulles Strategy

Kissinger's *Nuclear Weapons and Foreign Policy* was written at the height of the public debate over the Eisenhower strategy of "massive retaliation." And it was the Harvard professor's criticism of that strategy, together with his recommendations for an alternative policy, that first gained him broad recognition as an expert on national security.

The Eisenhower strategy had first been defined by John Foster Dulles on January 12, 1954, in an address before a generally hostile Council on Foreign Relations. The Secretary of State there indicated what he conceived to be the two indispensable elements of a defense strategy adequate to deter as well as to counter enemy aggression. The first requirement is, obviously, preparedness to meet every conceivable form and level of attack. But the second requirement is no less important if our preparedness is to have a deterrent power. The enemy must not be permitted to imagine, Dulles stressed, that he can always calculate in advance where and on what level of intensity we will respond to his aggressions. He must know for certain only that we will counter local as well as large scale attacks with adequate defenses, and that our defenses are to be, in every instance, "reinforced by the further deterrent of massive retaliatory power."

During his tenure as Vice President—which is to say, when he was still the old Nixon—Kissinger's new boss had often to stand up in defense of that Eisenhower strategy. Among its chief critics in those days was young Sen. John F. Kennedy. And in retrospect, it is particularly significant that the Kennedy assaults usually drew their main arguments from Kissinger's criticism.

In *Massive Retaliation: The Policy and Its Critics* (1959), Professor Paul Peeters focused attention on Kennedy's use of Kissinger's arguments in the debate that finally discredited the term if not the strategy. "If Senator Kennedy quotes Kissinger about our alleged 'Maginot-line reliance upon massive retaliation,'" Peeters noted, "it is because, with Kissinger, he identifies massive retaliation with overwhelming air-atomic superiority, a misconception for which there is no excuse whatsoever." Dulles had repeatedly explained in public that the nation's preparedness to respond to enemy aggression "at places and by means of *our* choosing" did not mean that "any local war would automatically be turned into a general war with atomic bombs being dropped all over the map." The basic idea, he had stressed, "is that we and our allies should have the means and the will to assure that a potential aggressor would lose from his aggression more than he could win. This does not mean that the aggressor had to be totally destroyed. It does mean a capacity to inflict punishing damage. We believe that we and our allies have the power to do that."

The meaning of the policy was thus made abundantly clear. Yet, as Peeters has demonstrated, Kissinger chose instead to accept the crudest partisan misconception, which was that the policy threatened "instant and massive thermo-nuclear retaliation" as the sole response America was prepared to make to any form of enemy aggression. With Kissinger's *imprimatur* of academic respectability to back it up, that crude view eventually prevailed. The Dulles strategy, as James Burnham has observed, was thus "never given a critical testing." Pinpointing the responsibility, Peeters has written:

> *No author is more frequently quoted by critics of massive retaliation than Henry Kissinger, and none has bothered less about understanding what he criticizes. We invite the reader to count the number of times Kissinger quotes Mr. Eisenhower or Mr. Dulles. It seems to us that his thesis is directed against the United States pre-Korea strategy and has been hastily recast in an effort to apply it to massive retaliation. Valid criticisms of pre-Korea defense thinking applied to massive retaliation (itself misunderstood by Mr. Kissinger) make an awkward ensemble.*

Published under the auspices of the Council on Foreign Relations, Kissinger's book soon came to be regarded as that Council's official rebuke of the "militancy" of Dulles—a circumstance that greatly enhanced its partisan value.

THE LIMITED-WAR STRATEGY

The alternative policy advanced by Kissinger in 1957 was his own "flexible" doctrine of limited war—or, more precisely, of the kind of war that a major power can "afford to lose." As first defined the "new" strategy was essentially a "nuclear strategy," calling for tactical use of low-yield nuclear weapons in response to enemy aggression; so that it differed from the real Dulles scheme, if at all, only with respect to the topmost limit of deterrence. Dulles had counselled that, when we are drawn into war, we must maintain the ability and the will to strike back at the enemy wherever we deem necessary and with whatever force suffices to frustrate his aggression. The ultimate deterrent for the enemy must be his knowledge of our determination to use the ultimate weapons, if need be. Kissinger advised, instead, that our local defenses in limited nuclear war be backed up, in the last resort, not by our determined will to use the ultimate weapons, but rather by a mutual fear—the common will, so to speak, of ourselves and our enemies—that the "unthinkable" holocaust might conceivably occur.

Liberal critics of Kissinger's first book on nuclear strategy had expressed dismay over its tolerance of the existence of the ultimate deterrent and its counselling of the use of tactical nuclear weapons in limited war, and some of them felt relieved, therefore, when Kissinger, in 1961, revised his limited war strategy. Though "the need for forces capable of fighting limited nuclear war remains," he cautioned in *The Necessity for Choice,* "several developments have caused a shift in the view about the relative emphasis to be given conventional forces as against nuclear forces." The new book called for the strict exclusion of nuclear weapons from limited war. Limited war of the kind a major power could "afford to lose" was to be waged exclusively with conventional weapons and with elaborate precautions to eliminate all danger of nuclear provocation. Under such circumstances, "we could reasonably announce," Kissinger assured his liberal friends, "that we would employ nuclear weapons only as a last resort and even then in a manner to minimize damage."

One must study those words carefully to make out the pattern of de-escalation proposed. From Dulles' determination to use ultimate weapons if need be, we have descended first to the notion of limited nuclear war and then to that of limited conventional war, in which the last resort is a threatened use of nuclear arms in a manner pre-announced to minimize damage. Our enemy need fear nothing beyond that, and he can thus proceed to escalate or de-escalate his own threats accordingly.

That was Kissinger's view in 1961. That was the year his Harvard-MIT colleagues McGeorge Bundy and Walt Rostow took over as chief foreign policy planners of the Kennedy Administration. Those two "civilian strategists" had immediately plunged our government into what has since been called their "great act of persuasion"—a policy designed to eliminate the threat of nuclear war by relieving Russia's fears of our military power and her envy of our economic wealth. Kissinger approved the general aim of the policy. But he warned his colleagues against undue haste and excessive enthusiasm. It was fatuous, Kissinger argued in those days, "to draw so much comfort from the hope that when the Soviet Union equals our economic performance it will become as consumer-oriented and as bland as we are. This is hardly a heroic attitude, nor likely to appeal to a world where millions strive for a new sense of direction."

Against the "haste" of the Rostows and Bundys, Kissinger advised a gradual step-by-step approach to the same goal. He warned that there was such a thing as moving too fast and too directly toward a detente with the communist powers. Atlantic unity should be used, he reasoned, to prepare Americans for a new status, even if such unity were originally sought out of fear of communism. In his own words: "In the past the Soviet threat has often produced Atlantic unity. It may again."

The superficial reader is apt to be pleased and the intelligent dove alerted by the diverse implications of that last statement. Is Kissinger counselling us to go back to the constructive realpolitik of the 19th century nation-builders? Is he another Demosthenes summoning the proud and the free to unite in the face of imperialist aggression? Just as fear of Nazi Germany sufficed to unite the Soviets with the hated capitalist democracies in World War II, so now fear of the Soviets may suffice to unite the proud western nations. The words can bear such an interpretation. But Kissinger hastens to assure attentive readers that, despite his almost Bismarkian talk, he remains a forward-looking, though cautious, internationalist. Fear of a common enemy may help to unite the Western nations, he explains, but "the ultimate unity of the West depends on what we affirm, not on what we reject. We of the West, who bequeathed the concept of nationalism to others, must summon the initiative and imagination to show the way to a new international order. Nothing is more crucial than for the West to develop policies which make for true community."

Beyond The Nation State

By 1965, Kissinger was prepared to put caution aside and argue unambiguously that, while preparedness for limited war was still to be preferred to "other even starker alternatives," no strategy of limited war could be effectively implemented so long as the Western nations retained their sovereignty. In *The Troubled Partnership* (New York, 1965), he focused his analysis on the difficulties the NATO allies were experiencing, and his anti-nationalist conclusion was that

> *institutions based on present concepts of national sovereignty are not enough. The West requires a larger goal: the constitution of an Atlantic Commonwealth in which all the peoples bordering the North Atlantic can fulfill their aspirations. Clearly, it will not come quickly; many intermediate stages must be traversed before it can be reached. It is not too early, however, to prepare ourselves now for this step beyond the nation-state.*

Half a page later, Kissinger explained how he (like Marx, we may add) was by no means insensitive to the "glorious achievements" of the nation-state system in the past. The fact to be faced, in his view, was simply that history had superseded the old arrangements. "For a while longer," he wrote somberly,

> *the West can continue along familiar lines. The traditional machinery of the Atlantic Alliance is well designed to produce the appearance of amity. But if the Alliance continues to confuse form and substance, energy will increasingly have to be spent in reconciling illusion with reality. Each nation will be thrown on its own resources and will emphasize policies that magnify divisions. At each previous critical juncture the West–though with much travail–found political forms adequate to its needs. It made the transition from feudalism to the nation-state. Its challenge now is whether it can move from the nation-state to a larger community and draw from this effort the strength for another period of innovation.*

Beyond the nation-state, Kissinger envisions an Atlantic Commonwealth of shared sovereignty; and from the effort to form that commonwealth will come, he hopes, the strength for greater exertions. And in the end . . . But Kissinger does not tell us much about how things will be in the distant future. His avowed object is simply to get us to take that first necessary step beyond the nation-state–the step which may prove to be, in the long run, the hardest of all, for it runs counter to the instinct for national survival in a people who have already shown how determined they can be to preserve at all cost the integrity of their national union.

The Kissinger Riddle

But if his object is to get us started on the way toward a regime of enforceable peace for all mankind, why doesn't our presidential advisor on national security affairs just come straight out and say so with the candor of a J. William Fulbright, or a Robert Hutchins, or a Norman Cousins?

Kissinger no doubt has all sorts of good reasons for not being frank on the subject. But perhaps the best reason is one hinted at long ago by Arthur Schlesinger, Jr., in *The Vital Center.* "In the long run," Schlesinger there confessed, "the supporters of world government are right; but in the short run, their efforts too often serve to distract men of good will from the urgent tasks of the moment." The notion that all it takes to establish a world government is a written constitution, of the kind drawn up for Robert Hutchins at the University of Chicago, is rejected by Schlesinger. The tensions between the major powers, he explained, "are much too deep to be waved away by constitutional formulas, however learned and ingenious." In his view, we must keep our hearts and minds fixed on the ultimate goal of genuine world unity; but, "in the meantime, we had better do what we can do to foster community where we can, through regional federations and through the United Nations, and not ignore these small gains in pursuit of a pot of legalisms at the end of a rainbow."

Schlesinger tells us in *The Vital Center* that he took his cue on this subject from Reinhold Niebuhr's "penetrating statement of the case against immediate agitation for world government," paradoxically entitled "The Illusion of World Government." (*Foreign Affairs,* April, 1949). In my book *War, Peace and The Presidency,* I have examined that Niebuhr essay at some length, pointing out the subtleties of passionate advocacy veiled under that deceptive title. And I am persuaded that a careful reading of Schlesinger and Niebuhr on the subject can help us to resolve the riddle of Henry Kissinger as propounded in the *Time* cover story.

Who is finally right: the superficial readers who see Kissinger as a hawk, or the intellectual doves who see him as Nixon's most astute appointment? If we really want an answer, we have only to read Kissinger's words as no doubt Schlesinger and Niebuhr have read them. Take, for instance, Kissinger's limited-war strategy. Is it a strategy designed to provide "national security" in the traditional sense? Kissinger knows how to field such a question. "National security policy in the nuclear age," he has explained in *Problems of National Strategy* (New York, 1965), "goes far beyond the traditional concept. . . . In its widest sense, it comprises every action by which a society seeks to assure its survival or to realize its aspirations internationally." One needs to read that twice to recognize that Kissinger is proposing an *alternative to survival* under the traditional name of national security!

"It is easy to understand the objections of the traditionalists," Kissinger acknowledges in *The Necessity for Choice;* the idea of an alternative to survival does indeed go *far beyond* the traditional sense of security. But Kissinger goes on to say that he finds "the violence of the criticism of some of the other groups" extremely puzzling. The worst attacks on his strategy have come, he complains, from "individuals who rebel against the very notion of strategy, such as the advocates of universal or even unilateral disarmament." Urging patience, he chides such critics for their shortsightedness. They pretend, he says, that

> *those who urge a greater reliance on limited war wish to bring it about. They give the impression that the choice before us is peace or limited war and they then proceed to demonstrate the easy proposition that peace is preferable.*

> *However, our alternatives are quite different. . . . Since surrender is not our national policy, it is important to get our choices straight. Limited war is palatable only when compared with even starker alternatives. . . . It is preferable not to peace, but to surrender or all out war. It is, to be sure, a subtle task.*

Kissinger hastens to assure his impatient liberal critics that he does not look upon his limited-war strategy as a "substitute for constructive policy." Its object is to give vent to otherwise uncontrollable passions and thereby purchase time for further negotiations to "avoid catastrophe." But his scheme can work, he warns, only if the government approaches each limited-war confrontation (as in Korea and Vietnam) "prepared to negotiate and to settle for something less than our traditional notion of complete victory."

Against the pacifist advocates of unilateral disarmament, Kissinger argues that the American people need to be led slowly, and ambiguously, to the same goal. Matching the profoundest subleties of Niebuhr on this point, Kissinger electrifies us with this startling piece of candor on why he wants Americans to fight no-win wars a while longer. "A nation which cannot be trusted when strong," he writes, "will hardly be able to deal with the much more difficult task of living in dignity when impotent."

To get the complete picture we have only to juxtapose its mosaic elements. Limited war is no substitute for constructive policy; but a constructive policy can be built upon it. Limited war will not provide national security in the traditional sense; but it will in Kissinger's new sense, which authorizes us to choose between survival and the realizing of our aspirations internationally. When we have fought our limited wars and have settled in each case for something less than the traditional meaning of security, the next step will be, as Kissinger says, the difficult one of perfecting ourselves in the art of "living in dignity when impotent."

Is that not, in sum, Kissinger's doctrine? Let the superficial reader judge for himself and then continue to marvel that the community of intellectual doves feels so much more secure with the New Nixon Administration than it did with the old Johnson Administration. "I think it's an excellent appointment," said Schlesinger, enjoying the first spoils of the victorious Dump-Johnson campaign; and, after acknowledging that it was very very encouraging, he added: "He's the best they'll get." Schlesinger is in a position to know, for he also has been trying to teach us how to live in dignity when impotent.

2. NIXON'S SUPREME STRATEGIST

Nixon's "State of the World" message, sent to Congress on February 18, 1970, is unprecedented in our history, both for its length (43,000 words, 119 pages) and its definition of global rather than national foreign-policy aims.

On both counts it represents–from an internationalist point of view–a stupendous victory for Henry A. Kissinger, the cosmopolitan peace-strategist who is Nixon's chief advisor for national security affairs. For conservatives who helped to elect Nixon in 1968, on the other hand, it represents a major setback. They had hoped Nixon would succeed, where Johnson had failed, in reversing the internationalist policies of the Kennedy strategists. That hope is now proved to have been utterly in vain.

No one can seriously doubt that Kissinger is the "principal author" of this latest policy statement. The *New York Times*, carrying the complete text, observed: "The long message bore the signature of the President and the stamp of Mr. Kissinger as well." "It has become increasingly evident that they think alike on the grand designs of American foreign policy. Kissinger is the man Nixon relies upon to pull together the policy judgments, as he did in today's message. In forming an overview of foreign affairs, Kissinger is the paramount strategist."

Liberal journalist Joseph Kraft adds admiringly: "By no mere accident the document was put together while the Secretary of State was off in East Africa and the Secretary of Defense in East Asia." "Kissinger has clearly superseded both in importance as a framer of national security policy. He is probably the second most powerful man in the world." And with less irony than truth, Nixon himself has told reporters: "The report is worth reading. I have read it myself."

Kissinger's rise to eminence as the most influential "civilian" strategist of our time began in December 1968, when Nixon first offered him his present job. The offer came as a surprise. Kissinger and Nixon had rarely met before, and politically, they had usually been ranged on diametrically opposite sides. Nixon, for instance, had defended Dulles' "massive retaliation" policy, whereas Kissinger, as spokesman for the Council on Foreign Relations, had literally led the attack on it, providing John F. Kennedy with some of the sharpest arguments he was to use against Nixon in the fateful T.V. debates of 1960. In 1968, with Nixon leaning to the right for his second try, again Kissinger was ranged against him, serving as chief foreign policy advisor for the party's leading internationalist, Nelson Rockefeller.

But politics makes strange bedfellows. After much consultation with friends, Kissinger accepted Nixon's offer. Internationalist Arthur Schlesinger, Jr. later boasted to reporters about his part in the decision: "Kissinger asked my advise about it a few weeks ago, and I urged him to accept. I find it very very encouraging." Other "high ranking former members of the Kennedy Administration" also approved. Kissinger, they agreed, would bring to the Nixon Administration a much-needed "force for reason, balance, and discretion in foreign affairs and arms control." That is to say—the former New-Frontiersmen claimed him as one of their own.

The conservative wing of the Republican Party voiced no objections—perhaps because the feeling was in the air that Nixon might be planning to "use" Kissinger with Machiavellian cunning. William F. Buckley's *National Review* ran an editorial suggesting that, in fact, Kissinger might prove to be more conservative, than liberal. *Time* magazine, on the other hand, ran a cover-story emphasizing the anomaly of the new association, and remarking cryptically: "A superficial reading of some of his works makes him seem like a hawk, but intelligent doves regard him as Richard Nixon's most astute appointment." Which means that, like Nixon himself, Kissinger is a man of studied ambiguities.

Certainly "studied ambiguity" is what most characterizes this first Nixon-Kissinger "State of the World" message. Its very length is an ambiguity, suggesting that exceptionally complex matters are being elaborated, when in fact the bulk of it is rhetorical padding, reiterating again and again that the past is dead, the future yet to come—all useless, except to obscure rather than clarify.

Take, for instance, the official title—"United States Foreign Policy for the 1970's: A New Strategy for Peace." Originally it had been simply: "A New Strategy for Peace"; but then, as the *New York Times* relates, "someone reminded the President that the brief title was strikingly similar to a collection of John F. Kennedy's speeches," including the key speech of June 10, 1963, which is now revered by many internationalists as a classic statement of their ideal. "And so," the *Times* concludes, the Kissinger team "agreed to downgrade the brief title to sub-title," adding seven words to five to obscure an otherwise striking similarity.

A similarity which—one hastens to emphasize—is even more striking when we pass from titles to contents. What we in fact have in Nixon's "New Strategy for Peace" is a return to the Kennedy-Rostow strategy of 1963, which the "dump Johnson" people accused Johnson of having betrayed and which the majority of Americans rejected in 1968 by refusing to support internationalist party platforms or candidates. Kennedy's speech had stressed the global rather than merely national concern of American Policy. "Peace," he had begun, "is the most important topic on earth." And after spelling out a commitment to "build new institutions for peace that would take the place of arms," he concluded: "While we proceed to safeguard our national interests, let us also safeguard human interests. And the elimination of war, and arms, is clearly in the interests of both."

Underlying all the arguments of the speech was Walt Rostow's teaching that "war, ultimately, arises out of the existence and acceptance of the concept of national sovereignty," and that, if war is to be finally eliminated, our government, sooner or later, must declare that it is "a legitimate American interest to see an end to nationhood as it has been historically defined."

After that speech, Kennedy found himself facing unexpected and fierce nationalist criticism, led by Barry Goldwater on the Senate floor. The President's ratings in the polls hit a new low. Thereafter, to the day of his assassination, he toured the country making patriotic speeches, particularly to Southern and Catholic working-class audiences, in the hope of recovering their electoral support.

The Kennedy "Strategy for Peace" speech had backfired—its internationalist admirers soon realized—because it had been too direct and too brief. In the Kissinger "New Strategy" those faults are remedied—which accounts for the unprecedented length and ambiguities. Echoing the Kennedy speech in his earlier "State of the Union" address, Nixon had thus defined his foreign-policy theme: "When we speak of America's priorities, the first priority must always be peace for America and for the world," And in the "New Strategy" message, we get this elaboration:

> *Building a lasting peace requires a foreign policy guided by three basic principles* . . . partnership . . . strength . . . *and a* willingness to negotiate. *All nations—and we are no exception—have important national interests to protect. But the most fundamental interest of all nations lies in building the structure of peace. . . . This vision of peace built on partnership, strength, and willingness to negotiate is the unifying theme of this report.*

Strength, needless to say, has always been a principle of national strategy, for war as well as peace. The novelty here lies in its being sandwiched between and subordinated to *partnership* and *willingness to negotiate,* with no explicit reference to a *willingness to wage war,* as a matter of principle, if need be. Would modern Israeli, or Soviet, or Red Chinese leaders fail to include willingness to wage war in a serious statement of their principles of national strategy? And what about the "old" Nixon who fought Alger Hiss and stood up for "massive retaliation" against its rejection by Kissinger and the Council on Foreign Relations?

But that old Nixon is gone, and he says so himself. In a recent press briefing, he went out of his way to point out that his new strategy statement "shows a significant shift from the policies of the past" which he and Secretary Laird had "supported when we were Congressmen together" and also "under the Eisenhower Administration from 1953 to early 1961." Dates precise enough for a tombstone!

Yet we must not imagine that what is new for Nixon is new also for his supreme strategist. On the contrary, Kissinger has been defining and refining this so-called new strategy since the mid-fifties. Each of its three basic principles, in fact, has been the subject of a major Kissinger book. The first was *Nuclear Weapons and Foreign Policy* (1957), devoted to strength for peace. It attacked Dulles' unlimited willingness to wage war, even on the level of thermonuclear retaliation, and recommended instead an unwillingness (shared fearfully with our enemies) to go beyond the level of "limited nuclear war." Next came *The Necessity for Choice* (1960), devoted to negotiation for peace. It urged lowering the level of willingness to fight from limited nuclear to limited conventional war and argued that such war must be waged only to purchase time for further negotiations with the enemy, never in the expectation of defeating him, in the traditional sense. Then came *The Troubled Partnership* (1965), subtitled *"A Reappraisal of the Atlantic Alliance."* It argued that, if strength for peace is not to culminate in war, partnership with our allies must take us "beyond the divisions of nation states" as soon as possible; for, if we cannot agree even with our allies to give up the prerogatives of sovereignty, which make wars possible, how can we ever hope to eliminate war universally, through negotiations with enemies as well as allies?

The ultimate goal for Kissinger is formation of a "creative world order" capable of enforcing peace without obstructing today's world-revolutionary drive toward "social justice" for all. The possibility of a nuclear war must be eliminated at all costs; but there is a risk, he holds, in pressing toward that goal too eagerly, as some advocates of unilateral disarmament tend to do: for their pacifistic talk, inexpertly advanced, could provoke a severe nationalist reaction. The approach most likely to succeed with Americans, according to Kissinger, is a cautious one, emphasizing not disarmament alone but also strength for peace; for, as he writes in *The Necessity for Choice* (p. 101), "a nation which cannot be trusted when strong will hardly be able to deal with the much more difficult task of living in dignity when impotent."

Of course, for the great majority of Americans who are grateful to Nixon for having given them Spiro T. Agnew, Kissinger hardly exists. Yet he has the President's ear. And a man in that position, long skilled in pleading the internationalist cause, with decades of experience as study director and spokesman for the Council on Foreign Relations, could very well manage to set the nation on a course from which there might be, at some point, no turning back.

Yet there is a profound irony here. The talk is of peace, but the emotional tension is of war. The longing for a creative world order in which the lowly are to be raised and the arrogant humbled has always been superficially very attractive, especially to academicians; but the fact is that it has inspired the bloodiest wars of all times. It is not a remedy for what ails mankind, but rather a symptom. At the close of World War I, G.K. Chesterton put it this way:

> *I have lived through the times when many intelligent and idealistic men hoped that the World War would be an introduction to the World State. But I myself am more convinced than ever that the World War occurred because nations were too big, and not because they were too small. It occurred especially because big nations wished to be bigger, or, in other words, because each State wanted to be the World State. But it occurred, above all, because about things so vast there comes to be something cold and hollow and impersonal. This recent Great War was* not *merely a war of nations; it was a war of warring Internationalists."*

We are again on the brink of that kind of war. The fundamental point is this: whenever a great nation—whether it be Russia or the United States, Germany or Japan—wearies of the tense discipline of maintaining a balance of power, and makes an enforceable peace its first priority, to which all other values are to be sacrificed, then it must either surrender itself to a world conqueror or plunge headlong into the arena of unlimited war; for it is either in surrender or in all-out war, and not in the ambiguities of negotiation, that the supreme national sacrifices for an enforceable peace are ultimately made. The United States can avoid that pathetic choice only if it is persuaded that it does not need an enforceable peace, which is incompatible with true freedom. For freedom's sake, all it has ever needed, and all it needs now, is the tense discipline of the balance of power.

From this point of view, the Nixon-Kissinger "New Strategy for Peace" is not a foreign policy at all but an evasion of sovereign responsibilities.

3. OUR CAPTIVE PRESIDENT:
THE ASCENDANCY OF A
SUPRANATIONALIST PROFESSOR

Last year [1970] the *New York Times* gave complete coverage to the President's "State of the World" message, running ten pages of text and four of commentary. That was in recognition of the fact that its separation from the traditional State of the Union Address was a precedent-shattering event. It was no trifling matter that our President should have been induced to limit his assessment of the State of the Union to a projection of health, education, and welfare goals, while reserving consideration of the Union's safety for a later document bearing a supranationalist title and written from a perspective that is clearly global.

The message this year [1971] is 180 pages long as compared with 119 pages last year. But the *Times* coverage is markedly reduced: only two pages of excerpts and one of commentary. That doesn't mean the *Times* considers the content unimportant. On the contrary, it simply indicates a willing acceptance of Henry Kissinger's staff motto with respect to foreign policy, which is: Relax, and leave the driving to us.

The truth is that the *Times* had anticipated this year's message with a full commentary on its meaning a month ago. That commentary is available now in pamphlet form for $1; but originally it appeared as a series of front-page articles (Jan. 18-24, 1971), exploring in detail how American defense and foreign policy decisions are made and precisely who makes them. Mr. Nixon, at that time, was in the midst of explaining his domestic reforms to the American people. He was on TV declaring himself to be the head of a New American Revolution, pledging himself to "stop the killing in Vietnam," to guarantee a minimal income regardless of employment, to purify the air, cure cancer, and pay for it all through deficit financing, the way academic "good guys" have always advised Presidents to do.

Mr. Nixon's antics in those days dismayed many conservatives. William F. Buckley, for instance, felt constrained to write: "Whether Mr. Nixon is trying suddenly to co-opt the rhetoric of the hard left, one cannot know. But unless one does know that his intentions are crafty, one is left despondent." The high-level liberal response, on the other hand was far more complex. James Reston, who is able to recognize foreign policy disguised as welfare reform, cautioned his *Times* readers: "One should not be cynical about this. It is a great improvement on Mr. Nixon's narrow, divisive themes of the last election. No doubt it represents the growing influence of men like George Shultz at the Budget Bureau, Elliot Richardson at H.E.W., and Henry Kissinger, who has been arguing that it is hard to conduct effective foreign policy with a divided country."

Woodrow Wilson had his Colonel House, Nixon has his Professor Kissinger. Reston's point is that when Kissinger argues, the President acts. Kissinger is a big man in the White House. Though he began in the basement offices of his predecessors McGeorge Bundy and Walt Rostow, he has long since moved up into what the *Times* describes as "bright, swank, Hilton-style quarters on the ground floor near the President's Oval Office." where he "directs his growing staff" and ranks, as the gossips say, "next to God" in protocol. According to the *Times* report, his staff budget of $2.2 million is three times that of Rostow in 1968, and his operation far more ambitious than either Rostow's or Bundy's. Specifically: "The heart of the Kissinger system is the committee structure, stacked up like the decks of an ocean liner, with the National Security Council on top. Before the policy options go to the President, they are rigorously reviewed by one of the first-tier committees, all headed by Mr. Kissinger. . . . On crucial issues like the arms talks, Vietnam, or defense manpower, the working groups headed by Kissinger aides do the staff studies on which high-level debates are later based. 'With that setup,' a knowledgeable official commented, 'Henry has such a hammerlock on foreign policy that you don't get any options through that he doesn't think are reasonable.'"

And yet, as *Times* correspondent Hedrick Smith notes: "Mr. Kissinger's influence with the President really derives less from organizational position than from sheer power of intellect as well as from their unexpected affinity of view. . . . Almost daily—frequently three or four times a day—he sees Mr. Nixon alone. Sometimes they will converse for an hour or so on world trends. . . . 'Nixon may hear all the options,' a shrewd bureaucrat has commented, 'but he seems to listen most of the time to one voice.'"

Max Lerner of the *New York Post* is both convinced and pleased by what he has read about Kissinger in the *Times*. Passing the word along, he adds: "Never in American history has a President depended so strongly for his global policy on any one man. . . . I'm happy it is someone with Kissinger's knowledge, coolness, and sense of the limits of power [who pursues] long-range calculated policies. He quotes Metternich: 'Because I know what I want and what the others are capable of, I am completely prepared.' It is a better description of Kissinger than any I have encountered."

What Lerner has just begun to appreciate, and what the *Times* studies establish beyond the shadow of a doubt, is that Kissinger's compact White-House operation has completely eclipsed the Defense and State Department bureaucracies; that the former Harvard professor has just the right "hard-line" academic style to continue to delude Republican conservatives; and that, if the extreme left doesn't rock the boat excessively at home or abroad, the long-range hopes of supranationalist liberalism, which seemed dashed to pieces in August 1968, may yet be realized, and possibly even before the White House incumbent comes up for re-election in 1972.

The key to Kissinger's ascendancy appears to be his masterly style, characterized admiringly by Max Lerner as "almost intolerably brilliant . . . shot through with paradox and with sentences that balance contrasting phrases like a juggler." The foreign-born Harvard professor evidently developed it when he was employed by the Council on Foreign Relations back in the fifties to sum up the views of a committee which had undertaken an elaborate critique of the Eisenhower-Nixon-Dulles policy of Massive Retaliation. In his book on the subject, *Nuclear Weapons and Foreign Policy* (New York, 1957), Kissinger gives us page after page in the style praised by Lerner. Sentences start off apparently saying one thing only to end up saying the apparent opposite. The original *Time* cover-story on Kissinger (Feb. 14, 1969) had the effect of that style in mind when it remarked on the paradoxical unanimity of conservative as well as liberal approval that greeted Mr. Nixon's announcement of Kissinger's appointment in December 1968. William Buckley on that occasion had sent Kissinger a note, saying: "Not since Florence Nightingale has any public figure received such universal acclamation." Jacob Javits had joined in to say approvingly that Kissinger's appointment could prove to be the most significant Mr. Nixon had made, because "it is in foreign policy that the Nixon Administration will make its mark." And Arthur Schlesinger, long-range Fabian supranationalist of *The Vital Center,* had added: "I think it's an excellent appointment. He's the best they've got. He asked my advice a few weeks ago and I urged him to accept."

Buckley, Javits, Schlesinger? To explain the apparent paradox, the *Time* cover-story writer remarked wrily, at the expense of conservative intelligence: "A superficial reading of some of Kissinger's works makes him seem like a hawk, but many intellectual doves regard him as Richard Nixon's most astute appointment."

As an example of that brilliantly paradoxical style—which is now the style of our "State of the World" messages–take this estimate of Metternich's achievement in Kissinger's dissertation, *The World Restored* (New York, 1964, p. 8): "The success of Clemens von Metternich made inevitable the ultimate collapse of the state he had fought so long to preserve." Surely it takes paradoxical brilliance to couple "success" and "inevitable collapse" that way–and we wonder whether Kissinger may not be contemplating a similar "success" for himself in aiding our President to "preserve, protect, and defend" our nation's sovereign independence.

Or take Kissinger's "Definition of National Security Policy" under that heading in *Problems of National Strategy* (New York, 1965, p.7). "National security policy in the nuclear age," he begins, "goes far beyond the traditional concept." That is fairly plain: because of the development of nuclear power, the old concept needs to be updated. Then comes the new definition, which we must assume is operative in Kissinger's mind today when, as Special Assistant for National Security Affairs, he advises our President. "In its widest sense," he tells us, national security policy in the nuclear age "comprises every action by which a society seeks to assure its survival or . . . " [we pause on that fatal *or* to stress the paradoxical brilliance of it: our nation, under the new definition, is to have an alternative to survival] ". . . or to realize its aspirations internationally."

Imagine trying to sell that updated definition to Abba Eban or Golda Meier! The alternative to survival it proposes is precisely what Israel's enemies are urging on it: "Instead of seeking to survive as a nation state, why don't you Zionist Jews take the alternative course of seeking to realize your aspirations internationally." Is Kissinger operating with that alternative in mind for the United States? We say he is; we say that it underlies his whole concept of "options," and, most dangerously, his concept of an alternative to automatic retaliatory destruction of Soviet cities in the event of a nuclear first-strike against our land missile sites. Automatic destruction of Soviet urban and industrial complexes by our surviving submarine-based missiles (which cannot pinpoint strategic targets) was the basis of our ultimate deterrence policy up to January 1969, when Nixon and Kissinger entered the White House. The concept then was that a Russian decision to strike us was also a Russian decision to destroy her own cities. Now, instead, our President is to be forced to intervene with a choice. He may, for instance, decide that a counter-blow against city populations under the circumstances is not really worth it, since the Soviets would surely reciprocate, leveling our cities with their remaining land and submarine-based missiles. The President might therefore opt, as the *Times* suggests, simply to issue a warning, perhaps through "selective" bombing of an airbase, and then try to negotiate a cease-fire of some sort, while the Soviets were reloading their land sites with missiles of pinpoint accuracy!

That is the present policy. It literally invites the Soviet Union to risk a first-strike as a means of gaining an absolute preponderance in the nuclear sphere, and we must not permit Kissinger's paradoxical brilliance to conceal the fact. If we are committed to act as that policy prescribes, then our country is no longer a first-rate power and deserves to be guided by a disciple of Metternich. We must not delude ourselves that Kissinger is concerned with our national security in the traditional sense. Like Karl Marx, Walt Rostow, Arthur Schlesinger, and J. William Fulbright (to name but a few out of very many), Kissinger believes that the era of nation-states is about to be phased out by the march of history, and that statesmen in this nuclear age have a responsibility to facilitate that phasing out. Typical are his words in *The Troubled Partnership* (New York, 1965, p. 248):

> *Institutions based on present concepts of national sovereignty are not enough. The West requires . . . the constitution of an Atlantic Commonwealth in which all people bordering the North Atlantic can fulfill their aspirations. It will not come quickly; many intermediate steps must be traversed before it can be reached. It is not too early, however, to prepare ourselves now for this step beyond the nation-state.*

Anti-communists who occasionally talk of an alliance of free nations against world communism might be tempted to imagine that Kissinger has something of that sort in mind in projecting a supranationalist Atlantic Community. But that is hardly the case. As our cosmopolitan "strategist" explains elsewhere: "in the past, the Soviet threat has often produced Atlantic unity. It may again. But ultimately the unity of the West depends on what we affirm, not on what we reject. We of the West, who bequeathed the concept of nationalism to others, must summon the initiative and imagination to show the way to a new international order."

How in the world did our President get saddled with such a counselor? One day that whole tale must be told. But this is neither the time nor the place. In a recent issue of the YAF *New Guard,* there was a pessimistic editorial entitled "Should Conservatives Support Richard Nixon?" The only optimistic word in it referred to Bill

Buckley's having said that, in Nixon, we at least have a President "who will listen to conservatives who can get his ear." To such conservatives I direct this plea: Tell the President that, for his own sake, for our sake, for our posterity's sake, and even for Kissinger's sake, he must send that supranationalist, double-talking, self-styled 20th century synthesis of Disraeli and Metternich back to the academy where he belongs and where he has always had a legitimate place.

A wise old European, who is a match for Kissinger in paradoxical brilliance, observed recently that Washington's most eligible bachelor, against whom revolutionary priests and nuns allegedly conspire, has all the earmarks of an easy scapegoat. He warns, compassionately, that if our governing class doesn't collapse prematurely (bombs have already struck the Senate!), Kissinger may end up getting hanged—in effigy, if not literally—from the top of the Washington Monument, like an expendable Turkish vizier or some daring, crypto-Jesuit counselor to a Protestant Queen.

4. THE LAST WAR?

Mr. Nixon has said that he is a pacifist and that he believes he can eliminate war by a pragmatic application of pacifist principles in American foreign policy.

These disclosures were made in an exclusive interview with C.L. Sulzberger of the *New York Times* (March 10, 1971). Early in the interview, the President said: "I rate myself as a committed pacifist, perhaps because of my Quaker heritage from my mother. . . . This war is ending. In fact, I seriously doubt if we will ever have another war. This is probably the very last one." Toward the close, he said again: "I can assure you that my words are those of a devoted pacifist."

That is an extraordinary assurance to receive from the Commander-in-Chief of our armed forces! By definition, a pacifist is one who advocates "suppression of war through individual or collective obstruction of militarism." By definition, refusal to bear arms, engage the enemy, accept the legitimacy of acts of war, or provide in any military way for the common defense, is consistent with pacifist, and especially Quaker-pacifist principles. The effect of the President's public commitment to pacifism could therefore be to destroy military discipline from top to bottom.

It will be argued, of course, that Mr. Nixon didn't mean what he said to Sulzberger, that he was merely trying to "improve his image" with his critics. The deplorable irony of such an assessment is that a William F. Buckley and an Allard Lowenstein can agree in making it. But whereas Buckley will want the President to prove in the end that he has been a tricky politician, disposed to lie about his ideals, Lowenstein will be able to plead with Nixon to prove by deeds that he is in fact the pacifist and puritanic moralist he professes to be.

Conservatives must not delude themselves as to where the moral advantage lies in this situation. President Nixon is evidently determined to prove that he is not a tricky politician. According to the High Command at the *New York Times,* he is seeking public recognition for having served liberal internationalist ends during the past two years, while managing to keep his old-time conservative supporters silent if not pacified. Sulzberger himself has made the point, writing: "The most interesting thing about President Nixon is that he regards himself as a genuine but practical pacifist who is slowly building up a world which may never see another war. . . . For his political opponents, editorial writers and cartoonists, he is a right-wing war-monger. . . . But the Nixon seen by the President himself is a pragmatic Quaker who not only wants peace but is patient enough to do something about it in a realistic way, even if it takes a long time."

News analyst Max Frankel is more explicit. Nixon's talk with Sulzberger, he says, "amounted above all to a reassertion of the faith of the World War II generation of American 'internationalists' against the challenge and disillusionment of the war in Vietnam." But Frankel knows that internationalists and pacifists are not to be confounded. As the Columbia Encyclopedia tells it, a line may be drawn "between the advocates of absolute peace (the pacifists) and those who seek to prevent war by international cooperation (the internationalists). . . . Recent pacifist movements have tended to concentrate their efforts on urging unilateral or multilateral disarmament and the cessation of nuclear testing. A number of these groups are suspect of political propaganda goals other than genuine world peace." With some such distinction evidently in mind, Frankel looks to '72 from the vantage point of the Sulzberger revelations:

> *The air is charged now with denunciations of "militarism" and "neoisolationism," while the real debate lies ahead. If the politics of the Democratic contenders for the Presidency are any guide, it will be a debate not only among the old "internationalists" but between them and their postwar sons and daughters, many of whom have been moved by the Vietnam issue to question the morality as well as the wisdom and effectiveness of recent American exertions abroad. . . . It has been suggested here that the President's new willingness to divulge some of his inner feelings bespeaks either a sense of confidence or of political vulnerability.*

Nelson Rockefeller obviously smells political vulnerability. He has begun to talk of running for the Presidency again in '72. Perhaps he has an inside word from Henry Kissinger that Nixon is cracking under the strain, cares only for his "moral" image, and may follow Johnson's example in not seeking a second term.

But the essential point is this: Two years of the Nixon Administration have eliminated virtually all conservative influence on the conduct of American foreign policy. It is as if Rockefeller himself had won in '68—or, rather, much worse, for Rockefeller could never have silenced his conservative opposition as Nixon has managed to silence Strom Thurmond, Barry Goldwater, *Human Events,* and *National Review.* If the *Times* High Command is not grossly mistaken about the President's state of mind, America's fate is now to be decided in a debate between the internationalists of the old left and their sons and daughters on the new left, with Mr. Nixon confiding that his Quaker heart beats in rhythm with the leftist sons and daughters!

Nixon's profession of pacifism helps to explain why he has failed to maintain superiority or even parity for the United States in nuclear missile strength, and why, on top of that, he has abandoned the nuclear deterrence policy of assured destruction inherited from the Johnson Administration. *Assured destruction* was the one element of the Eisenhower-Dulles policy of nuclear deterrence which neither the Kennedy nor Johnson administrations presumed to abandon, though repeatedly urged to do so by the Bundys and Rostows. Robert S. McNamara was certainly an internationalist of the old left. He led the way in depriving this nation of its nuclear superiority. But he respected the limit of *assured destruction* as the sole justification for his military cut-backs in first-strike nuclear capability. As he expressed it after leaving office in 1968 (*The Essence of Security*, p. 53):

> *If the United States is to deter a nuclear attack on itself or its allies, it must possess an actual and a credible assured-destruction capability. . . capable of damaging the aggressor to the point that his society would be simply no longer viable in twentieth-century terms. That is what deterrence of nuclear aggression means. It means the certainty of suicide to the aggressor, not merely to his military forces, but to his society as a whole.*

Certainty of suicide to the aggressor: "that is what deterrence of nuclear aggression means." Such was our policy as late as January 1969! But then Nixon and his newly discovered alter ego Kissinger entered the White House. In the "State of the World" message of 1970, Nixon referred explicitly to the inherited policy of assured destruction, remarking that, "once in office, I concluded that this strategic doctrine should be carefully reviewed." He went on to say that, as part of that review, Kissinger and his staff would explore the following question: "Should a President, in the event of a nuclear attack, be left with the single option of ordering the mass destruction of enemy civilians, in the face of the certainty that it would be followed by the mass slaughter of Americans?"

That was a rhetorically loaded question. The certainty formerly applied to the suicidal consequences of an aggressor's first strike is there applied instead to the consequences of our retaliatory strike, in which "mass destruction" of the enemy is to be followed by "mass slaughter" of Americans. The question is answered in the 1971 message, where Nixon says: "I must not be—and my successors must not be—limited to the indiscriminate mass destruction of enemy civilians as the sole possible response to challenges. This is especially so when the response involves the likelihood of triggering nuclear attacks on our population."

That is a policy of "sufficiency"—but only according to pacifist-Quaker standards. What internationalist McNamara defined as the essence of nuclear deterrence—"the certainty of suicide to the aggressor, not merely to his military forces, but to his society as a whole"—has been abandoned by the Nixon-Kissinger administration. What we have instead is a policy of double talk about "strength" (in partnership, in conventional arms and in negotiating positions) to keep the loyal "superhawks" quiet till all the bridges are crossed and burned behind us.

Here is how Nixon put it to Sulzberger: "You must look at the facts. The soviets have three times the missile strength (ICBM) of ourselves. By 1974 they will pass us in submarines carrying nuclear missiles. . . . But each has a kind of sufficiency. The Soviets are a great land power opposite China as well as having far-reaching interests elsewhere. We are a great sea power, and we must keep our strength. I am a strong Navy man myself. I believe in a strong conventional navy which helps us to play a peace-keeping role in such areas, for example, as Latin America."

What it all amounts to, at best, is that, in this nuclear age, America is to serve the world hegemony of the Soviet Union in precisely the same way that Metternich's Austria was allowed to serve the hegemony of Great Britain in the post-Napoleonic era. It is to be Kissinger's diplomatic gift to American Quaker pacifism.

How long will our Republican conservatives remain silent? Will they persist in risking the safety of our nation to guard their partisan political advantage? The pathos of their situation is well expressed by James J. Kilpatrick in a column entitled "What Happened to Our Skipper?" Kilpatrick writes: "A series of worrisome developments is causing increasing concern among Mr. Nixon's friends and supporters on the political right. We are not ready to abandon ship: Where do we swim to? But it would be reassuring, all the same, to know where in hell we are going. . . . The dismal thought is beginning to take hold that Mr. Nixon has jettisoned his charts and compass of 1968—tossed them over the rail—and now is steering by the seat of his pants. . . . The rueful notion will not go away that we preferred our skipper then, to our skipper now."

I must say that I was not a Nixon supporter in 1968. Back in

1966 I wrote an article for *National Review* in which I warned that the heads of the "dump Johnson" movement were determined to elect even a Richard Nixon, if need be, to have their way in foreign policy. After the 1966 elections, Nixon had said: "The peace party always wins. I know my own party. If the war is still going on in '68, there is no power on earth can keep them from trying to outbid the Democrats for the peace vote."

That statement had gratified leftist I.F. Stone as much as it ought to have alerted conservative Republicans. Stone devoted an entire newsletter to it and took ads in all the major liberal newspapers to publicize it. His conclusion was: "Many of us will see a Republican victory again—as in 1952—as the only way to end an Asian war. . . . Even another interlude of social stagnation will not be too high a price to pay for peace if Johnson does not change course." In my *National Review* article, I argued that the stage was thus being set for a Nixon comeback and warned:

> *What a tragic irony it would be if the growing conservative movement allowed itself to be used at this time to frustrate its chief end. That end must be to stiffen this nation's will to survive as a sovereign state under the pressure of enemies foreign and domestic who would prefer to see it dead and buried, whether through Trotskyite subversion, Maoist violence, or liberal euthanasia. To survive, this nation must stand firm where its troops and its will have been committed, resisting communist imperialism as well as American one-worldism in its many varieties. If it stands firm, it can eventually tame not only the Russians and the Chinese but even the African peoples into accepting civilized membership in the family of sovereign nations that recognize the right of each to defend its integrity. . . . Johnson should not be forced, by a political squeeze-play from left and right, into getting out of Vietnam before '68, like a repentant aggressor.*

What Johnson refused to do to get himself re-elected in '68, Nixon is clearly determined to do now—if not for a second term (he may be despairing of that) at least to prove to the *Times* people that he really is the decent Quaker pacifist he claims to be. Conservative nationalists really have only one alternative under the circumstances. They must begin now to mount an all-out drive for the nomination of Governor Ronald Reagan in 1972, or at least for a prominent conservative to challenge Mr. Nixon (and Congressman McCloskey) in the Republican primaries.

5. KISSINGER, POOR RICHARD, AND *NATIONAL REVIEW*

Not since 1493, when Pope Alexander Vl conferred with the Kings of Portugal and Spain on how they might best split up the world between them, has a supranationalist diplomat advanced such plans for global reapportionment as Henry Kissinger apparently has in his secret Peking talks and doubly-secret SALT negotiations.

Some say that a new Tordesillas "line of Demarcation" has already been projected for tomorrow's world, to run, probably between Moscow's India and Peking's Pakistan, the way the old line ran between Spain's America and Portugal's Brazil. In 1493, the issue was how best to Christianize a vast new world; today, apparently, it turns on how a half-subverted Christendom can best be communized.

At any rate, on the strength of his spectacular Peking mission, the *New York Times* has hailed Kissinger as the "Inscrutable Occidental," with assurances that only an occidental of his special breed of inscrutability "could have slipped into mainland China, arranged a chat for President Nixon with Premier Chou En-lai and Chairman Mao Tse-tung, and kept it all secret."

Inscrutable is a good word for Poor Richard's Kissinger. Back in '67, it was he who managed to send two mysterious Frenchmen to Hanoi to "open clogged communications" between LBJ and Ho Chi Minh. The Frenchmen went briefed in depth "on what to say and what to look for in response." Now an American President is being sent to Red China; and he too will be well briefed. For, as Arthur Greenspan of the *Post* tells it: "When Richard Nixon goes to Peking, he will come with dozens of options clearly spelled out for him, all prepared by Kissinger and his staff of experts."

But Kissinger's inscrutability didn't really become a public concern till his appointment to take Walt Rostow's place was first announced in December 1968. At that time, newsmen wondered: Why has Nixon chosen another liberal; and why haven't the Goldwaters and *National Review* protested? An answer was sought in the apparent inscrutability of Kissinger's writings which—colleagues admit—mean one thing when carefully studied and quite another when read quickly for a general impression.

Adding to the image of inscrutability was Kissinger's reply when a *Time* cover-story writer asked him (Feb. 1969) about his ideological orientation and what he hoped to achieve as a Nixon advisor. Discussing ideology, he said cryptically: "If I were in 19th century Great Britain, I might be a Disraeli Conservative in domestic affairs, but not in foreign policy." Paraphrased, his own clarification read: "Disraeli was an unabashed imperialist. Kissinger, by contrast, believes that U. S. power must not be spread too thinly, especially in politically underdeveloped areas that Americans little understand." In retrospect, it is easy to see here a central guideline for the Nixon policies that have most dismayed right-wing supporters; for being a Disraelian on the home front means trying to beat liberals at their own game, with deficit spending, etc., while being a non-Disraelian in foreign policy means trying to escape sovereign responsibilities through unilateral disarmament, precipitous negotiations, and cowardly retreat in the face of a determined enemy.

Discussing ultimate goals, Kissinger had waxed philosophic with the *Time* reporter. "Nothing is more difficult for Americans to understand," he said, "than the possibility of tragedy." One lesson he particularly wanted to teach Americans was, therefore, that "great states disintegrate, and so can theirs."

Kissinger has been trying hard to teach us that lesson. And, judging from the President's speech of July 6, 1971 (delivered in Kansas City, Mo., while Kissinger was en route to Peking), he has found at least one apt pupil. In that speech, Nixon despaired publicly of this nation's capacity to keep from disintegrating, the way ancient Rome disintegrated. On his return, Kissinger stressed that Chou En-lai had shown great interest in that speech, and that an English text was used, for accuracy, while Chou subjected him to "very intelligent questioning" about its meaning.

Chou En-lai is, of course, a veteran of fifty years' service in the communist drive to overwhelm the security of the Western nations, and particularly of the United States. He must have thought it fascinating, if not inscrutable, that Kissinger himself–central coordinator of our national security intelligence–should have come in person to arrange a "chat" for Nixon with the Red Chinese leaders. But, as Edgar Snow reports in *Life,* those Red Leaders were most eager to meet with our top security man. "Kissinger?" one of them reportedly said. "There is a man who knows the language of both worlds–his and ours. With him, it should be possible to talk."

What Chou and Kissinger talked about–whether they touched at all on the pros and cons of our security, for instance–remains concealed from us, as also from the governments of our anti-communist Asian friends. But since those talks, there has been no concealing the fact that, here in America, "the liberals," as William Buckley has summed it up, "are jumping for joy." Through reiteration in the news media, the feeling has become contagious. And yet, when liberals jump for joy, the very least a Buckley conservative can do is to think twice before jumping in with them.

Bill Buckley hasn't rejoiced with the liberals. In his *New York Post* column of July 20, 1971, he asked bitterly: "One wonders, what did Chou En-lai say to Henry Kissinger? . . . Did he say that, what the hell, we could keep Formosa?" And his ironic reply—"Perhaps someday Dan Ellsberg will tell us"—passed beyond bitterness to the edge of rage. Those words are, to my knowledge, Buckley's first criticism of Kissinger. And from their mood, it must have been but a short step to the "Declaration" of July 26, 1971, in which he and eleven conservative colleagues (including other editors of *National Review*) resolved to suspend support of Nixon's policies.

That wasn't an easy move, least of all for Bill Buckley, who has had an almost quixotic sense of loyalty toward the old prosecutor of Alger Hiss. Till now, it has seemed that, so long as Nixon could get himself despised and distrusted by even one prominent liberal, the myth of his "indelible conservatism" would hold. Regardless of policy, Buckley conservatives would rush to his defense—*noblesse oblige*. And a grateful Nixon has usually responded in kind, with assurances that he much prefers conservative loyalty to the "contempt" and "distrust" of liberals who, it seems, will never be satisfied, no matter how much the Administration does for them.

If the myth of Nixon's indelible conservatism has been broken, that's welcome news. Still, as it stands, Buckley's suspension of support misses the mark. It demands too much of Poor Richard in deliberately ignoring the fact that, so long as he remains in the tutelage of the inscrutable Henry Kissinger, he cannot really be held accountable, in a personal sense, for his deeds in office. The *National Review* editors and their conservative colleagues elsewhere know this. It explains why their July 26 Declaration is hedged with reaffirmations of personal respect and affection for the man, and why it ends with these poignant words: "We consider that our defection is an act of loyalty to the Nixon we supported in 1968."

Nothing Nixon can do will ever free him from the contempt and distrust of the liberal establishment, for that establishment knows that Kissinger, not Nixon, is "the one." Conservatives like James J. Kilpatrick complain that Nixon "has jettisoned his charts and compass of 1968–tossed them over the rail–and is now steering by the seat of his pants." But, in fact, the man at the helm has all along been Kissinger, not Nixon. And Kissinger has kept on a steady course, with charts carefully plotted through long years of service as top brain of the internationalist wing of the Republican Party, as also of the Council on Foreign Relations and the Rockefeller Brothers Foundation.

With Kissinger constantly at his side, Nixon has indeed changed; but only to become an imitation of what Kissinger has long been: a half-measure Disraelian internationalist, skilled at giving pseudo-conservative excuses for moves which, when linked together, will lead the nation irreversibly down a suicidal course, toward a cosmopolitan new world order situated, as Kissinger likes to say, somewhere "beyond the nation-state."

Overwhelmed by what the *Times* has called the "sheer power" of Kissinger's intellect, Poor Richard Nixon has been taken in and made to feel self-righteous about it. But, unhappily for America, long before Poor Richard was taken in, the editors of *National Review* appear to have suffered the same fate.

And there's the crux of this whole inscrutable business. Nixon and Kissinger met for the first time during the campaign of '68. In a normal course of events, Nelson Rockefeller ought to have made the introductions. Nixon had been unabashedly a compromise candidate. Rockefeller could therefore have presented Kissinger to him as the price the moderate and conservative Republicans would have to pay, if the liberal internationalists were not to withhold their support, as they had in '64.

But it didn't work out that way. Instead of coming to Nixon as Rockefeller's man, under unmistakable internationalist-liberal auspices, Kissinger managed somehow to come to him with a personal introduction, glowing endorsements, and a chorus of blessings from the editors of *National Review*. How he did it was, in its way, a more remarkable more inscrutable feat than even his spectacular mission to Peking, which has so dismayed the conservatives. For the hard truth is that Kissinger could never have gotten to Peking, if the Buckley conservatives hadn't opened a way for him into the deepest recesses of Nixon's confidence.

The same liberals who are now jumping for joy over Kissinger's Peking escapade had also jumped for joy when the news first broke that their long-time friend and academic colleague had been appointed by Nixon to serve as chief presidential advisor for national security affairs. That was on December 2, 1968. Dozens of leading liberal internationalists were questioned about it, and they all responded with mixed surprise and delight. Arthur Schlesinger was explicit enough when he said: "I think it's an excellent appointment. . . . Henry asked my advice several weeks ago and I urged him to accept." And Adam Yarmolinsky expressed the feeling of scores of colleagues when he said: "I sleep better with Henry Kissinger in Washington."

At that time, in liberal intellectual circles, there was not the slightest doubt about Kissinger's past or ideological bent. He was Rockefeller's man, unmistakably a man of the liberal internationalist left. But then came the December 17 issue of *National Review*, and all was suddenly changed. In a brief but emphatic editorial, the leading journal of conservative opinion dismissed the unanimity of liberal approval of Kissinger's appointment as irrelevant, remarking: "Let us leave it that Mr. Kissinger is a practiced diplomat, a finished scholar, a member of the faculty of the country's senior university, that he has stood at the right hand of Nelson Rockefeller; so that the profile is almost universally pleasing." But then came this extraordinary commendation, hinting at some privileged new insight:

> *Mr. Kissinger is . . . unusual, and we choose to believe that it is this in him which above all commended him to the attention of Mr. Nixon: he is a realist, a patriot, he sees a problem whole, is sometimes maybe a little dreamy on disarmament matters—but one cannot walk away from any of his books or articles, or know something about his contributions to American strategic thinking, and be less than grateful for his appointment, and confident that he will render great service.*

That editorial dismayed me. In its cryptic phrases the scrutable had suddenly become inscrutable. Kissinger was thereafter to be a man of puzzling ambiguities who could manage to wink knowingly at a Buckley while giving Arthur Schlesinger a confidential squeeze on the arm. I had read all his writings. He was unmistakably an anti-nationalist. My book *War, Peace, and the Presidency* had just been published, and, while the focus there is on Rostow's anti-nationalism, I knew that Kissinger shared Rostow's notion that it had become a "legitimate American national objective" in the nuclear age "to see an end to nationhood as it has been historically defined." His accession to Rostow's post could mean, in my judgment, only that the old Harvard-MIT anti-nationalist bias would continue to guide presidential thinking—with the added weight, this time, of having been endorsed by *National Review*.

But that was long ago. Since then, Bill Buckley and I have had a sometimes strenuous, but always friendly tug of war on the subject.

My judgment has been and is that Kissinger has abused Buckley's friendship to give himself conservative credentials with Nixon which he could not otherwise have acquired. Buckley has now criticized Kissinger for the first time. I therefore presume to ask him publicly to make a full break, and thereby start the laborious process of freeing our President from Kissinger's inscrutable guidance. It may be that, once the incubus is lifted, Nixon may again show himself to be (in Bill Buckley's phrase) "one of us."

6. CONCLUSION

In the final weeks of 1971, Walter Lippmann came out of his semiretirement to rejoice publicly over the Kissinger feat which had brought Red China into the UN, kicked Nationalist China out, and gladdened the hearts of anti-Americans all over the world.

Like Moses dancing before the Ark of the Covenant, the old liberal journalist explained to a host of admirers how the thing could only have been done with a man like Nixon in the White House. "The theory when I was young," he said "was that you always got Conservatives to do the liberal things and liberals to do the conservative things. In Nixon's case it's very dramatic because he was such a violent, unscrupulous anti-communist. . . . The reason there has been no outcry about the reversal is that it was made under the auspices of a certified anticommunist like Nixon."

Ignoring Nixon as a mere front-man, John Kenneth Galbraith has thrown a party in honor of Kissinger at Harvard. In a more practical spirit, but equally confident that Kissinger has scored a touchdown for the internationalist cabala, I. F. Stone has sold his lucrative leftist newsletter to the *New York Review of Books* and hung up his gloves for the season. Even James Reston has put down his guard long enough to call for prayers of thanksgiving. "Pray silence, then," he wrote on November 30, 1971, "for the bold professor. . . . He has played a valiant role in private for the President, and nothing proves it more than his deft handling of the difficult opening to China."

But we must not imagine that the cat is now forever out of the bag, that Kissinger must hereafter stand exposed for what he really is, and has always been. After the Pentagon papers scandal, we would be naive to imagine any such thing. Publication of those papers by the liberal press served to "prove," as we all know, that the Bundy-Rostow-McNamara conspiracy of doves was somehow "really" a conspiracy of hawks. And so now, to "prove" the same about Kissinger, we have the Jack Anderson "revelations."

Only a Jack Anderson, long schooled in Drew Pearson's art of journalistic duplicity, could have been expected to handle so complex a propaganda assignment. Now that the United States has been committed to give up in Asia, to force West Germany into the world communist embrace, to bolster the Soviet Economy with a $6 billion "loan," and to "negotiate" its own unilateral disarmament at secret SALT and Pugwash conferences, the time fast approaches when Kissinger will have to head for cover. It becomes urgent, therefore, to arrange for his going out like a "hawk," like a foreign-policy hard-liner, who schemed in secret to accomplish conservative ends, and failed only because the wave of the internationalist future and the righteousness of the antinationalist cause at home and abroad have proved irresistible, etc., etc.

Anderson boasts that, if he revealed how he got his anti-Kissinger top-secret National Security documents, it would embarrass the White House more than the publication of them. I hold, instead, that Kissinger wouldn't be in the least embarrassed any more than he was embarrassed by publication of *The Pentagon Papers,* which he himself had helped to compile.

Leftist hatchetman Anderson cries, "Down with Kissinger." But it is a case of *cui bono.* Conservatives who ought to have raised the roof long ago for Kissinger's dismissal are confounded into silence. If Kissinger weren't on our side, they reason, why would Anderson attack him?

The ruse has obviously worked. The liberal press has poured out thousands of articles on Kissinger in recent weeks, pre-empting almost every possible position, pro or con. The editors of *National Review,* on the contrary, have kept their lips shamelessly sealed, as if struck dumb by the wheels within wheels of such brilliant cosmopolitan pyrotechnics.

But our supermarkets are still overflowing with goodies, and we can all, by one means or another, still get our hands on money to indulge our vices. And so we endure the shame of it. We see American officers on our TV screens in their North Vietnamese captivity poked in the ribs to make them walk, and tucked under the chin, like animals, to make them show their faces, and there is no outcry. We stare impotently. We turn the dial to catch a glimpse of the same incredible sight on another channel.

Acting more and more like an imitation of himself, the Commander in Chief of our armed forces continues to run for re-election as a middle-of-the-road Republican. Party stalwart Barry Goldwater continues to back the boss on the assumption that in election campaigns there can be no substitute for a Republican Party victory, no matter what. It is conceivable that, after the primaries, Nixon may tour the country campaigning with one arm wrapped around Ashbrook and the other around McCloskey, even as he simultaneously embraced Goldwater and Rockefeller in '68, to rout the awful Democrats.

Blinking behind his horn-rimmed glasses, the inscrutable Henry Kissinger, or the "bold professor," as Reston called him—observes it all. He knows that there is a powder-keg of latent popular resentment in this country, which may suddenly blow up, sending him and his anti-nationalist colleagues to a much merited hell of everlasting nuclear fission, if not of mere "fire burning with brimstone." But there is no turning back for him at this late date. Having conned the editors of *National Review*, he must count on their intellectual vanity, at least, to hold back the wrath of the American right-wing.

Kissinger to-date has had only superficial acquaintance with such wrath. After his first secret talks with Chou En-lai, he told reporters: "I have received many amazing letters. It has been my first real exposure to right-wing extremists. They sound very much like the left-wing extremists, only their vocabulary is not so good."

It is much too late, of course, for America to be saved by good or bad vocabularies. We have been backed into a national-security corner from which we cannot escape without bloody recriminations. National redemption will come hard. We must learn to pray, as President Lincoln prayed, for God-fearing strength to do the awful deeds that may have to be done to defend our national integrity against the contemporary anti-nationalist challenge.

It is worse for us today than it was for Lincoln on the eve of the Civil War. Patriotism was then still a living force in the schools, pulpits, and local governments of both the North and South. Today, on the contrary, a thoroughly alien-minded intelligentsia, contemptuous of country, has saturated our schools, pulpits, and local governments with its anti-nationalist ideology. And it has placed its Rostows and Kissingers in places of incalculable power.

Still, if we act, as patriots, not with malice, but "with firmness in the right as God gives us to see the right," and if we pledge ourselves, in that spirit, to "strive on to finish the work we are in," God may yet answer our prayers.

NOTE TO THE ORIGINAL EDITION (1980)

Most of the chapters included here were originally published in Henry Paolucci's monthly political newsletter, *State of the Nation*. Chapter 7 ("Introduction The Kissinger Legacy"), Chapter 13 ("Kissinger's War: A Revisionist Perspective"), and Chapter 15 ("From Kant to Kissinger and Brzezinski") derive from papers originally presented at the 1978 and 1979 annual meetings of the American Political Science Association (APSA).

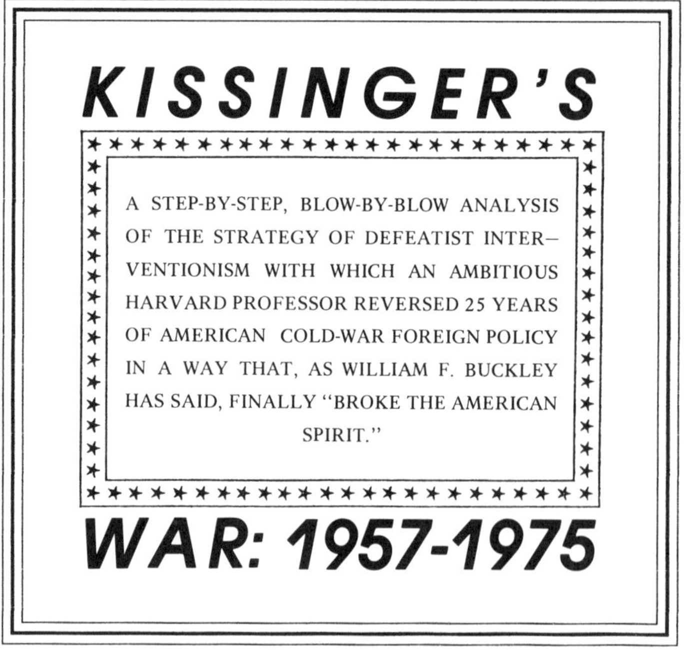

(From the cover of the original edition of
***Kissinger's War: 1957 – 1975* (1980)**

7. INTRODUCTION: THE KISSINGER LEGACY

> *"The war in Vietnam was, in a sense, a theorists' war* par excellence. *The strategists of the late nineteen fifties were only slightly interested in the question of which country or countries might be the scene of a limited war . . . Kissinger had warned in his 1957 book that the policy he was proposing would require 'a public opinion which had been educated to the realities of the nuclear age.' . . . One might say that the plan was to pay for nuclear peace with limited war . . . and that it was in the very nature of the doctrine that it had to be presented misleadingly to the public and the world. For to explain the policy fully would be to undermine it."*
>
> JONATHAN SCHELL, *THE TIME OF ILLUSION* (NEW YORK, 1976)

Kissinger's war began as a theorist's war with the publication of *Nuclear Weapons and Foreign Policy* (New York, 1957), and it remained a theorist's war—a textbook war—until its author was appointed to the post of Special Assistant to the President for National Security Affairs by President-Elect Richard M. Nixon, on December 2, 1968.

After that, Henry A. Kissinger—young Harvard theorist and Rockefeller Brothers Foundation research-director—quickly found opportunities to turn theory into practice. He rose rapidly from the status of mere coordinator of National Security Council deliberations to that of chief White House military strategist and tactician for a very real war. Rising higher still, he had the extraordinary experience, as Secretary of State, of receiving in his very own hands a presidential letter of resignation, the first ever submitted in American history.

With the man who originally appointed him driven from office, Henry Kissinger went on to exercise a virtual monopoly in the conduct of America's side of a war which had already become for him an almost total fusion of theory and practice. That was the time of the Ford-Rockeller *interregnum*—a period of more than two years during which the top elective posts of the American Government, both the Presidency and the Vice Presidency, were occupied by non-elected appointees. Then it was that Secretary Kissinger, still holding his cards very close to his chest, maneuvered spectacularly to bring the war to a close.

The end came abruptly in April 1975, while the American Embassy in Saigon was in full operation. Henry Kissinger had decided not to "panic the natives" by signalling the precipitous and total flight of the American presence he had designed. Thus, American newsmen were on hand to photograph the efforts of many local clients of our Government to cling to the landing gear of the "last" American helicopters fleeing from the scene. Even so, it could not be said that the war had ended haphazardly. Certainly Henry Kissinger gave none of us the impression that as its supreme theorist and strategist, he had lost control of the war. On the contrary, those who knew his "theory" of limited war in the nuclear age, could see at once that he had obviously brought the thing to an end quite in accordance with the theoretic prescriptions of 1957, not the least of which was, in his own view, the following:

"A doctrine of limited war will have to discard any illusion about what can be achieved by means of it. Limited war is not a cheaper substitute for massive retaliation. On the contrary, it must be based on an awareness that with the end of our atomic monopoly it is no longer possible to impose unconditional surrender at an acceptable cost. . . . The argument that neither side will accept defeat, however limited, without utilizing every weapon in its arsenal is contradicted both by psychology and by experience. There would seem to be no sense in seeking to escape a limited defeat through bringing on the cataclysm of an all-out-war, particularly if all-out war threatens a calamity far transcending the penalties of losing a limited war. It simply does not follow that because one side stands to lose from a limited war it could gain from an all-out war." (1957 ed., pp. 123-124)

The War in Theory: Kissinger's Apprenticeship

In early January 1969, shortly after Kissinger's appointment to the office his Harvard-MIT colleagues McGeorge Bundy and Walt W. Rostow had held under Presidents Kennedy and Johnson, the Council on Foreign Relations published a second, abridged edition of *Nuclear Weapons and Foreign Policy*. Gordon Dean had written a publisher's foreword for the original edition and he here supplied a revision of the same in which he summed up the reasons for the "immediate and profound impact" the book had previously made "both here and abroad." A first reason, he said, was that it had "succeeded in articulating with great clarity the fears and reservations that many Americans had been feeling about certain of our postwar policies and failures–especially about our reliance on massive retaliation." Another was that "readers found in Dr. Kissinger a first-rate intelligence which had succeeded in cutting through many false assumptions and contradictions in our policies to propound a fresh conception." But, speaking for those who had originally employed young Henry Kissinger to write the book for them, Gordon Dean had not hesitated to conclude:

"Finally, the book carried added weight, perhaps, because it was the outgrowth of a study conducted by the Council on Foreign Relations, which called together a panel of exceptionally qualified individuals to explore all factors involved in the making and implementing of foreign policy in the nuclear age. Thus, although the book is the work of an individual, Dr. Kissinger had the benefit of the wisdom and experience of experts and men of affairs in all relevant fields, such as government, diplomacy, science, engineering, the military services, and weapons production."

The immediate impact of the book in 1957 had been to establish Henry Kissinger as the leading academic critic of the way President Eisenhower, with Richard M. Nixon as his Vice President and John Foster Dulles as his Secretary of State, had brought the Korean War to an end in 1953. Eisenhower had campaigned for the Presidency the year before on a pledge that he would quickly end the stalemate in Korea. Truman's administration had failed to convince the aggressors, "in advance," that their aggressions would not be a profitable operation; "a wholly new Administration" was required "to bring the Korean War to an early and honorable end," because the "old Administration cannot be expected to repair what it had failed to prevent."

After the July 27, 1953 Truce Treaty was signed, and he was asked "what it was that had brought the Communists into line," President Eisenhower had replied without equivocation: "Danger of an atomic war. We told them we could not hold it to a limited war any longer if the Communists welshed on a treaty of truce. They didn't want a full-scale war or an atomic attack. That kept them under some control."

At about the same time, in his "historic" address of January 12, 1954, before the Council on Foreign Relations, Secretary Dulles formulated the national security principle that had guided Eisenhower in terminating the Korean war. The containment policy inherited from the Truman administration, Dulles had said, remained in force; but with this difference: henceforth potential aggressors would have our assurances in advance that their aggression would backfire on them, that we would strike back to contain it, not necessarily on the spot, to their perceived advantage, but "at places and with means of our own choosing . . . reinforced by the further deterrent of massive-retaliatory power."

That was the Eisenhower-Dulles policy against which Kissinger had purportedly written his *Nuclear Weapons and Foreign Policy.* Between 1957 and the 1960 election, Nixon had often spoken in defense of what Kissinger criticized; and, as it became clear that Nixon would be the leading Republican presidential contender after Eisenhower, the Democratic contenders began to identify him with the massive retaliation policy and attack him for it. Professor Paul Peeters very ably documented the phenomenon at the time in *Massive Retaliation: The Policy and its Critics* (Chicago, 1959), where we read: "No author is more frequently quoted by critics of massive retaliation than Henry Kissinger, and none has bothered less about understanding what he criticizes. . . . If Senator Kennedy quotes Mr. Kissinger about our alleged 'Maginot-line reliance upon massive retaliation,' it is because, with Kissinger, he identifies massive retaliation with overwhelming air-atomic superiority, a misconception for which there is no excuse whatever."

Perhaps if the United States had been at war somewhere in 1960, as it had been in 1952 and would be in 1968, Richard Nixon might have won the Presidency that year. During John F. Kennedy's three years as President, at any rate, it was not the Eisenhower-Dulles strategy for handling limited wars but one very like Kissinger's— advanced and implemented by McGeorge Bundy, Walt Rostow, and Robert McNamara—that was operative. By then Henry Kissinger had in fact written a second important book on the subject, *The Necessity for Choice* (New York, 1960), refining his earlier doctrine. In 1957, he had argued that, in waging a limited war, a threat to use tactical nuclear weapons might be admissible, provided the enemy were assured that it would not lead to our employment of strategic nuclear arms, or other means of all-out war, simply to avoid limited defeat. In 1960, on the contrary, he argued that nuclear weapons of any kind, tactical or whatever, had no place at all in his refined doctrine of limited war. To be truly limited in his sense of the term, a war would have to be fought exclusively with conventional weapons, he explained, from beginning to end, since it would be virtually impossible to authorize our field commanders to use tactical nuclear weapons, and then expect them to pull back intentionally, and lose, if the enemy persisted in his resistance. Kissinger therefore argued in 1960 that no nuclear weapons, not even such as might have a force yield *less* than conventional weapons, should be in the possession of any American unit committed to combat in a limited war. Summing up his "reversal" on this position since 1957, Kissinger wrote:

"Some years ago this author advocated a nuclear strategy. It seemed then that the most effective deterrent to any substantial Communist aggression was the knowledge that the United States would employ nuclear weapons from the very outset. [That was, of course, the Eisenhower-Dulles view rejected by Kissinger; Kissinger's "nuclear strategy" proposed to go as far as to use the threat of tactical nuclear weapons, not "massive retaliation," as a last resort.] The need for forces capable of fighting limited nuclear war remains. However, several developments have caused a shift in the view about the relative emphasis to be given conventional forces as against nuclear forces. . . .

"To be sure, troops can be trained to use both nuclear and conventional weapons. They should be aware of the elementary forms of protection [!] against nuclear attack. But once committed to combat, the units actually engaged in military operations must choose one mode of warfare or the other. . . . If nuclear weapons become an integral part of the equipment of *every* unit, it will be next to impossible to keep a war conventional regardless of the intentions of both sides. Even if the plan is to employ nuclear weapons as a last resort (and "in a manner to minimize damage") this becomes empty when the responsibility of defining a last resort becomes too decentralized. A regimental or even a divisional commander should not be the judge. Lacking the over-all picture, he will always be tempted to utilize all weapons available to him. When he is hard-pressed, it would require superhuman discipline not to employ arms which he believes would solve his difficulties."

That was the Kissinger limited-war doctrine of 1960, which he further refined in several chapters of his *Troubled Partnership* (New York, 1965) and in his introduction to a book of "readings," titled *Problems in National Strategy,* published that same year. Basically, for all its apparent complexity, Kissinger's doctrine differed from the limited-war facets of the containment and massive retaliation policies in only one essential respect. As Acheson and Dulles defined them, limited wars were to be fought so as either to stop the aggressor on the spot or, by striking him elsewhere with means and at times of our own choosing, to compel his withdrawal to his starting point. Kissinger's limited war, on the other hand, was to be fought in such a way that, if the enemy refused to give up his local aggression, we could always be in a position to let our side lose—rather than threaten escalation as Eisenhower had done to end the Korean war.

President Kennedy's limited-war strategists, who later served President Johnson, fully accepted the Kissinger version of the limited war doctrine. Yet, as the subsequently published *The Pentagon Papers* prove, they never quite succeeded in getting their Presidents to accept the notion that, in Vietnam, losing might after all be preferable to winning. As late as March 17, 1968, just weeks before his announcement that he would not seek a second elective term, President Johnson pounded a lectern before a large audience to say: "Your President has come here to ask you people, and all other people of this nation to join us in a total effort to win the war. Make no mistake about it—I don't want any man in here to go home thinking otherwise—we are going to win!"

Those words of a beleaguered President—faced by a "dump Johnson" movement led by Allard Lowenstein and fully supported by the Eastern intelligentsia—had been rather a cry of defiance against what was for him an inexplicable yet determined effort within his own administration to drive him out of office by means of the war. And at the same time, the Republican Party strategists were predictably trying to take maximum political advantage of the intense opposition the incumbent Democratic President was facing in his own party. With that, we are plunged into the midst of the extraordinary presidential campaign of 1968, when Richard M. Nixon emerged from the political graveyard to gain the Republican nomination and win the November national election.

That he was preparing himself for a comeback, despite his narrow defeat for the Presidency in 1960 and his landslide loss by more than a million votes in the California gubernatorial race of 1962, the former Vice President had clearly signaled to attentive king-makers in 1966, right after the midterm congressional elections. The results in 1966 clearly presaged what the consequences of the internal Democratic party divisions might be for Johnson in 1968. In many parts of the country, anti-war Democratic liberals and Republican conservatives bent on defeating Democrats by hook or crook had joined forces to oust Democratic incumbents or defeat Democratic aspirants who openly supported "Johnson's war" in Vietnam. And Nixon did not blush at the time to indicate his availability as a candidate for high office ready to "serve" just such a coalition in 1969. Without mincing words he had said on November 11, 1966: "The peace party always wins. I know my party. If the war is going on in '68, there is no power on earth can keep them from trying to outbid the Democrats for the peace vote."

That Nixon statement was widely publicized. I.F. Stone's weekly

Washington Newsletter ran a banner headline on it, and then placed ads in the major newspapers, including the *New York Times* and *Washington Post,* calling attention to I.F. Stone's readiness to draft Nixon, if need be, as the Republican candidate to stop Johnson in 1968. Stone wrote: "Many of us will see a Republican victory again—as in 1952—as the only way to end an Asian war. The price will be the end of that progress on the home front which began under Kennedy and took on real momentum under Johnson before he made his error in February 1965, in the skies over North Vietnam. Even another interlude of social stagnation and lackluster leadership will not be too high a price to pay for peace if Johnson does not change course."

By the start of the 1968 campaign, Nixon was talking like Dulles and Eisenhower before the end of the Korean war. In one of his set speeches, he would typically identify the long-drawn-out Vietnam war as another "Democratic" war, like the Korean war, which could only be ended by a speedy return to the peace-strategy of General Eisenhower. "How do you bring a war to conclusion?" Nixon would ask rhetorically. "I'll tell you how Korea was ended. . . . Eisenhower let the word go out—let the word go out diplomatically—that he would not tolerate this ground war of attrition. And within a matter of months they negotiated."

It was candidate Nixon's way of saying that, while he would never have gotten us into the Vietnam war in the first place—fighting the enemy on his own terms on his own grounds—he would follow the example of his old commander-in-chief in getting us out. He would let the enemy know that he would not keep the war limited for their convenience, but would respond with means and at places and times of our own choosing—reinforced by the further deterrent of massive retaliation.

Nixon had apparently returned in principle to the Dulles doctrine against which Henry Kissinger had launched his *Nuclear Weapons and Foreign Policy* in 1957. Why would he then, just a few months later in 1968, turn to the author of that book to fill the post that McGeorge Bundy and Walt W. Rostow had held under Presidents Kennedy and Johnson? Coral Bell, in her highly sympathetic, pro-Kissinger study of *The Diplomacy of Detente: The Kissinger Era* (New York, 1977), put the question this way: "How did it happen that Mr. Nixon, who as vice-president seemed to out-Dulles Dulles in his readiness for war in the 1954 Vietnam crisis, and who held the angry 'Kitchen Debate' with Khrushchev in 1959, chose a National Security Advisor of Kissinger's well-known views ten years later?"

Professor Bell surmises that it was a case of opposites trying to "use" one another. At any rate, Nixon's seeming acceptance of Kissinger's "concept of detente," she writes, "may have been rather more a tactic than a strategy: that the cold warrior of Mr. Dulles's time was still lying in wait behind the artful web of Dr. Kissinger's detente diplomacy." But finally Kissinger got the upper hand. Nixon may well have intended to use Kissinger's concepts as a cover while preparing to follow the Dulles-Eisenhower strategy in the end. Yet, as Bell puts it, "in his final phase of weakness he had to accept them." And that provided Kissinger with the one thing he could never have supplied for his doctrine on its own, or with the help of his patron Nelson Rockefeller: a conservative, hard-line anti-Communist cover.

Nixon's "credentials as a tough-anti-Communist," Professor Bell concludes, "operated as a sort of protective coloration or camouflage for policies that would probably have raised great alarm and resistance on the Republican right and in 'Middle America' if they had been sponsored by a liberal Republican, like Rockefeller, and still more if they had been sought by a Democrat. Even the eventual necessity of accepting the departure of American troops from Vietnam without victory might have been almost an impeachment matter for a different kind of President."

BACK DOOR TO NIXON

Walter Lippmann had justified his active support of Nixon straight through the re-election campaign of 1972 on the grounds that only such a man could have made the Kissinger reversal of the Cold War a reality without a tremendous "Middle America" backlash. In his interview with Ronald Steel, his biographer, published on October 16, 1971, we read: "Only Nixon, among the available public men, could have made such a reversal. . . . The theory when I was young and just learning about politics was that you always got Conservatives to do the liberal things, and liberals to do the conservative things. In Nixon's case it's very dramatic because he was such a violent and unscrupulous anti-communist, but nevertheless it's in the correct order of political progress that it's happening."

In the end—in his weakness—President Nixon tried desperately to give his intellectual critics the impression that he had really been playing the Lippmann role quite intentionally, that he had started *right off* as President with the intention of managing a Disraelian turnabout in the American political party system. He said, finally, that he was a "Disraelian"; but that was only after his top Harvard domestic policy advisor "Pat" Moynihan had given him a biography of Disraeli to read. Kissinger, on the other hand, had said quite frankly to a *Time* cover-story reporter before he took office in January 1969: "If I were in nineteenth-century Great Britain, I might be a Disraeli conservative in domestic affairs but not in foreign policy." As paraphrased by the *Time* reporter, Kissinger's own clarification of that self-characterization reads: "Disraeli was an unabashed imperialist. Kissinger, by contrast, believes that U.S. power must not be spread too thinly, especially in politically underdeveloped areas that Americans little understand."

In those days, Kissinger's views were so well-known, as Professor Bell says, especially in the academy, that, to explain why President-elect Nixon might have turned to him, the *Time* cover-story reporter inserted this purposively ambiguous comment: "A superficial reading of some of his works makes him seem like a hawk, but intelligent doves regard him as Richard Nixon's most astute appointment." What could not have been anticipated in January 1969 or October 1971 (when Lippmann rejoiced in the Kissinger-Nixon association) was that Kissinger could conceivably survive without *Nixon as his cover*–so as to avoid the risk of a Nixon reversion before America's self-inflicted defeat in the Vietnam "limited war" could be presented to a confused public (which had given Nixon a conservative landslide victory in 1972) as a *fait accompli*.

Professor Coral Bell acknowledged (in the book from which we have already quoted) that "there were a good many riddles and ambiguities in the relationship between Mr. Nixon and Dr. Kissinger," and adds that there "will perhaps continue to be even after both men have written their memoirs." That is certainly true. President Nixon's memoirs, to be sure, only compound the riddles and ambiguities; for the ex-President seems eager now to claim Kissinger's national security and foreign policy "triumphs" as his very own–as against the charge that he had really functioned finally (with respect to what Lippmann took delight in) only as some far-fetched Trilby to Kissinger's Svengali. But Kissinger's memoirs are something else. He comes close to telling us, in the first chapter of *The White House Years,* that he used *no* Disraelian maneuver to get himself hired by Nixon. He comes close to telling us that he *did not use* a most authoritative *conservative* advocate to facilitate the passage from Rockefeller to Nixon in 1968.

In a subsection of the first chapter titled "Nelson Rockefeller," Kissinger tells us of his bitter disappointment over Rockefeller's repeated loss to the "Nixon forces" of the Republican Party, which took its final toll in 1968. "I attended the gallant press conference in which Rockefeller conceded to Nixon," he writes, "and I was sick at heart." A few sentences later, we are in a subsection titled "The Phone Call," where we read: "Some months after that depressing day—with Richard Nixon now President-elect—I was having lunch with Governor Rockefeller and a group of his advisers in New York City in his small apartment on the fourth floor of the Museum of Primitive Art. It was Friday, November 22, 1968. . . . In this splendid setting we were discussing what attitude Rockefeller should take toward a possible offer to join the Nixon cabinet and what Cabinet position he should seek if given a choice."

Kissinger observed that Nixon would "almost surely carry out his announced intention to act as his own Secretary of State," and therefore urged Rockefeller to aim for Secretary of Defense, in which post he would be able to "implement his decades-long interest in national security." Given the example of Robert McNamara, it was likely, too, Kissinger had added, that "the Secretary of Defense could play a major role in the design of foreign policy." And then it happened. "We were debating these considerations in a desultory fashion," writes Kissinger, "when we were interrupted by a telephone call from the office of the President-elect." Who but the President-elect would be putting in a call to that exquisitely decorated Rockefeller apartment "designed by the architect Wallace Harrison, who had also built Rockefeller Center"? Kissinger at this point lets his old patron down gently.

"It was a poignant reminder of Rockefeller's frustrating career in national politics," the ex-Harvard professor writes, "that the caller was Nixon's appointments secretary, Dwight Chapin, who was interrupting Rockefeller's strategy meeting to ask me—and not Rockefeller—to meet with his chief. In retrospect, it is clear that this phone call made our discussion pointless. But we returned to it as if nothing had happened. No one at the lunch could conceive that the purpose of the call could be to offer me a major position in the new Administration."

Obviously Rockefeller had not been pressing the President-elect to give his man Kissinger a major position in the new Administration. Had Kissinger himself, perhaps, made a back door bid on his own? Had he been expecting such a call, having told the appointments secretary's staff where he might be reached? "I did not know the President-elect," he writes. "My friend William F. Buckley, Jr., the conservative columnist, had told me for years that Nixon was underestimated by his critics, that he was more intelligent and sensitive than his opponents assumed. But I had no opportunity to form my own judgment until after the 1968 election." Acting for Rockefeller at the Republican National Convention in Miami, Kissinger had earlier that year met members of the Nixon campaign staff, but only to "make sure," as he says, that the Republican platform planks on Vietnam "took account of the hopes for a negotiated settlement." It had been the convention victors' small concession to the vanquished, he adds, "which we in the Rockefeller camp—with little enough to celebrate—welcomed as a moral victory."

Was that all the contact that preceded what Kissinger calls "The Phone Call"? No. There had been one more thing. Kissinger had agreed in a general way that both the Humphrey staff and the Nixon staff could get answers on specific questions in the area of his expertise, if they wished. But, in any event, he hastens to add, "only one question was ever put to me by the Nixon organization." And here comes the second and only other reference to William F. Buckley, Jr. in the Kissinger memoirs.

"Early in October 1968," Kissinger writes, "Bill Buckley introduced me to John Mitchell, then Nixon's campaign manager. Mitchell asked me if I thought the Johnson Administration would agree to a bombing halt in Vietnam in return for the opening of negotiations before the election. I replied that it seemed highly probable that the North Vietnamese wanted a bombing halt on these terms, and that they would seek to commit both candidates to it. Therefore I believed that Hanoi was likely to agree to it just before the election. I advised against making an issue of it. [To make an issue of it would have been in conflict with the Rockefeller platform plank on the "hopes for a negotiated settlement."] Mitchell checked that judgment with me once or twice more during the campaign. At one point he urged me to call a certain Mr. Haldeman if I ever received any hard information, and gave me a phone number. I never used it."

THE BUCKLEY "PASSPORT"

In his *United Nations Journal: A Delegate's Odyssey* (New York, 1974), William F. Buckley, Jr.—who shows himself on the back jacket-cover in a group picture, standing behind Secretary of State Kissinger on the day when they both inaugurated their State Department careers at the United Nations General Assembly, where Kissinger spoke and Buckley, with many other staff members, listened—tells us about his having "introduced Kissinger to John

Mitchell," or rather, to intermediaries who provided the actual service. At the Miami Republican Convention, before the nomination, Kissinger had tried to negotiate a deal with Buckley to rally conservative support for Rockefeller, in the event that Rockefeller won. In Buckley's words: "My responsibility, Kissinger urged, was to demonstrate to American conservatives that the country would be better off with Rockefeller as President, than with a Democratic President." Buckley's response was that Rockefeller could not conceivably win the nomination unless Goldwater supported him *in advance,* which he would never do.

Then came the October intervention to which Kissinger refers. Kissinger "asked to lunch with me," writes Buckley. "He had a few ideas he thought would be interesting to Nixon, in framing his foreign policy speeches. But these ideas he must advance discreetly, as he would not wish to appear, having just now left the dismantled Rockefeller staff, to be job-seeking." Buckley called Frank Shakespeare at the Nixon Headquarters and recited Kissinger's qualifications. Shakespeare called them to the attention of "Len Garment and John Mitchell, neither of whom," as Buckley puts it, "had heard Kissinger's name before. They were impressed . . . and said they would introduce him to Nixon, except that Nixon was out of town campaigning. Kissinger's drafts were cordially received."

Kissinger has told us of the results of his contacts with John Mitchell. But he has said nothing about his final drive to reach Nixon through Buckley. That occurred, Buckley tells us, in late November— no doubt shortly before that November 22, 1968 advisory lunch in Rockefeller's Museum of Primitive Art apartment. "I was lecturing in Los Angeles," Buckley tells us, "and was staying with friends in Pasadena"–which, by normal standards, would have made him relatively inaccessible. Yet "Kissinger reached me by phone." This time there was no talk of proceeding discreetly. As Buckley recalls, Kissinger was concerned by what might happen to the limited war in Vietnam during the final weeks of the lame-duck Johnson incumbency. "Nixon must be told," Kissinger had said, "that it is probably an objective of Clifford to depose Thieu before Nixon is inaugurated. Word should be gotten to Nixon that if Thieu meets the same fate as Diem, the word will go out to the nations of the world that it may be dangerous to be America's enemy, but to be America's friend is fatal."

That biblically-phrased petition of late November 1968 moved the editor of *National Review.* He now intervened decisively. "I telephoned New York," Buckley writes. "A personal meeting was set up between Kissinger and the President-elect, and a week or so later, my phone rang." The caller said: "You will never be able to say again that you have no contact inside the White House." Thus, it was not as "Rockefeller's man" but as "Buckley's man" that Kissinger received "The Phone Call" at Rockefeller's apartment from Nixon's appointments secretary, Dwight Chapin, asking him "–and not Rockefeller–to meet with his chief."

THE CLARK CLIFFORD CONNECTION

From the standpoint of national-security ideology, rather than that of sheer political ambition, it may be said that Kissinger's last-minute warning, sponsored by Buckley, about the possible collapse of the war in Vietnam before Nixon's inauguration represented a desperate effort on Kissinger's part to "save" his kind of war from being aborted before its "strategic" lessons had been fully learned by the American people. Clark Clifford, to whom Kissinger referred in his urgent late-November call to Buckley, had replaced Kissinger's friend Robert McNamara as Defense Secretary on March 1, 1968. Long before that, McNamara had begun to compile his long "white paper" on the war, later called *The Pentagon Papers*. He had called in Henry Kissinger himself, as *Time* magazine later reported, to structure the project. McNamara's replacement by Clifford signaled the start of an all-out drive to "win in Vietnam."

As he later explained in detail in his much-publicized *Foreign Affairs* article of July 1969, Clifford had taken office on March 1, 1968, "with one overriding immediate assignment–responding to the military request to strengthen our forces so that we might prosecute the war more forcefully." The military in the field had called for some 206,000 additional troops, beyond the 525,000 level already being maintained there. And Clifford was directed, as his "first assignment, to chair a task force named by the President to determine how this new requirement could be met. We were not instructed to assess the need for substantial increases in men and materiel; we were to devise the means by which they could be provided."

The military request had not been something out of the blue. The military had known from the beginning what it would cost to "contain aggression" in Vietnam, given the restraints imposed upon them by the post-1961 limited war doctrine, to which Kissinger had contributed so much theoretically. Kissinger had said, for instance, that "any limited war must have some sanctuary areas," and that the old concept of destroying "enemy communication and industrial centers" would have to be greatly modified, if limited wars were to be kept limited in his sense. As against the massive-retaliation of striking "at places of our own choosing," Kissinger had proposed that, in his kind of limited war, "each side could be required" to list the towns and industrial and transport-communications centers, as well as bases that were vital to its viability as a society, and those "would then be immune from attack."

The restrictions placed on the American fighting forces in Vietnam had been from the beginning–under President Kennedy–of that order; and the Diem regime had balked at them, till it was over-thrown in 1963, because comparable restraints certainly had not been and would not be imposed on Hanoi by Peking or Moscow. The combined American and Diem forces in the South had the charge of securing the integrity of South Vietnam without pursuing the enemy into his Laotian, Cambodian, and North Vietnamese sanctuaries ["the danger of misunderstanding is least," Kissinger had written, "if the sanctuary follows national boundaries"], without min-ing his harbors, and without destroying his great industrial stores or manufacturing centers. Had such political restraints not been im-posed, President Johnson's escalation of the troop level during 1965 would have resulted, no military man doubts, in a complete collapse of the enemy's war effort in the south before the year was over. As for functioning under those restraints, "sound estimates of the cost and requirements were available," Hanson Baldwin would later write in *Strategy for Tomorrow, "before* the first U. S. combat troops were committed in March, 1965. Both the Army Chief of Staff and the Marine Commandment are on record in the early months of 1965 as estimating that victory in Vietnam would require 500,000 to 800,000 men and take years of effort."

Were those estimates ever passed on to President Johnson by the defense establishment he had inherited from the Kennedy adminis-tration? Hanson Baldwin writes: "It is hard to believe that the President received those estimates." Had Johnson received them, Baldwin continues, it is inconceivable that he would have "an-nounced a major build-up of combat forces in Vietnam" in the sum-mer of 1965 only to let it be altogether undermined "by the nation's failure to mobilize its reserve forces." And he concludes: "The mili-tary had anticipated and prepared for mobilization; again it is diffi-cult to believe that the President fully understood the inevitable consequence of his failure to utilize rapidly and decisively the nation's might. Somewhere between the responsible heads of the armed forces in the Pentagon and the Commander in Chief commu-nications broke down or meanings were obscured."

In the late 1967 and early 1968, the estimates Hanson Baldwin speaks of finally reached President Johnson. As a direct consequence he asked Clark Clifford to replace McNamara and work out ways for finally bringing the troop level up to the figure the military had requested from the outset. But, as Clifford later put it in his *Foreign Affairs* account of what happened to him during his first weeks in office, despite his most strenuous efforts to get his inherited task force to "stay with the assignment of devising means to meet the military's requests, fundamental questions began to recur over and over." What followed in his retrospective account are several pages of the kind of arguments against escalation of a limited war to a force level to secure victory that Kissinger advanced in his *Nuclear Weapons and Foreign Policy* and in *The Necessity for Choice*.

Clifford finally lost patience. He had helped to draft the official text of the Acheson-Truman doctrine of containment. How, he wanted to know from his inherited experts, are we going to contain the enemy aggression, finally? And it is here that he gives us what is surely one of the most startling revelations in American national-security history. "When I asked for a presentation of the military plan for attaining victory in Vietnam," he writes, "I was told that there was no plan for victory in the historic American sense." What was the point then of having fought to this point? What was to be gained by further fighting? Clifford, as he made clear, despised the academic notion of war fought merely to "lengthen the step," as Kissinger had said, between the stark "alternatives of surrender or all-out war." He rejected flatly the Kissinger notion of wars which, while they gave our "native belligerency" an outlet for a while, could nevertheless be rigorously scaled down to serve the very limited aims "of obtaining a breathing space for negotiations and of bringing home to the opponents the risk of all-out war."

In Vietnam, obviously, the "breathing space" that Kissinger's kind of war provided had served to persuade only the American public at home—not our military men in the field, and least of all the North Vietnamese—of the risk of all-out war. Clifford was told that, instead of any plan to defeat the enemy in any sense, the idea was to keep the present level of resistance constant in the hope that the enemy "would find it inadvisable to go on." Clifford then asked: "Does anyone see any diminution in the will of the enemy?" The consensus in that task force inherited from the Kennedy days was that "there appeared to be no diminution in the will of the enemy" and that, on the contrary, it was the great mass of Americans that was tiring of the war. That was the turning point for Clifford. "After those exhausting days," he then says, "I was convinced that the military course we were pursuing was not only endless, but hopeless." He had started with overriding the immediate assignment of strengthening our forces so that we might prosecute the war more forcefully; he had learned after a few days that the war had been architected during the Kennedy years on the Kissinger model so as to preclude so much as a plan for victory in the historic American sense; and so, he had quickly concluded, the time had come "to disengage."

Had Clifford been converted from hawk to dove? No. Rather, he had seen at once that the Vietnam war had been structured as a war we allegedly "could afford to lose," so as to "educate" us as a nation to the futility of the containment and massive-retaliation varieties of war which specified no fail-safe force levels of American local resistance. Eisenhower had threatened to generalize the war in Korea in order to contain the aggressor. If that was really out of the question in Vietnam, then the best thing, Clifford concluded, is to end the killing as quickly as possible, write the war off as a mistake, and gird ourselves to fight a proper kind of war in the proper place.

That is the advice Clifford gave President Johnson late in March 1968, and Johnson did not know what to make of it. He had hoped Clifford would say: Let's supply the troops requested; let's escalate to win. Pulling out would sound like surrendering! And his Harvard-MIT advisers who shared Kissinger's view of the utility of *some* fighting as a fail-safe alternative to starker choices agreed. Johnson was advised not to escalate to victory and not to pull out. And that was the *status quo* national-security policy he bequeathed to his Republican successor. The Kissinger-style limited war was thus destined to survive the collapse of the Johnson Presidency.

Johnson seemed to hope, during the nine months after his decision not to seek re-election, that his successor would be a tough Republican who would "clean the rascals out" of the national security and defense department establishments. But his successor had, before his inauguration as President, heeded the advice of the man who had come to him so highly recommended by "America's leading conservative journalist," if not by its leading capitalist-liberal Republican politician. With Henry Kissinger by his side at the Hotel Pierre in the weeks just prior to his inaugural address, Richard Nixon soon found himself maneuvered into saving Kissinger's war for Kissinger himself to handle in its long drawn-out final phase. That war, as we know, was then destined to end not like the Korean war, with our client-state's territory cleared of the enemy, but in a quite opposite fashion. And the end, as we saw it on TV in April 1975, came only after 26,000 additional American soldiers had died, after 200,000 more had been wounded, and after the spirit of the American people back home had been broken. We say nothing here of the price paid by the Vietnamese.

Nixon's Inaugural: The Pledge to Negotiate

According to Raymond Price, principal writer of Nixon's inaugural address, the sentence in that address which Henry Kissinger particularly urged on the President-elect was the one that reads: "After a period of confrontation, we are now entering a period of negotiation." Kissinger had submitted a three-page draft of what he titled his "Proposed Foreign-Policy Section of Your Inaugural Address." His cover-memo made clear that his overriding concern was that some statement of commitment to the Rockefeller plank of the Party Platform—the plank on the hope of a negotiated settlement in Vietnam—be included. "Some version of the underlined sentences on page three," he had written, "should be in for the reasons we have discussed. I shall be happy to explain the grounds for the other passages."

Raymond Price writes of this in *With Nixon* (New York, 1977), where he is at pains to indicate just what influence Kissinger had been able to exert on the Nixon administration even before actually assuming office. "In passing the Kissinger material along" to Price, as principal speech writer, "Nixon explained to me," Price writes, "that [the underlined sentences in Kissinger's draft] had been worked out with Soviet representatives as a public signal to confirm private indications he had given that he really did want an 'era of negotiation.' But that—or some version of it—was the only part of the Kissinger material that was sacrosanct." In Kissinger's draft, the underlined sacrosanct sentences read: "To those who, for most of the post-war period, have opposed and, occasionally, threatened us, I repeat what I have said already: let the coming years be a time of negotiation rather than confrontation. During this administration the lines of communication will always be open."

That was the tiny seed out of which the great tree of the "detente reversal" of twenty-five years of American cold-war policy was to grow. The lines of communication between the White House and the Kremlin were to become so open during the Nixon-Kissinger years that the continuing war in Vietnam took on an aspect altogether unprecedented in military history. Between 1969 and 1975, the

United States transformed its war effort in Vietnam into what has been aptly characterized as "one of the most savage retreats in modern history." Kissinger wanted the retreat, to be sure; but he wanted it to be savage, as he repeatedly said, to prevent a "Middle America" backlash on the home front. That was the cover for all-out detente with Moscow.

In *The Time of Illusion* (New York, 1976)–a remarkably impartial book to be discussed at length later in these pages–Jonathan Schell (a journalist of impeccable liberal-intellectual credentials) says at one point: "If the President was going to risk American credibility by withdrawing from the war . . . it would have to be accompanied by many awesome displays of unimpaired resolve." Displays, he specifies, "such as the invasion of Cambodia" when half our troops were out, "the mining of the ports of North Vietnam" when almost all our troops were out, and later, "the carpet-bombing of North Vietnam in the Christmas season of 1972" when the so-called peace accords, or terms of only lightly-disguised American surrender, were about to be initialed by Kissinger and Le Duc Tho in Paris.

All that while, Kissinger was pursuing Soviet-American detente, the crowning moment of which was the Moscow Summit meeting of May 1972. General John D. Lavelle, commander of all U.S. air operations in Southeast Asia had just been relieved of his command and stripped of two of his four stars for having conducted "unauthorized" strikes against staging areas for mass invasions from the North which Kissinger's strategy had declared to be "immune from American attack" while detente negotiations were going on with Moscow. Jonathan Schell thus represents the apparent paradox for us: "For a moment, as President Nixon proclaimed that 'America's flag flies over the ancient Kremlin fortress' while Americans were dying in Southeast Asia in an attempt to counter the Kremlin's influence, the fighting in Vietnam came to look like something without precedent in military history: a war in which generals on the opposing sides combined into a joint command."

Mr. Schell, it appears, had read Kissinger's theoretic accounts of how limited wars ought to be fought in the nuclear age only after the Vietnam war had taken its full toll at home as well as abroad. Thus he could say: "In the framework of Kissinger's thinking, it made perfect sense to move toward the summit, and so toward peace, in the sphere of direct relations with the Soviet Union, while simultaneously moving toward . . . intensified war in the sphere of Vietnam." In *Nuclear Weapons and Foreign Policy* Kissinger had argued that, since "the goal of war can no longer be military victory, strictly speaking, but the attainment of certain specific political conditions which are fully understood by the opponent . . . it will be necessary to give up the notion that direct diplomatic contact ceases when military operations begin. Rather, direct contact will be more than ever necessary to ensure that both sides possess the correct information about the consequences of expanding a war. . . . If our military staffs could become clear about a doctrine of limited war, we could then use the disarmament negotiations to seek a measure of acceptance of it by the other side."

With even greater frankness he had added elsewhere in the same 1957 volume: "A limited war can remain limited only if at some point one of the protagonists prefers a limited defeat to an additional expenditure of resources or if both sides are willing to settle for a stalemate in preference to an assumption of increased risk." Such are indeed the matters to be discussed by cold-war adversaries in the nuclear age when their leaders meet in summit conferences. Kissinger made that one of the central arguments of his 1960 volume *The Necessity for Choice*. His kind of limited war, as contrasted with the open-ended varieties of limited war comprehended in the massive retaliation and containment policies, he wrote in 1960, "is based on a tacit bargain not to exceed certain restraints. One side's desire to keep the war limited is of no avail unless the other cooperates: it takes two to keep a limited war limited. . . . It is often argued that, if both sides could agree on anything as complicated as limited war, they would probably agree on keeping the peace in the first place. But this is essentially a debating point. . . . Limited war is not a substitute for constructive policy. It does offer the possibility—not the certainty—of avoiding catastrophe."

Kissinger there reminds his readers that "if we reject the concept of limited war," as he defines it, then "our only options will be surrender or all-out war." And "since surrender will not be our national policy," he adds, "it is important to get our choices straight. Limited war is palatable only when compared with even starker alternatives." But that, in his view, puts large demands on policy makers. If they are not to go astray, as Acheson and Dulles went astray, they must stand with him in the conviction that, to be certain of avoiding catastrophe in a limited war, we "must enter it prepared to negotiate and settle for something less than our traditional notion of complete victory."

It is not difficult to understand, after reading the passages just cited from his books, why Kissinger should have been so anxious to prevent a unilateral, unnegotiated American withdrawal from the fighting in Vietnam—such as Clark Clifford had urged on Johnson in

1968. From the standpoint of Kissinger's limited-war theory, the controlled fighting must be continued until the risks of escalation are sufficiently appreciated, at least by one side, to make it ready to accept defeat if the other side won't settle for a stalemate. Clifford's proposed unilateral retreat would have returned the United States to precisely where it had been in the very first stages of its involvement in Vietnam back in the mid-1950s. That fighting had to continue, according to Kissinger, until the Soviet American detente he had been negotiating was signed, sealed, and institutionalized; and then, with Soviet intervention, motivated by its desire to enjoy the advantages of detente, Hanoi would be forced to settle; or, if that couldn't be brought about even with Soviet intervention, then we would wisely settle, accepting limited defeat–in the spirit of Kissinger's *Necessity for Choice*–rather than risking the survival of mankind once more with another massive-retaliation threat, like that of Eisenhower in 1953.

What Price Kissinger?

But how exactly did Henry Kissinger's ascendancy over Richard Nixon starting in January 1969 actually affect the conduct of our limited war in Vietnam? General William C. Westmoreland, who commanded our forces in Vietnam from 1964 to 1968, and then continued in service as Army Chief of Staff through 1972, has suggested that it is a question warranting at least as much in-depth investigation by our Congress as the Watergate scandal and at least as much news media curiosity as was shown in the public exhibition and endless discussion of *The Pentagon Papers*. We know all about Nixon's doings in the White House with regard to almost all matters except those that fell under Kissinger's care. Has that been because of news media respect for the alleged "confidentialities of foreign relations"? Jonathan Schell reminds us of the absurdity of such a suggestion by drawing this contrast: "The underground record of the executive branch in foreign policy during the Kennedy and Johnson years was made known through publication of the Pentagon papers, but the underground record in foreign affairs of the Nixon Administration remains mostly undivulged."

That contrast is the theme of a later chapter in this book. Here we want to consider briefly General Westmoreland's complaint against the congressional and newsmedia persistence in trying to sweep the facts about a national disgrace of the proportions of our conduct of the war in Vietnam–especially since 1969–under a rug, as he put it.

As an interested party, even, in some measure, as a responsible party, General Westmoreland has called our government's "handling of the Vietnam episode," especially since the Tet offensive of 1968, "a shameful national blunder." In an article dated March 26, 1978, Westmoreland acknowledges that military intervention in Vietnam had been from the very beginning a blunder from the military stand-point. The military had told their commander-in-chief exactly that, at the very start–though, in keeping with their oath, they responded loyally to White House orders. But what added national *shame* to the blunder, in his view, was what happened after 1968, which is to say, after Henry Kissinger entered the White House with Richard Nixon.

Bad as things were, down through 1968, President Johnson at least had not contemplated subjecting our troops to a slow withdraw-al, punctuated by virtually meaningless military ventures that could serve no real military purpose when most of our troops had already been withdrawn. That came with Kissinger in 1969 when, in the General's words, "the United States resorted to a withdrawal strate-gy, and omitted any demand for a *quid pro quo* from Hanoi." That made a shameful end to the war inevitable. And he concludes: "Our country, once an honorable ally, had betrayed and deserted the Republic of Vietnam after we had enticed it to our bosom. It was a shabby performance by the United States. That unhappy experience should not be swept under the rug and forgotten."

Is Henry Kissinger to remain *forever* immune from serious news-media and congressional scrutiny? It is inconceivable that any other public figure of such notoriety could have gotten away with blocking public access, in our day, to the records of "telephone conversations that Kissinger conducted from his White House and State De-partment offices," simply by removing them *illegally,* for safe-keep-ing, to "the late Nelson A. Rockefeller's estate in Pocantic Hills, N. Y. and later donating them to the Library of Congress under a deed that bars public access." The Supreme Court has ruled that, had the transcripts of the phone conversations not been removed illegally from the White House and the State Department offices, they would have been accessible, to be sure; but, the only public recourse now is for the White House and State Department to charge Kissinger with theft and get the courts to convict him and then order restoration. The whisper against that in public corridors and major editorial of-fices has been: Lese Majesty. Kissinger's connections apparently make him "too powerful to be hurt by public action."

But Kissinger's long-time friends are something else. Many of them fear that, with his Disraelian efforts to get himself another "conservative" presidential sponsor, he may be going too far. It is the fate of Disraelians out of office that what they say—no longer contradicted by their deeds—has to be taken literally. If Kissinger fails to push himself back into high office, his "cavorting like a hawk," his "playing tough," to ingratiate himself with right-wing Republicans is apt to ruin things he supported in the past with his Disraelian deeds. Some of his long-time friends have therefore been conducting pre-emptive strikes against him, and revealing "secrets" in the process, to secure a hold on him for the future.

Typical of this is the book *Uncertain Greatness: Henry Kissinger and American Foreign Policy* (New York, 1977), by Roger Morris. Roger Morris had been a member of Kissinger's innermost circle of aides during the first year and a half in the White House. At the time he wrote his book, he was director of humanitarian policy studies for the Carnegie Endowment for International Peace. His concern in the book is plainly to protect the cause of peace in the nuclear age, which Kissinger had so "ably served" in practice, from the consequences of his play-tough rhetoric to attract a new conservative Republican prospective presidential employer. He finds an opportunity to do that very typically in a passage where he explores the reasons for Alexander Haig's rapid rise in Kissinger's service from lowly staff-colonel to four-star general.

"Kissinger," Morris writes, "needed Haig to provide reassurance, as well as to act as a litmus test on the right in a government where Kissinger was unlikely to be attacked successfully from the left. For the most controversial policies Kissinger planned—initiatives in arms control and ending the war—he would be, he believed, most vulnerable to criticism. Haig the decorated combat veteran, the leathery soldier of stern opinions, would help clothe those actions. Jealous of the relationship as well as of Haig's power, Helmut Sormenfeldt would joke in acid terms that Kissinger the German-Jewish immigrant kept on Haig, the all-American colonel from Philadelphia, to testify at some imagined right-wing trial, if Henry went too far with detente."

But, as Professor Coral Bell has observed on another level of discourse, the "eventual necessity of accepting the departure of American troops from Vietnam without a victory"—the fail-safe ending to the war that Kissinger's limited war doctrine forced on the country— might indeed "have been an impeachment matter for a different kind of president." Impeachment proceedings were finally started against Nixon, but not for the "impeachment matters" to which Coral Bell refers.

The chapters that follow are a month-by-month account of the

Kissinger legacy. (The first was written in March 1975.) Kissinger's doctrine of limited war, as Jonathan Schell so aptly put it, was supposed to "provide the United States with an effective means of promoting its interests and ideals at levels of violence below the brink of nuclear war; instead, it provided the notorious quagmire in Vietnam into which the United States poured its energy and power uselessly for more than a decade . . . and precipitated a wave of disrespect for a particular President which resulted in his forced resignation from office." The consequences of Kissinger's theory of war as applied to Vietnam are here examined in detail in all their dramatic implications. The pattern that emerges is a grim account of the Kissinger strategy as it was carried into practice. I have traced the theoretic formulations of that position in *Who is Kissinger?* and in related articles, many of which were published on the *New York Times* "Op-Ed" page between 1971 and 1974. Here I have carried the examination into the final phase of the process: Kissinger's prolonged effort to keep a "fixed fight" in Vietnam fixed to the end, while gaining time to prepare the home front for what he has called the "much more difficult task of living in dignity when impotent."

8. THE DETENTE POWER-VACUUM

At Nuremberg, Nazi war leaders were charged with many crimes. But scheming with the enemy to fix the war's outcome the way criminal gamblers fix prize fights was not one of them. International war codes were often ruthlessly violated in vain efforts to ward off defeat; but always the Nazi forces, like the Viet Cong and North Vietnamese and our own zealous Calleys and Lavelles (not to mention Israeli and Arab zealots of recent Middle East wars), fought to win. Scheming not to win no matter how bravely one's soldiers fight is something relatively new in major power history. The civilian policy-planners who have staged our bloody Vietnam adventure on the pattern of a fixed fight are thus clearly not war criminals in the Nuremberg sense. Even with his latest plea for U.S. aid to prolong the no-win fighting a month or two, Kissinger hardly qualifies. What he has been patching together with his sham-war in Vietnam, his studiously bungled Interventions in the Pakistan-India, Greece-Turkey, Arab-Israeli conflicts, and his detentes with Peking and Moscow, is something sui generis. *Perhaps after the feared recriminations have come and gone, historians will conjure up an appropriate name for it.*

In his March 26, 1975 news conference on the failure of his Middle East diplomacy, Secretary of State Henry Kissinger prepared a way for eventual escape from personal responsibility by invoking his old theory of diplomatic linkage. Israel's apparent loss of confidence in American guarantees was due largely, he insisted, to its perception of congressional failure to support Kissinger initiatives elsewhere—particularly, as he specified, in Portugal, Greece, and Turkey, as well as in Southeast Asia.

As anticipated, congressional leaders hastened to reject Kissinger's suggestion of linkage between their attitudes on Vietnam and Israel's loss of confidence in his personalized diplomacy. Senator Birch Bayh called it a grossly self-serving argument unworthy of the Secretary; and he insisted further, before the TV cameras, that he, for one, had no intention now or in the future of treating Israeli interests the way the interests of incompetent and cowardly client-states in Asia have lately been treated.

Israel, with its tough elastic strength, is not likely to be inordinately alarmed, therefore, by this apparent breach in American executive and legislative branch relations. Kissinger's chiding is apt to elicit many more congressional assurances of support for Israel, backed by substantial appropriations; and his striking acknowledgment of the failure of unilateral American peace efforts will ease the way, finally, for Israelis to negotiate Israeli interests directly with the Soviet Union without serious risk of being accused of de Gaullist desertion of "Western solidarity."

We begin to glimpse here something of the real significance of these simultaneous failures of unilateral American military intervention in Vietnam and unilateral American diplomatic intervention in the Middle East. Both failures are a consequence not of last-minute cutoffs of aid to client-states or of local intransigence but of Kissinger's own grand design for detente at all costs with Peking and Moscow. The very logic of such detente requires eventual dissolution of anticommunist alliances everywhere and immediate abandonment of support to client-states that are not in a position to negotiate detentes of their own. In the early sixties, when the Bundys and Rostows were guiding us on a parallel course, General de Gaulle quickly grasped the logic of the situation. Rather than risk seeing his France offered up to Moscow by the Kennedy administration as a detente trade-off, he hastily withdrew her from the perils of client status and moved to negotiate directly with the communist powers.

Under President Johnson in the mid-sixties, it seemed for a time that de Gaulle's move had been premature. But then came that fateful March of 1968, on the Ides of which a presidential task-force headed by newly appointed Defense Secretary Clark Clifford refused, in effect, to implement a presidential order on how the Vietnam war was to be conducted. Rather than face up to the prospect of having to purge top advisors, President Johnson chose to pass the buck on to his successor—a choice he revealed on March 30, 1968, with a public confession of his incompetence to govern under the circumstances. Johnson's failure of nerve made possible the election of Richard Nixon and the start of the Kissinger-Watergate era, the detente policies of which, shrouded in secrecy at first, have long since amply justified de Gaulle's worst fears.

KISSINGER'S "DETENTE OR BUST" POLICY

In 1968, shortly before his appointment as Walt Rostow's successor, Henry Kissinger published an essay summering up the deficiencies of the Bundy-Rostow approach to detente and suggesting how such deficiencies might easily be supplied, through seemingly slight policy adjustments, under a new presidential administration. The essay comes to focus pointedly in its final pages on "why, in the past, every period of detente has proved stillborn." [*Agenda for the Nation,* K. Gordon, ed., New York, 1968, pp. 585-614]

Since 1917, there have been, Kissinger noted, "at least five periods of peaceful coexistence," each hailed by many in the West as signifying a "final change in Soviet purposes," only to be "ended abruptly with a new period of intransigence." While rejecting simplistic explanations, Kissinger's concern was nevertheless to underscore the mistakes of the West which, in his view, had virtually constrained the Soviets to exploit the advantages of running alternately hot and cold.

To illustrate his argument, Kissinger cited the mistaken response of most Westerners to the Soviet invasion of Czechoslovakia, which had just occurred. While the mood of outrage prevails, there is a tendency, he noted, "to focus on military implications or to speak of strengthening unity in the abstract. But if history is a guide, there will be a new Soviet peace offensive sooner or later. Thus, reflecting about the nature of detente seems most important while its achievement seems most problematical."

As Kissinger argues the case, America's chief mistake in all this has been to require too much of its adversaries and too little of its allies as prerequisites for genuine detente. For instance, popular American feeling as reflected in our statecraft tirelessly requires of our Soviet adversaries that they demonstrate an internal, "change of heart." That is a grave error, in Kissinger's judgment, since it merely tempts them to make sham professions of change, thereby postponing "the choice which they must make sooner or later: Whether to use detente as a device to lull the West or whether to move toward a resolution of outstanding differences." We have there a clear anticipation of Kissinger's current insistence on detente with no strings attached, despite pressures to lift Soviet restrictions on Zionist emigration.

With respect to our allies, the matching error has been, in Kissinger's view, a cold-war disposition to "pose false inconsistencies between allied unity and detente," when in fact "a true relaxation of tensions presupposes Western unity." There we have a foretaste of Kissinger's current insistence that nothing we may have to do to guarantee a Soviet-American detente could conceivably undermine any alliances worth maintaining in this nuclear age.

In office, behind the shield of Nixon's sham-conservatism, Kissinger moved quickly to introduce the seemingly slight policy adjustments that would insure success for future detente efforts. Hereafter, as the original Guam statement of the new strategy emphasized, our government would pursue peace by doing slightly less to gratify allies and slightly more to woo adversaries than it had formerly done. A definitive statement of principles for Kissinger's fail-safe pursuit of Soviet-American detente was reserved, however, for the first of the annual book-length "State of the' World" messages he drafted for Nixon, where we read: "Building a lasting peace requires a foreign policy guided by three basic principles: . . . *partnership . . . strength . . .* and *a willingness to negotiate.* [The] most fundamental interest of all nations lies in building the structure of peace. . . . This vision of peace built on partnership, strength, and willingness to negotiate is the unifying theme of this report."

The novelty here is the sandwiching of *strength* between *partnership* and *a willingness to negotiate,* omitting any principled declaration of *willingness to wage war* standing alone, if need be, as a free people's alternative, even in this nuclear age, to accepting a coward's peace imposed by alien masters. We need to ask: Would modern Israeli or Soviet or Red Chinese leaders fail to include a declaration of willingness to wage war (even when bereft of partners) in any serious statement of their principles of foreign policy?

Strength only in partnership and partnerships maintained only to sustain a willingness to negotiate is thus the sum and substance of Kissinger's foreign policy. The line is obviously direct from its principles to the current debacle in Southeast Asia, where partnerships and strength have been thoroughly consumed on the altar of a shameless willingness to negotiate to the point of unconditional surrender. It is no wonder therefore that old-time partnerships elsewhere in the world—from Thailand through the Middle East to Portugal—are rapidly unraveling, as one government after another rushes to the communist negotiating tables to settle for whatever sort of peace may still be possible, with or without a semblance of honor.

C. B. MARSHALL ON THE LOGIC OF DETENTE

Because of Nixon's feigned conservatism and the partisan acquiescence of many old Republican conservative leaders, Kissinger's pursuit of detente at all costs has gotten by with virtually no serious criticism from the right. His Jewish origin has no doubt been an added restraint, especially on criticism from the so-called respectable right of the Buckley-conservatives where fear of accusations of anti-semitism often rises to the level of paranoia. For an intelligent analysis of the errors and duplicities of the policy itself, as distinct from its author, we can do no better, therefore, than to assume the perspective of the Truman-era foreign policy planners who knew the limits of detente diplomacy even as (unlike the Old Nixon) they knew also the limits of responsible military action.

A man of that perspective, whose counsels on our sovereign national interests ought to be heeded today, is Charles Burton Marshall. He was a top Acheson advisor in the days when Portugal, Greece, Turkey, and the Islamic countries, as well as Israel, could count on our determination to contain communist aggression. Late in 1965, after the Bundys and Rostows had temporarily lost control of presidential decision-making and before Dr. Kissinger could have so much as dreamed of succeeding to Rostow's place under conservative auspices, Professor Marshall had very rigorously defined the logic of detente in terms obviously relevant today.

"From adversary relationships in international affairs to normal business dealings," Marshall wrote in his *Exercise of Sovereignty,* "is a great leap—one not to be accomplished by merely verbalizing. Of itself, the cited assertion of 'no reason why, with proper caution and much patience, we cannot arrive at agreements of this kind' does not bridge the gap. The past has shown manifold reasons. They are not susceptible of being overridden by declaration. As a central point of difficulty in the past, the purpose of the other side in the bargaining attempts has been to eliminate the basis from which to approach bargaining on this side. By logic, the likelihood of finding opportunity for mutual gains in such a circumstance is ruled out. The analogy to 'normal business transaction' is inapplicable. A more apt analogue would be that of a trading relationship between a gunsmith and a customer imbued with intentions of subsequently holding up the gunsmith."

Since the secretly negotiated Nixon trip to Peking (which marked the abrupt end of our communist-containment policy of 25 years standing), we have had no end of trading relationships on the pattern of Marshall's more apt analogue. Helmut Sonnenfeldt and Henry Kissinger have sat across a table from the masters of world communism to negotiate "deals" for the American people that have amounted quite literally to selling arms to a customer who intends to hold you up. Subsidized by vast direct U.S. Treasury credits (and, where needed, also by much vaster rotating private-bank credits), the Sonnenfeldt-Kissinger type deals have resulted in food shortages at home and in the sort of unemployment linked with skyrocketing inflation that usually plagues nations defeated in war. The communist powers, on the other hand, have come out of such deals with a vastly increased competence to topple pro-American governments not only militarily, as in Southeast Asia, but also politically, as in Portugal.

The Soviet Union, Marshall reminds us, is a special breed of political enterprise. It is ruled by a party of men "who reached power through conspiracy and, having achieved power, have not dared to risk their hold on it by resort to a valid procedure of consent. They have remained conspirators after becoming governors, combining the usages of conspiracy with the prerogatives of the state. Both at home and in the world at large, the conspiracy that walks like a state requires tension and conflict to maintain its grip. It uses in the service of this aim a political doctrine emphasizing the pattern of violence–class conflict, subversion," wars of national liberation, and so on.

What can be the object of American negotiations with the heads of a conspiracy that walks like a state, which is to say, with a state that does not hold itself to be a true state in the traditional sense? The sole rational object must be, as Solzhenitsyn so passionately and correctly advises, to get that conspiracy to give up the aims and usages that enabled its conspiratorial founders to seize power. Kissinger has insisted, on the contrary, that our object must be detente at all costs, regardless of the usages of conspiracy. For him, apparently, the prerogatives of statehood represent a greater threat to the "cause of peace" than the usages of conspiracy or of his own secretive brand of supranationalist Disraelian diplomacy. Professor Marshall thus helps to clarify this all-important point:

"If there is to be a relaxation of tensions otherwise than on terms of capitulation, it will be only in the inward sense: a reassertion of captaincy over our own spirits and resolving to live calmly in danger for a long time to come. . . . The problem is how to restore balance to our side, how to dispel the beguiling notion that negotiation of itself is a means of redressing dangers and achieving harmony of interest, rather than merely an avenue along which one may proceed to success, impasse, or catastrophe, depending on the ratios of will and resources between the adversary parties. To counter the surge of demand for negotiation under conditions of high disadvantage to our side it will be necessary to abandon the secondary and unattractive propositions that clutter up the American case and to concentrate on a few basic and sound propositions: a proper insistence on the baleful character of the adversary, the necessity of American interposition, in fact and not merely in promise, on the continent, and the indispensability of NATO."

In the parallel discussion of the logic of detente with Peking,

Marshall stresses how the "domestic needs and ambitions" of Mainland China "are intertwined with its world outlook and its historic goals. . . . Chineseness is intertwined with Marxism. The regime is at once dogmatically communist and unequivocally racist."

On the domestic side, the Red Chinese rulers have imposed a discipline geared ruthlessly, as Professor Marshall says, "to change the face of the land and to bring it by rigorous effort abreast of the industrialized countries of the West, in the shortest possible time." Balancing this domestic effort is an external drive "to reconstitute the Chinese family of nations—an historic expression representing a ring of protectorates ranging over Mongolia, Korea, Vietnam, Tibet, Bhutan, Burma, Malacca, Java, Luzon, and Ceylon. This purpose in turn intertwines with that of eliminating all western influence from Eastern Asia—especially United States influence, for the United States, as leader among nations opposing the march of communism and as helper and ally to those disposed to stand independent of Red China, has been singled out as a supreme enemy to be humiliated, isolated, and brought to defeat. . . . This in turn relates to an ambition to establish Chinese preeminence in the Communist collaboration which, in the regime's view, is destined by a dictate of historic laws for worldwide triumph."

Again we need to ask: What can be the object of serious American negotiation with such an imperialist racist regime whose founders, like their counterparts in Moscow, seized power on the strength of the conspiratorial usages of Marxist supranationalism? The obvious answer is that we must seek to induce them, or successors however distantly removed, to comport themselves responsibly, in the sovereign political sense, as representatives not of a conspiracy that walks like a state, but of a genuine state: a state which, like our own as projected in the Declaration of Independence, claims for itself only a separate and equal station among the powers of the earth, in a *systematized* juridical relationship of mutual recognition with all other such states.

Henry Kissinger's strategy for peace runs in precisely the opposite direction. The object of his sensationally publicized negotiations with Peking, as also of his lengthy policy-declarations on the subject, has been detente at all costs for the sake of peace at all costs. The Communist Chinese have responded accordingly with imperial contempt. The United States for which Kissinger is permitted to negotiate must certainly be a paper-tiger headed by supranationalist plutocrats who work secretly through lackeys to arrange plutocratic deals around the world, while their common soldiers by the tens of thousands (to say nothing of the soldiers of trustful client-states and allies) are left in the fields to bleed and die for nothing.

If we reversed our present supranationalist course and directed our negotiations toward getting Red China to assume the responsibilities as well as the prerogatives of sovereign statehood, what are the chances that we might succeed? "Time," writes Professor Marshall, "may work its changes on Communist China–perhaps for the worse but maybe for the better. We can best hope for the latter and be prepared to exploit whatever breaks come our way–in the meantime taking care to keep our guard up, not expecting too much, but taking care never to do too little." On the level of ultimate cultural differences, Marshall suggests that we would do well, realistically, to look for guidance not to our immediate past, but to "such historical processes as the long confrontation between Christendom and Islam."

We dwell here on this foreign policy perspective of C. B. Marshall because it is deeply rooted in the finest American political tradition, running back to the founding of the Republic. It can therefore help to guide us now as no supranationalist perspective, detached from living national traditions, conceivably can. When Kissinger speaks of the need for a "renewed sense of national purpose" to get us through this moment of global retreat so fraught with the threat of populist recriminations, he is, of course, prolonging the purposive ambiguities of the six and a half years of Disraelian double-talk through which he has already led us. Kissinger has given up on the nation-state system. His strategy is to purchase peace at all costs, and then to negotiate secretly, no doubt with moralizing pleas for "good will on both sides," in the hope of getting Peking and Moscow to give the world a more benign forced peace than Hitler might have been disposed to give it had his Nazi regime won the Second World War.

The Marshall perspective, which was also the basic Truman-Acheson perspective, had critics on the right, of course, as well as on the left. The image of the Old Nixon making a career of hard-line anti-communism at the expense of genuinely patriotic, responsible statesmen is not apt to be forgotten. Once in office, under Kissinger's tutelage and tempted by hints that the supranationalist educational establishment might one day celebrate him as the great peace-maker of the terminal years of our Republic, that Old Nixon soon proved how hollow his anti-communism bellowed from the housetops had really been. To the delight of the Lippmanns, Lerners, and Schlesingers (to name but a few), the hardliner completely reversed himself. It was a contemptible opportunistic reversal. And he has had to pay for it quite fittingly with total personal disgrace.

Henry Kissinger has been the sole survivor of the Nixon administration's Watergate debacle. That was possible because (despite William F. Buckley's enthusiastic endorsement) Kissinger was never really a part of that administration. When it sank, he floated off on his own. Now our entire nation seems threatened by a comparable total collapse. Will Kissinger again manage somehow to float away in safety?

We need to recall in this connection two highly relevant judgments Henry Kissinger pronounced long before he entered the White House with Nixon to set us on our present disastrous course. The first assessed for readers of his *A World Restored* the "success" of the linkage diplomacy of his nineteenth century counterpart and model: "As in Greek tragedy, the success of Clemens von Metternich made inevitable the ultimate collapse of the state he fought so long to preserve." The other judgment, from *The Necessity for Choice,* applies quite directly to our own American destiny, as Kissinger, with his vaunted "tragic sense of history," manifestly conceives it. Chiding radical colleagues who pressed for unilateral American disarmament, as against his own Disrealian recommendations for an indirect approach to the same end, Kissinger cautioned: "A nation which cannot be trusted when strong will hardly be able to deal with the much more difficult task of living in dignity when impotent."

Diplomatic success that makes political collapse inevitable; strength to facilitate our learning how to live in dignity when impotent. They are the notions that precisely sum up the cabaret-statesmanship of our Secretary of State.

Kissinger has survived the disaster of the first resignation of a President in American history; let us act in time to prevent his surviving the collapse of our state, which his past "successes" threaten to make inevitable. His supranationalism, aspiring to build a creative world order upon the ruins of a system of sovereign nation-states that has now become worldwide in scope, may be tolerable still in American university classrooms; but it has long since ceased to be tolerable, in terms of the exercise of, sovereignty, in top decision-making posts of our government.

9. OUR VIETNAM DEFEAT:
WHY THE SIX-YEAR DELAY?

Secretary of State Henry Kissinger has offered a two-fold excuse for the failure of his "peace-with-honor" Paris accords signed in January 1973. In the last weeks, while assuring us that honor was still salvageable, Dr. Kissinger blamed congressional recalcitrance in denying final pittances of aid that might have made a difference. And while our abandoned clients in Saigon were laying down their arms in unconditional surrender, he added a suggestion that the Watergate scandal, coming on the heels of the January 1973 accords, deprived the settlement terms of respected force on our side.

Yet to many of us it was obvious even before the Paris accords were signed that the Kissinger Vietnam peace plan was, on its own terms, an American surrender (see my June 30, 1972 OP-ED article, "The Thin Line: Settlement or Surrender"). The question then was: Why the long delay in negotiating a settlement so obviously favorable to Hanoi? When the accords were signed, former Under Secretary of the Air Force Townsend Hoopes, who favored a U.S. pullout, thus summed up the view from the sympathetic left: "The January 1973 accords achieved only what could have been achieved in 1968 or 1969: the withdrawal of American forces and the return of American prisoners. The cost of deferring this necessary but unspectacular achievement until 1973 was about $50 billion in additional direct war costs, at least 20,000 additional American combat deaths, and hundreds of thousands of Vietnamese, Laotian, and Cambodian casualties."

At the time of the accords, Mr. Kissinger ascribed the delay in working out an "honorable" settlement to North Vietnamese intransigence. Before October 1972, he explained, Hanoi had demanded that we topple the Thieu regime as a precondition for settlement. Once the communists gave up that demand, peace with honor was possible.

Mr. Kissinger never explained what *quid pro quo* he had offered to break Hanoi's intransigence. But an 8-column *New York Times* headline (Jan. 24, 1973) spoke plainly enough: "North Vietnamese Viewed The Costly Spring Drive As Crucial For A Settlement." That 1972 Spring Drive had enabled the North Vietnamese to place at least 145,000 and perhaps is many as 300,000 regular troops-in South Vietnam. We need to recall that General John D. Lavelle had tried, without Washington authorization, to stop the communist build-up for that Spring Drive. For that he was relieved of his command of American air power in Indochina and later demoted two ranks. Will history have to record that Gen. Lavelle was fired because a successful Hanoi drive into South Vietnam was essential to make Kissinger's "pull-out peace" acceptable to Hanoi?

According to the terms negotiated by Kissinger, the Thieu government was to survive as, at best, a transitional regime. It was to have no permanent U.S. guarantee. Once all our troops were out, the advantage of Hanoi's having hundreds of thousands of regulars in place would be obvious.

Our retreat to that point had been punctuated by shows of strength. When half our troops were out we invaded Cambodia; when all were out we mined Haiphong; and when Kissinger was about to initial the conditional capitulation, we had a flurry of massive bombings in the north. Why that periodic show of military firmness when all the while we meant to give up?

In the past, Henry Kissinger has not shrunk from answering that kind of question. His object all along, he has periodically admitted, has been to get the U.S. out of Vietnam on terms acceptable to Hanoi, yet in such a way as to avoid a popular backlash on the home front. In a press briefing back in December 1969 he put it this way: "Anybody can end the war. Our problem is to keep the society together."

Urging anti-war critics to be patient with his indirect methods, Mr. Kissinger once warned that a settlement arrived at without displays of American "firmness" could turn our society "into a group that has nothing left but a physical test of strength, and the only outcome of this is Caesarism. . . . Upper-middle-class college kids will not take this country over. Some more primitive and elemental force will do that if it happens."

Thus the cause of Kissinger's long delay in closing down the Vietnam war may have been all along his fear of a right-wing American backlash. Over 26,000 Americans died and over 150,000 were wounded after the Kissinger-Nixon strategy for "controlled" peace negotiations went into operation in 1969. Has that awful price been paid simply to forestall, by a Disraelian maneuver, the wrath of the silent majority that gave Mr. Nixon his landslide re-election in 1972?

Back in January 1973, many of us asked: Will the communist powers permit us to "enjoy" for long the illusion that we have not lost a war in Vietnam? And worse, will our intellectuals in the news media and at the elitist universities prostitute their intelligence to sustain that illusion on the grounds that to do otherwise might precipitate what Kissinger has worked so shrewdly to avoid?

We have had the Communist response–a resounding No! No acceptance even of unconditional surrender until every last American is out! So far, the response of the education communications elite has been typical Watergate-era cover-up solidarity. The intention seems to be to "stonewall" it with a confident line till the threat of recriminations blows over.

KISSINGER'S LIMITED-WAR DOCTRINE

Our defeat in Vietnam is a direct consequence of our government's adoption of the so-called Limited-War Doctrine, of which Henry Kissinger has been since 1957 the principal architect and chief advocate. In the early sixties, McGeorge Bundy and Walt Rostow (who had earlier labored with Kissinger on its theoretic formulation) very nearly succeeded in committing the Kennedy Administration to its implementation as official U.S. military policy. But an assassin's bullet cut their maverick patron down and raised the gruff Texan who simply could not be induced to fathom its subtleties. And so it was left to Kissinger himself to implement his own design for the conduct of a war which, in his judgment, *we could afford to lose*–deliberately lose–once it was clear that the only alternative to losing was to risk escalation to the level of a nuclear holocaust.

President Eisenhower had risked turning the Korean war into a holocaust by threatening the North Koreans and Red Chinese with the use of our most advanced weapons–which is to say, our nuclear arsenal–if they persisted in their aggression. The subsequently formulated Dulles doctrine of massive retaliation defined the rationale of the threat that ended the Korean war. Charging that the threat and its rationale were both irresponsible, the Bundys, Rostows, and Kissingers hastened to develop an alternative strategy for ending local wars without risking a nuclear holocaust. The result was the Limited-War Doctrine which, since January 1969, has in fact determined in every detail the conduct of our tragic pseudo-war in Vietnam.

In Vietnam, Henry Kissinger has simply applied to the bloody, bitter end the lesson which, in his judgment, we ought to have learned and applied in the Korean War, namely that (as he phrased it in *Nuclear Weapons and Foreign Policy,* New York, 1957, p. 48) "we could not afford to win in Korea, despite our strategic superiority, because Russia could not afford to lose."

Kissinger's point is that President Eisenhower ought to have been willing to lose outright in Korea rather than risk, as he did, a nuclear holocaust. As he explains (p. 146): "There would seem to be no sense in seeking to escape a limited defeat through bringing on the cataclysm of an all-out war, particularly if all-out war threatens a calamity far transcending the penalties of losing a limited war. It simply does not follow that because one side stands to lose from a limited war, it could gain from an all-out war."

In his *Necessity for Choice* (New York, 1960), Kissinger refined his notion of the *desirability* of accepting defeat in a limited war when the alternative is all-out general war. General war is defined there as "aggression which, if not resisted, will lead immediately to the collapse of the victim. The victim is reduced to impotence; he can survive only at the aggressor's pleasure." It is the kind of war, therefore, that a major power obviously *cannot afford to lose.*

By contrast, as Kissinger goes on to explain, a limited war is one that a major power like the United States *can* afford to lose. "It is a threat," he acknowledges in carefully measured words, "which jeopardizes survival *ultimately.* Victory for an aggressor will lead to a deterioration of our international position but it will not jeopardize our existence immediately."

In other words, as designed and implemented by Henry Kissinger, our acceptance of defeat in Vietnam, after ten years of fighting a "limited war," rectifies at long last the mistake of President Eisenhower in Korea. The defeat we have purchased there at such a frightful cost in lives, maimed limbs, and shattered hearts, is preferable, in Kissinger's forecast judgment, to the risk we might have run in trying to win a war which the communists obviously felt they *could not afford to lose. Ultimately,* as Kissinger boldly emphasizes in the words last cited, such a defeat, accepted as a matter of policy, jeopardizes our very existence, but *not immediately.*

The proper response here is of course that of General Douglas MacArthur when the debate over the Korean War was at its height. "You have got a war on your hands," MacArthur told a Senate hearing in 1951, "and you can't just say, 'Let that war go on indefinitely while I prepare for some other war. . . .' I do unquestionably state that when men become locked in a battle, there should be no artifice under the name of politics which should decrease their chances for winning." MacArthur was dismissed by President Truman; but President Eisenhower later applied precisely that MacArthur criterion to end an ugly Asian war without ultimately jeopardizing our national existence.

10. THE CRIME
OF NO-WIN
BELLIGERENCY

When Kissinger cavorts like a hawk these days pleading for a last spasm of aid to "our" side in some distant troublespot, we can be sure the cause he purports to defend is lost. He did it in the last days of Vietnam. He is doing it again as the curtain falls in Angola. His plea is invariably for insufficient *aid: enough to prolong the fighting but not to avoid defeat, since defeat, by the logic of detente, is the price he has committed us to pay for Soviet supported global peace. Kissinger had been arguing since 1957 that, if forced to choose between all-out war and passive surrender, Americans would choose the former. He therefore urged President Kennedy's advisers to forestall such a choice by pursuing a fail-safe alternative: his own limited-war strategy which, by definition, rules out both passive surrender and open-ended military escalation to avoid defeat. That has been our policy since 1961. It has cost us a protracted surrender in Vietnam, concessions of arms superiority to the enemy, and collapse of three successive presidencies. Yet, as Mr. Moynihan acknowledges, the designers of our defeatist interventionism are still in place. They are now political desperados, caught up in an on-going situation from which there is for them no turning back. All who sense this and keep silent are accomplices.*

What are the lessons Henry Kissinger would have had us learn from the Vietnam surrender to communist force he negotiated for us? Kissinger has no doubt already prepared a long memorial on the theme for Mr. Ford to read to Congress as his Bicentennial report on the State of the World. Meantime we have a first White Paper: the official State Department transcript of the December 23, 1975 Kissinger press conference on "Angola and Detente."

For Kissinger, Angola is a test case. It asks: Are Americans finally resigned to the idea that serious resistance to communism is no longer feasible in the nuclear age? Vietnam had not supplied a conclusive answer. Till the very end there was a feeling that, had he remained President, Nixon might have balked at surrender. Before Soviet-built tanks could have been filmed battering down our Embassy gates in Vietnam, before scornful red guards could have seized our Ambassador's desk with his personal things—including a signed picture of the President—still on it, a relapsed Nixon might have shouted some obscenity for the tapes to record, fired Kissinger, and called upon the Joint Chiefs to start World War III, if necessary, to prevent our national humiliation.

Nothing of the sort happened, of course. While Kissinger and four-star General Haig were persuading Nixon to resign, Defense Secretary Schlesinger (history will record) effectively blocked all presidential communication with the armed forces. What happened instead was what might have happened to Abe Lincoln had he, for pseudo-pacifist reasons, given up on the Civil War, only to face impeachment for violations of the Constitution which could be justified only by a decisive victory for the Union. Because of doubts about the meaning of our Vietnam surrender, Kissinger offers us Angola—a carefully contrived laboratory experiment, mounted solely to illustrate the prescribed lesson.

ANGOLA AND WATERGATE

When news of a covert American intervention against the Soviet-backed MPLA in Angola was first leaked, Clayton Fritchey, a loyal Kissinger admirer, hastened to exonerate the Secretary of State by blaming it on Ford's election-year eagerness to "propitiate the ultraconservative wing of his party." Kissinger knows there are no sound foreign policy reasons for the intervention, said Fritchey; and he concluded that, "if the sharp reaction on Capitol Hill effectively puts a stop to further escalation, it could be a blessing in disguise for the Secretary of State, for he will be rescued from an ill-advised venture without having exposed himself to blame by the pro-interventionists."

But Kissinger's news conference on the subject was by no means a merely partisan exercise. Propitiation of conservatives quickly gave way to a professorial lecture on the need to resist communist military expansion despite Vietnam. We surrendered there, but—unless, Congress votes us down—we will go on resisting communism wherever we are challenged. That, on the surface, is Kissinger's Angola stand. "If the Soviet Union continues action such as Angola," he said, "we will, without question, resist." And again: "There is no question that the United States will not accept Soviet military expansion of any kind."

Resist *without question,* then; but how, and to what end? For detente's sake, Kissinger hastened to qualify, our resistance must, of course, be *manifestly inadequate.* "We are talking," Kissinger stressed, "about trivial sums." In addition, if the Soviet-backed MPLA prevails over the other Marxist-revolutionary factions contending for succession to Portuguese rule in Angola, "we can live with it"—our Secretary of State assured reporters—since we "have no permanent interests in Angola." Asked whether intervention with trivial sums might not, nevertheless, escalate into another Vietnam, Kissinger replied confidently:

"Let us not fool ourselves about what happened in Vietnam. We did not start in Vietnam with a few hundred men and wake up one morning and have 500,000 troops there. Every step in Vietnam was a conscious decision that was publicly known and to which there was no significant objection when there was still time to do something about it. There is no possibility that the same thing could happen in Angola, when even the first step has produced such an intense debate."

Kissinger's point is that our Vietnam intervention was dangerously open-ended (sometimes aiming at military victory, sometimes not), whereas our Angola intervention is strictly controlled in concept as well as means. Since we have "no national objectives in establishing a pro-American or pro-Western government in Angola," we have not intervened to win. On the other hand, if the trivial sums requested are withheld, Kissinger argued, "if we do not succeed in convincing the public or the Congress" that our limited intervention must continue, "then we will certainly lose on this issue" and probably face a contingency of "more serious dislocations . . . further down the road." We have intervened, said Kissinger, "to avoid that contingency. If we turn out to be wrong and the Congress is right, I will be delighted."

A friendly reporter then asked the obvious question: If Angola is really a test between the USA and the USSR, "why not go to the heart of the issue on a question like the grain shipments to the Soviet Union and things like that, in which the Soviet Union has a direct interest and some pressure can be brought to bear?" Without a blush, Kissinger offered this non sequitur: "I think it is a rather curious method to say 'you go ahead and take over Angola with 5,000 foreign troops, but in the meantime we will start harassing you with some other things.'" Our detente-era resistance to communism, Kissinger would have us understand, must be on-the-spot resistance, so as to leave no doubt that we are opposing aggression, not detente. How we resist Soviet-backed aggression in Angola, he stressed, must be viewed "within the context of our overall relationship. And there is no question that our overall relationship will suffer if we do not find an adequate solution to the Angola problem. Where it will suffer and in what ways, I am not prepared to say."

While our national security bureaucracy is thus kept busy covertly resisting communism in distant places, Kissinger labors overtly to give us an institutionalized, irreversible Soviet-American detente, whatever it may ultimately cost us as a nation. In this respect, his anti-communist gesture in Angola is on a par with the White House "plumber" initiatives that sent minor intelligence operatives deep into the Watergate hotel and Ellsberg's psychiatrist's office to fight communism on the eve of the 1972 re-election campaign. With Gordon Liddy at CREEP headquarters dropping hints that the White House was still covertly financing the good fight, Watergate surely gave the 1972 re-election campaign a strong undercurrent of right-wing promise. Walter Lippmann fully appreciated the importance of such undercurrents to the success of the Kissinger-Disraelian reversal of the cold war. "Only Nixon," Lippmann had written in 1972, announcing his decision to support the re-election of a man he otherwise despised, "could have made such a reversal. . . . The reason there has been no serious outcry is that it was made under the auspices of a certified anti-communist like Nixon."

Nixon must have believed till the end that his own indelible anti-communist certifications were indispensable to Kissinger's political survival and that by raising his Special Assistant to the high office of Secretary of State he had bought himself some very heavy personal insurance. It didn't work. Kissinger's private constituency soon showed how ably it can select survivors when it topples an administration. But, having survived Nixon, Kissinger has now to try his own hand at tossing anti-communist sops to the right.

Take, for instance, the very serious recent criticism of the SALT negotiations which is on the verge of openly charging Kissinger with a treasonable cover-up about Soviet violations. It is now known that not only Paul Nitze but Admiral Zumwalt too resigned high office in protest against Kissinger's apparent willingness to sacrifice security for his detente "successes." Kissinger's typical response to such charges has been to beg the question: "I believe it is a good working hypothesis to assume that government is not run by conspiracy but by serious people trying to come to serious conclusions about difficult topics." He has even suggested that the Nitzes and Zumwalts are themselves undermining our security by creating the "impression that the U.S. Government would make a serious agreement on a matter affecting the survival of the United States and that its senior officials would then collude in a violation of this agreement"–which is indeed precisely what is charged!

It is at such moments that timely leaks and public discussion of Kissinger-directed covert anti-communist intervention in places like Angola can provide an extremely valuable cover. Compliant doves are bound to raise a furor while pliant Ford loyalists pretend to have understood the necessity for such operations. And when the Senate has rescued Kissinger by voting down support, one can imagine the expected confidential phone call received at the editorial offices of *National Review:* "Don't blame me, Bill. God knows how I pleaded for at least a show of fighting spirit. But what can you do with a cowardly people and an even more cowardly Congress? Your friend Whittaker Chambers was right. They don't even want to save face!"

THE SOFT CORE

Another questioner at the December 23 press conference asked pointedly: "Mr. Secretary, when you say you consider the Soviet actions in Angola incompatible with detente, what does that mean? What is the 'or else,' and how incompatible." Kissinger's reply, elaborated at some length, needs close reading, for it takes us directly into the soft core of his so-called national security strategy for our future. We must first of all, he says, "separate two things: The relationship with the Soviet Union that is inherent in the relation of the two superpowers; and, secondly, those relations that are subject to decisions and that we can regulate in terms of Soviet behavior." About what is inherently settled, he then proceeds to say:

"The basic problem in our relations with the Soviet Union is the emergence of the Soviet Union into true superpower status. That fact has become evident only in the 1970s. As late as the Cuban missile crisis, the disparity in strategic power between the United States and the Soviet Union was overwhelming in our favor. In the 1970s and 1980s the Soviet Union will have achieved, and is on the road to achieving, effective strategic equality, which means that, whoever may be ahead in the damage they can inflict on the other, the damage to the other in a general nuclear war will be of a catastrophic nature.

"This being the case, in the past the emergence of a country into superpower status–such as, for example, imperial Germany vis-à-vis Great Britain–has generally led to war. Under the conditions of the nuclear age, it must not lead to war. That is a fact of the period that any administration, and any opponent of the administration, would have to face if it had to assume responsibility. . . . That part of the Soviet-American relationship cannot be abolished. That is inherent in the relationship."

Before the 1970s, in other words, Soviet military expansion could still presumably have been stopped the way German military expansion had twice been stopped in the 20th century–by recourse to a general war. Now, according to Kissinger, a general war to stop the Soviets is out. That's settled. But we can, "by conscious acts of policy" short of general war, still do something. "This," says Kissinger, "has been called detente." General war is a unilateral means of imposing restraints upon an aggressor; detente is a bilateral means, requiring "conscious restraint on both sides." Needless to say, detente or bilateral restraint had been the object of the Munich Pact with Hitler. When Hitler failed to restrain himself, the Allied Powers restrained him by means of general war. What happens now when the Soviets fail to exercise self-restraint? "The situation," Kissinger replies, "becomes inherently tense." But–"it must not lead to war." We must remain self-restrained. The best we can do is show our displeasure firmly in one place while offering generous concessions elsewhere. That is the essence of detente. And "the danger to detente that we now face," according to Kissinger, "is that our domestic disputes are depriving us both of the ability to provide incentives to moderation, such as the restrictions on the trade act, as well as of the ability to resist military moves by the Soviet Union, as in Angola."

KISSINGER'S PROTRACTED DECEPTION

We must counter by asking: Is it true that developments of the 1970s projected into the 1980s have backed us into the corner Kissinger has described for us? Or is he rather merely exploiting the stunned American acceptance of defeat in Vietnam, on the heels of Nixon's resignation, to saddle us with a plan for defeatist interventionism which he first advanced in the mid-fifties and has been developing and refining ever since? Back in January 1969, when Kissinger originally joined Nixon in the White House, I wrote an article assessing his published views on national security policy, where I concluded:

"Against the pacifist advocates of unilateral disarmament, Kissinger argues that the American people need to be led slowly, and ambiguously, to the same goal. Matching the subtleties of Niebuhr on this point, Kissinger electrifies us with this startling piece of candor on why he wants Americans to fight no-win wars a while longer: 'A nation which cannot be trusted when strong will hardly be able to deal with the much more difficult task of living in dignity when impotent.'

"Limited war will *not,* Kissinger admits, provide national security in the traditional sense; but it will in the *new* sense he means to define for it, which will authorize our nation, through its ruling elite; to choose whether 'to assure its survival or to realize its aspirations internationally.' When we have fought our limited wars and have settled in each case for something less than the traditional meaning of security, the next step will be, as Kissinger says, to perfect ourselves in the art of 'living in dignity when impotent'."

Kissinger says now that the Soviet Union's effective strategic equality with the United States is a policy-shattering development of the 1970s. Yet if we turn to his *Nuclear Weapons and Foreign Policy,* published in 1957, we read in the Foreword by Gordon Dean: "For all practical purposes we have in terms of nuclear capabilities reached a point which may be called 'parity.' We have known that such a time would come. It is now upon us. I do not mean necessarily parity in numbers of large bombs. Numbers become less important when the point is reached where both sides have the capability to annihilate each other."

That effective strategic equality had been reached at the time of the Korean war was indeed the basic assumption of Kissinger's book which he had been commissioned to write in the mid-fifties by a panel of the Council on Foreign Relations chaired by Gordon Dean. The Council panel had met for over a year to explore the "deficiencies" of the Eisenhower policy of massive retaliation, and Kissinger was commissioned to write an assessment of their deliberations.

The book's central point was that Eisenhower and Dulles ought to have realized back in the early 1950s that "we could not afford to win in Korea, despite our strategic superiority, because Russia could not afford to lose." Eisenhower had instead risked an all-out nuclear war by threatening to use our most advanced strategic arms if North Korea, backed by Peking and Moscow, persisted in its aggression. According to Kissinger and his Council peers, that had been an irresponsible act. Truman had dismissed MacArthur for proposing to generalize the war. Eisenhower ought therefore to have kept it limited to the end, even if that meant (in a strictly limited sense) losing it. "There would seem to be no sense in seeking to escape limited defeat through bringing on the cataclysm of an all-out war," wrote Kissinger in 1957, "particularly if all-out war threatens a calamity far transcending the penalties of losing a limited war."

But why send troops to die in a war you don't mean to win? Kissinger gave his frankest answer to that question in his second major book on the subject, *The Necessity for Choice,* published in 1960.

Urging unilateral disarmers to support his limited-war strategy as an alternate route to their own goal, he cautioned them that, in the face of Soviet aggressive behavior, "if we reject the concept of limited war, our only options will be surrender or all-out war. . . . Since surrender will not be our national policy, it is important to get our choices straight." And he concluded:

"The *worst* that could happen if we resisted aggression by means of limited war is what is certain to happen if we continue to rely on the [Eisenhower] strategy of the past decade. Limited war is based on a kind of tacit bargain not to exceed certain restraints. . . . We must enter it prepared to negotiate and to settle for something less than our traditional notion of victory. . . . Limited war is palatable only when compared with other even starker alternatives. . . . It is, to be sure, a subtle and complex task, and it presupposes a rare blend of psychological, political, and military skills."

Kissinger has certainly proved since 1969 that he has the rare blend of skills required to get a mighty people to lose a limited war as a bloody alternative to popularly-unacceptable outright surrender. Yet think of the millions of Americans who went to Vietnam since 1969 not knowing it was a fixed fight? When he entered My Lai for combat, did Lieutenant Calley, for instance, know that he was in a war programmed to end in a stalemate at best and in voluntary defeat, if need be, to prevent open-ended escalation? When My Lai occurred in mid-March 1968, Clark Clifford was our newly appointed Defense Secretary. Did he know that victory had been ruled out in Vietnam? As he later acknowledged, he had entered the Pentagon on March 1, 1968, assuming that his defense-establishment council was as determined as he, President Johnson, and the Joint Chiefs were to win the war. But by mid-March he was faced with an astounding revelation. As he later pin-pointed the moment in *Foreign Affairs:* "When I asked for a presentation of the military plan for victory in Vietnam, I was told that there was no plan for victory in the historic American sense."

Clifford, an insider, had to be "told." President Johnson was never told. He was dumped as a war-monger instead. Then came the Nixon-Kissinger administration with its doctrinal reversal of the cold war. Kissinger got his President to go to Peking and Moscow to end the era of confrontation and initiate the era of detente. Calley was soon tried, as a sort of stand-in for Johnson. Then *The Pentagon Papers,* which Kissinger had helped to compile, were published, showing that not only Johnson but Kennedy too had hoped for military victory in Vietnam. Kissinger could then claim for Nixon that he was indeed the first President of the nuclear age to reject victory in war, as an instrument of policy, when its pursuit entailed a risk of nuclear holocaust.

Next came the John D. Lavelle case. A four-star commander of all U.S. airpower in Southeast Asia, General Lavelle had presumed without specific authorization to order attacks against an obvious North Vietnamese build-up to invade the South in the spring of 1973. That spring drive in fact placed at least 200,000 regular North Vietnamese troops in the South in time for Kissinger's cease fire. For having tried to stop it, Lavelle was relieved of his command and reduced two ranks. Kissinger had decreed severely that, to avoid any risk of openended escalation, all shows of U.S. strength in Vietnam had to be carefully monitored to serve a single end—that of providing a "cover" for our headlong retreat. Thus, when half our troops were out, Kissinger joined Nixon in authorizing a temporary invasion of Cambodia; when all our troops were out, our air and naval forces were authorized to mine Haiphong harbor; and when terms of conditional surrender were being initialed in Paris, orders were given for a uselessly bloody bombing of Hanoi. Final capitulation brought us a cover in the form of the Mayaguez rescue. And now Kissinger offers us Angola.

Defeatist intervention in Angola is clearly something very close to the bottom line for the limited-war alternative to surrender. Our arms have sustained both sides in the Greece-Turkey dispute, as in the India-Pakistan dispute, all to the Soviet Union's advantage, as Senator Stevenson has lately pointed out. We arm both sides in the Middle East, and, through our oil cartels and aid to Moscow, also all sides in Angola. Kissinger calls it policy. History, however, is bound to record it as a protracted crime against the American commonwealth which the ex-Harvard professor has been able to pursue with impunity thus far only because so very many persons in high places have too long collaborated with him.

Kissinger's long-term collaborators know only too well that, when he takes a final fall, they can hardly exonerate themselves without offering him up as a scapegoat. It must be for them a distressingly unpleasant thought. But precisely that thought must have been a large factor in the logic or cunning that permitted his relatively swift rise to apparent dominance of our foreign policy. Yet when and if that painful time comes, we can be sure that the powerful Trilateral Commission and the peer organizations represented in its membership will already have surfaced with a bright and bravely serviceable Brzezinski to take Kissinger's place, and perhaps also an Elliot Richardson to maintain more than a semblance of continuity.

11. AN EXEMPLARY DEBATE ON ANGOLA: TUNNEY, STEVENSON, GOLDWATER AND HELMS

> *We may be entering an era when congressional debates will acquire a greater significance in our governmental process than they have ever had before. In England, with the rise of party discipline, the once widely read Commons debates have steadily lost significance, since, as Walter Bagehot long ago observed, an intelligent reader soon notes the change when otherwise honest men are obliged by partisan pressure "not only to employ arguments which they do not think conclusive, but likewise to defend opinions which they do not believe to be true." The reverse is happening in our post-Watergate Congress. Party loyalty, if not discipline, still determines much that is said. Yet even a glance at the Congressional Record suffices to suggest that a new frankness reigns on the floor. If that frankness could be brought to our citizenry daily, it would break the monopoly-control our newsmedia now exercise on public information. We have the electronic means for it.*

The Senate debate over the so-called Tunney amendment to the House Defense Department appropriations act for the current fiscal year (H.R. 9861) lasted five days: December 15-19, 1975. At issue was a small-scale covert American intervention in Angola ordered by Henry Kissinger at a time when it was obvious that a Soviet-Cuban takeover, already in progress, could hardly be prevented by anything less than an overt rupture in detente relationships or direct military intervention on a massive scale. In the wake of newsleaks, the Senate by unanimous consent called for closed-session clarifications. Two closed sessions were held. But, as Kissinger's purpose was not thereby clarified, the Senate voted finally against permitting any funds appropriated for defense to be used covertly in Angola for any purposes other than gathering intelligence.

Regardless of what one may think of the vote that concluded it, there can be no doubt that the substance of that Tunney-amendment debate was very important. At its height, Senator Robert Morgan of North Carolina rose to say (Dec. 18, 1975): "While I think sometimes we are attempting to conduct the foreign policy of this country for and on behalf of the President rather than by consulting and advising the President, I do believe that this debate has been as informative and helpful as any debate that I have heard on foreign policy since I have been in the Senate."

The pity is that the substance of that debate never reached the American people. The media focused instead on Kissinger's account of what a vote against support of his Angola maneuver was supposed to mean. TV screens flashed glimpses of him hawkishly denouncing "congressional interference," while admirers in the major newspapers hinted, with cryptic analyses, at the subtle ambiguities in Kissinger's policy statements which enable him to get what he wants while feigning not to want it. Had the debate itself been adequately reported, the general public impression would have been altogether different.

Of course, one may read it all in the tiny print on coarse paper of the *Congressional Record.* And perhaps some dozen people in a million may actually take the trouble to do so. But trouble is the word for it. The *Record* is a jumble of things said or purportedly said, strung together without directive headlines, or intelligible indices, or significant topical divisions. Compare it with any issue of the *Washington Post* or *New York Times* (to say nothing of the slick TV network news marathons) and it is at once obvious that, when ignored by the media, our Members of Congress have little recourse. They can circulate an occasional newsletter to local constituents, but, except through the cumbersome *Record,* there is simply no way their joint deliberations can be made known to the national constituency for whose unity of government they are charged to conduct those deliberations.

America has witnessed advances in communications technology that boggle the mind. Yet nothing has been done to bring that technology to bear on the processes of our representative government. Its "immense power to influence and shape public opinion" has accrued by public default to a handful of oligarchs who now exercise it, as Malcolm Muggeridge recently observed, "with little regard for any consideration except profit and self-importance." How anomalous it is to have to endure endless investigations of CIAs and FBIs when there is a power in our midst which can, "with the same sublime unction . . . destroy a presidency and recommend the magical qualities of a new detergent, lose a war and promote a cakemix." As Mr. Muggeridge aptly admonishes:

"Future historians, if there are any, will surely marvel at the tolerance accorded this instrument of persuasion, so immensely more powerful than anything of the kind which has ever existed before, and at the manner in which its pundit salesmen have been able, with equal impunity, to topple institutions and undermine authority, and to sing the praises of some potion or pill capable of delivering us from pain, anxiety, body odor, acidity, and other infirmities."

To get themselves noticed by the so-called free press, our legislators must vie not only with detergent, cinema, and 8-track tape ads, but also with every self-appointed marginal interest-group leader who has studied the latest learned-journal article on how to "make news" at minimal private expense. The result is a scandalous blackout of real news of the kind that could give us a genuinely well-informed public opinion. In the debate on the Tunney amendment, many senators on both sides spoke exceptionally well. Had they been seen and heard or read at length, our nation would certainly have been healthier for it.

Senator Byrd On The Role of Congress

When the House Appropriations Act for the Defense Department reached the Senate floor, Harry F. Byrd of Virginia cautioned his colleagues (Dec. 15, 1975) that "we must debate these issues with full awareness of the restraints imposed by the capacities of the national economy and national will." Setting a statesmanly tone for the ensuing debate he then added: "Secretary of State Kissinger has from time to time suggested that the Congress interferes unduly with foreign policy, and that this interference undermines the flexibility needed by the executive branch in conducting diplomacy. But that is part of the American system. Congress has a role to play in the conduct of foreign relations. To cite only the most obvious points, the Senate must ratify treaties and the Congress as a whole must approve any commitment of funds. And beyond the strictly legal requirements, there is the important point that in an open society, no foreign policy can be successful which lacks a consensus. Surely recent history has taught us that.

"There can be no scheming Metternich, no juggling Tallyrand, in the United States. This country's ability to deter aggressors and to negotiate with firmness depends in no small degree upon our national unity of purpose. But we cannot impose unity, as totalitarian governments do. Instead, we must arrive at our foreign policy–I speak of policy now, not the mechanics of its execution–through democratic means."

Having defended congressional prerogatives at the "outset of the foreign policy debate," Senator Byrd next offered an introductory comment on matters of substance. He wished to stress, he indicated, the difference between genuine detente, which he favored, and the spurious detente pursued by Secretary Kissinger, which has served only to dim "popular awareness of the existing military and political threats to the United States." Recalling that he had been the "first Senator to applaud former President Nixon's trip to China," he added that he certainly favored "keeping the lines of communication open to Moscow." Yet, however desirable it may be to have a genuine detente—a genuine relaxation of tensions—"what has happened in practice is that Secretary Kissinger has used it in an effort to buy Russian friendship with more and more concessions." Americans must not forget, he amplified, that "while moods and methods, words and gestures, may change in Moscow, the underlying goal of the Communist dictatorship remains constant. That goal is the world-domination of the Communist system. Russian actions in Angola give fresh proof. . . . The United States cannot afford to accept a 'detente' which paves the way for global domination by the Soviet Union."

Senator Byrd noted that Kissinger himself, when he taught at Harvard, had repeatedly warned against any idea that the Russians would "abandon their drive for world domination in the name of detente." G. Warren Nutter, a former State Department advisor, and professor at the University of Virginia, had recently pointed this out in a monograph on the Secretary of State, and Byrd quotes his words: "Kissinger the public official could find no more severe critic of his policy of detente than Kissinger the scholar, who would say that the search for a no-risk policy is self defeating, that a so-called no-risk policy incurs the greatest risk of all."

It is, of course, true that Kissinger the scholar was aware of the dangers of pursuing a no-risk or "fail-safe" national security policy. But, as we have often stressed, it by no means follows that Kissinger the scholar opposed adoption of such a policy by his colleagues in the Kennedy administration. On the contrary, he urged its adoption and implementation and has himself been implementing it for the past seven years, in full awareness that the price of persistent imple-mentation must be a series of "limited" surrenders till all is irre-versibly lost. Vietnam was unmistakably such a surrender. Would Kissinger's no-risk intervention in Angola prove to be another? That was precisely the issue raised in the Senate debate over the Tunney amendment. By misrepresenting it to the American people, the media gratified Kissinger's mounting need for a cover of purposive ambiguities. But we have, fortunately, the unambiguous directness of the *Congressional Record.*

TUNNEY CITES TAFT

The Senate debate on Angola passed through four dramatic phases. John V. Tunney began it by calling for closed session briefings on the purpose of the covert intervention. Citing Senator Robert Taft's classic objection to half-hearted military interventions, he warned that we have let ourselves be involved in such interventions "for the past 30 years . . . and where has it gotten us? I will state that it has gotten us thrown out of Southeast Asia and has brought about the collapse of three pro-western regimes. It has gotten us hundreds of billions of dollars in debt . . . and has cost us 55,000 American lives." Rejecting more of the same in Angola, Tunney concluded:

"If the Soviets are taking advantage of the Angolan situation, as indeed I believe they are, then let us go to the heart of the problem, the leadership of the Soviet Union. Let us make it clear to them that we view their interference there as inconsistent with detente, that . . . if they want American technology and investments and, most important, if they want American grain now or any time in the future, they had better seriously weigh the cost of intervention in Angola. And the same is true of the Cubans. . . . In short, let us take action to stop the Soviets and the Cubans. But let us have no more Vietnams. We, in this country, are prepared to fight to defend freedom . . . not to squander the lives of our young men and our treasure in foreign policy adventures that bear no true relation to our national security."

What were the national security implications of Kissinger's adventure in Angola? Tunney had several times asked State and Defense department officials for a clarification, only to be told that, while they were free to discuss with him what the Soviets were doing in Angola, they could not discuss what we were doing there. Why such a provocatively unacceptable insistence on secrecy? Did Kissinger perhaps *want* a Senate rejection? That was when Tunney called for a closed session to elicit clarifications, failing which, he would move to block funds for any activities in Angola other than intelligence gathering.

THE STEVENSON-GOLDWATER RESOLUTION

Senator Adlai Stevenson III of Illinois, a Marine Corp veteran and a long-time critic of Kissinger's conduct of foreign affairs, then intervened to say that, while he shared "all the reservations which have been eloquently expressed today about the dangers of U.S. assistance for any party," he did "not want to vote for an amendment which terminates all support for the anti-Soviet side in Angola without any alternative response to this Soviet challenge." There is no doubt, he specified, that the "Soviet Union is testing detente . . . to the limit–and we have defined no limit." The central fact is that "Soviet arms on a massive scale and a Cuban expeditionary force have landed on the shores of a newly dependent African state in naked pursuit of strategic advantage." The Tunney amendment, implying American acquiescence, forces upon us the question: "'Have we been so traumatized by the tragic American adventure in Vietnam that henceforth we are to accept Soviet military arrogance wherever it shows its head?" But Kissinger's token intervention, programmed explicitly *not to upset detente,* is surely no answer.

"What does detente mean anyway?" Stevenson asked. To mean anything, he urged, "it must be a two-way street. If the Soviet Union is to enjoy the benefits of trade in commodities which are valuable in the improvement of its standard of living, and other advantages of detente, then it must also meet certain standards of civilized international behavior. The implausibility of continued U.S. aid to the Soviet Union in the form of technology, capital and wheat, irrespective of its conduct in the world, is brought inescapably to the attention of the Senate. The United States has just committed supplies of grain to the Soviet Union for 6 years–not withstanding its transgressions in Angola or anywhere else. The agreement cannot mean what it says. All such agreements are subject to abrogation by one party if conditions are changed materially by another."

Senator Stevenson then introduced a resolution (S.R. 333) to counteract any adverse impression the Tunney amendment might make. Its terms specified that the President should (1) call upon all nations to stop intervening in Angola, (2) order the U.S. Ambassador at the U.N. to lay the matter of Soviet aggression before the Security Council, (3) urge the Organization of African Unity to act decisively, (4) curtail exports to all countries that persist in intervening, (5) ask other nations to apply similar sanctions, and (6) "pending efforts to seek an end to all foreign intervention in Angola, suspend further assistance to any faction."

At this point, Senator Barry Goldwater intervened. "I want to commend the Senator from Illinois," he said, "for this resolution. I think it is the first thing that has made any sense in a long day. While it may shock the Senator from Illinois to find the Senator from Arizona agreeing with him, I think this resolution comes at a proper time. I am particularly interested in the paragraph where he urges the President to use his authority under the Export Administration

Act of 1969 to curtail exports to countries which persist in intervening in Angola. We have never, as a nation, used the instruments of national policy that we have available to us short of the instrument of war itself. . . . I am thinking particularly of the Soviet Union's need for wheat." Urging that we use every economic and diplomatic weapon available to us, Goldwater concluded: "I want to again commend the Senator from Illinois, and, if he does not think it would be detrimental to his interests at home or here, I ask unanimous consent, if he agrees, to have my name included as a cosponsor, and I will ask forgiveness of my saints in heaven." [Laughter.]

In the same vein, Stevenson replied: "I am delighted by the Senator's comments, and I hope it does not shock him to find me agreeing with him . . . to the extent that I will probably vote against the amendment, and for the reasons he suggests, namely, that the United States should not deprive itself of any weapons with which to pursue any legitimate foreign policy objective." After a unanimous-consent vote adding Goldwater's name as cosponsor of his resolution, Stevenson observed that the United States "loses its credibility in the world when, on the one hand, it seeks to oppose Soviet intervention in Angola with aid to tribal factions in that country, and, on the other hand, aids the intervenor with not only food but also with capital and with technology. . . . Detente is a legitimate objective of the United States. But pursuit of detente by such methods . . . produces the reverse of detente. It produces tension, confrontation, and is doing so today in Angola."

Goldwater then added: "Maybe I am a bit harsh in including food in economic warfare, but it is a very effective weapon. War is far worse and, with the proper use of the weapons we have had available, political, economic, etc., I believe war can be avoided. . . . I am glad the Senator has introduced this resolution and made the comments he has made, and I think it will provide very interesting reading to those who follow the *Record*." Goldwater and Stevenson here asked unanimous consent for a vote on their resolution. Bob Packwood of Oregon pressed for postponement till after the scheduled closed session and a vote on the Tunney amendment, and his objection sufficed to have the resolution "placed on the calendar" for later consideration.

GARN AND DOMENICI

The closed session brought no significant clarifications from Kissinger's people. In open session once again, Senator Garn of

Utah rose to say that what most troubled him was the "secrecy of the U.S. contribution to the anti-communist resistance in Angola." Secrecy, he warned, "led to our defeat in Vietnam, which in turn has contributed to our paralysis in Angola. . . . If we are unwilling to intervene directly, we should immediately raise the diplomatic costs to the nations that do intervene. Such a course should be obvious, and would be if we were not blinded by the rhetoric of detente. Secretary Kissinger . . . has shown an almost amazing tolerance of offensive and insulting action by the Soviet Union and her client states. Now, all of a sudden, he is upset about Soviet intervention in Angola. Well, a number of us who have never understood his passion for accommodation are strongly opposed to the . . . constraints imposed on us by our blind adherence to the policy of detente."

In a colloquy with James McClure of Idaho, Senator Pete Dominici of New Mexico agreed that Angola and detente are inseparably related, and urged that the "sale of technology, trade relationships, cultural exchanges, SALT II, and all these kinds of negotiations" be used, therefore, as a "leveraging mechanism." With Senators McClure, Robert C. Byrd of West Virginia, and William L. Scott of Virginia concurring, Domenici then asked that his and their names be added as cosponsors of the Stevenson-Goldwater resolution.

But the immediate business on the floor was a vote on the Tunney amendment. In a final appeal, Senator Tunney argued that Kissinger could hardly be serious about resisting a Soviet takeover in Angola since, while pleading for trivial sums to opponents of the MPLA, he had done nothing to stop Gulf Oil from pouring huge sums into MPLA coffers. "There really does not seem to be any centrally controlling objective of American policy in Angola"; and that, Tunney concluded, "is what I consider dangerous." At which point Senator Jesse Helms of North Carolina took the floor to restate the dilemma Stevenson had originally posed.

Helms' Rejection of Negotiated Settlements

The Tunney amendment and the administration's position framed by Kissinger, Helms explained, offer us the "choice of outright abandonment of our responsibilities or a negotiated abandonment of our responsibilities. . . . The first is quick and cheap; that is the Tunney amendment. The second is long, protracted, painful and expensive. Both arrive at the same ultimate end." He was "presently inclined," he said, "–oh, so reluctantly–to vote for the Tunney amendment in order to let it be known that I will have no part of wasting money when the goal is to negotiate a settlement of the type which has always left the communists in place. . . . Is there anyone in this Chamber or in the cloakrooms or in the offices of the Dirkson or Russel building who does not believe that a 'negotiated settlement' is negotiated surrender?"

Helms stressed that the Soviet Union's shipment of "new armaments of a high quality . . . to Angola with no payment asked, and the presence of hundreds of Soviet personnel, are an entirely new development, based on a new world strategy," in the face of which Kissinger's covert intervention coupled with uninterrupted detente-negotiations is shamelessly, not to say treacherously, inadequate. "To put it bluntly," Helms concluded, "detente is the rationalization of surrender, just as our negotiations have been a protracted process of confirming the Communists in positions of strength in various places around the world. . . . No negotiation, not even a SALT negotiation, is important if it allows the Soviets to take the world piece by piece. I do not believe there is a Senator in this place who will deny that that is precisely what is going on. I hope that whatever else the Senate may do in this matter, we will at least endeavor to make sure that the American people understand what is at stake."

After several other senators had spoken for and against, the vote was finally taken on the Tunney amendment: yeas 55, nays 22, not voting 23. The *New York Times* alleged, after the fact, that a vote *against* Tunney was a vote *for* Kissinger's covert intervention. But that is patently false. As the *Record* shows, the severest critics of Kissinger opposed the amendment or abstained from voting, while his ardent supporters, for the most part, voted yea, no doubt believing (as Clayton Fritchey noted at the time) that a Senate restraint on anti-Soviet aid was what Kissinger *really* wanted.

When Kissinger first joined the Nixon administration in January 1969, he boldly declared himself to be a Disraelian in politics. He and Daniel P. Moynihan later taught President Nixon how best to use Disraelian conservative atmospherics as a cover in pursuing supranationalist ends. Poor Nixon is gone, now, but the master Disraelian of our time clings to office. No doubt the heads of international communism who deal with him and his friend Helmut Sonnenfeldt in major "negotiations" about America's future must wonder what marvel of collective stupification can have made such a thing possible. Yet the answer is now fairly obvious. Kissinger and his peers are sustained in office by the power of America's newsmongers.

The hyper-constitutional power of our news conglomerates to influence and shape public judgment is so immense that it dwarfs that of all other sectors of our society combined. Using the most advanced technology, it "sells" itself night and day to the American people in what amounts to a nationwide crimewave of incessant "jury tampering." Our Federal legislators must act to protect us against the non-representative oligarchy that now monopolizes our most advanced means of news dissemination and persuasion. They owe it to our gravely endangered 200-year old "experiment in government by discussion." And they can best begin to do it by getting their legislative sessions televised daily, and adequately reported to their national constituencies.

12. THE "SECRET" KREMLIN SPEECH

In the late fifties, Henry Kissinger took the lead among the many academic war-theorists who criticized President Eisenhower for having ended the Korean war by threatening the enemy with "massive retaliation" if he persisted in his local aggression. Eisenhower's threat, Kissinger had said, risked mankind's nuclear self-destruction, which was averted, it appears, only by a timely exercise of Soviet "nuclear-age prudence." Kissinger has since then had his chance to reverse Eisenhower's approach in practice. As chief of our Vietnam war effort in its final phase, he was able to end it without risky threats, though not without an American defeat. But would such an ending have been acceptable to John F. Kennedy, had he lived? The Pentagon Papers strongly suggest the contrary: that he would have rejected it as President Johnson later did. And we have Kissinger's word for it that, had Nixon remained President, nothing like what happened in the final days of our little Dunkirk would have been thinkable. We know what happened. Hanoi's Soviet-made tanks were permitted to rumble unopposed through hapless Saigon for a symbolic smashing-down of the U.S. Embassy's gates, while our last helicopters were lifting off with local clients clinging to their landing-gear. Did Kissinger, chief theorist of fail-safe wars, perhaps help history along a bit to get us our first non-elective interregnum just in time for termination of the war in a way that no elected American President could have allowed? Jonathan Schell's The Time of Illusion *doesn't, quite raise that question. But it does pursue the "logic" of Nixon's disgrace (foreshadowed in Kissinger's cryptic Kremlin speech of 1972, divulged by William Safire) back to Kissinger's limited-war doctrine.*

Richard Nixon and Henry Kissinger both tried very hard to shield the inner workings of their exercise of power from public scrutiny—with obviously unequal success! Jonathan Schell calls attention to the disparity in his excellent book *The Time of Illusion* (New York, 1976), "Never in American history," he writes in its Prologue, "had as much information about an Administration in power been held in secrecy as was held in secrecy during most of the Nixon years. But never in the history of the world, perhaps, had as much been revealed about the workings of a government as was revealed about the workings of the Nixon apparatus during and after its fall."

There is no denying that the measure of Nixon's failure as a keeper of secrets is unprecedented in our history. But what about that large part of the Nixon government that was from the beginning in Kissinger's almost exclusive charge? In a note at the book's close, Mr. Schell underscores the fact that, despite widespread impressions to the contrary, very few "internal documents of the Nixon Administration concerning foreign affairs" have so far "seen the light." Is it because the powerful investigative forces of our society still draw a deferential line when it comes to the confidentialities of foreign relations? The absurdity of such a suggestion is impressed upon us by Schell with this striking reminder and contrast: "The underground record of the executive branch in foreign policy during the Kennedy and Johnson years was made known through publication of *The Pentagon Papers,* but the underground record in foreign affairs of the Nixon Administration remains mostly undivulged."

Many of the very same people who compiled and published *The Pentagon Papers* also worked hard at dismantling the "Nixon apparatus" to make its inner-workings public. Kissinger was, of course, never a part of that apparatus. From the time of his first strategy meetings with the President-Elect, Morton Halperin, and Lawrence Eagleburger at the Hotel Pierre in December, 1968, he had applied his best talents, and those of his most trusted friends, to developing an apparatus of his own. Will the inner-workings of that apparatus ever be given a Pentagon-papers treatment? How unlikely that seems to be for the moment may be judged from the circumstances of publication of the one significant "internal document" of the Kissinger record that has so far surfaced.

A "NIXON PROFILE" FOR THE KREMLIN LEADERS

The document in question was published by William Safire of the *New York Times,* first in a *Harper's* magazine article and then in his best-selling book *Before the Fall: An Inside View of the Pre-Watergate White House* (New York, 1975). It is identified as the "fourth and final draft" of a Kissinger speech—"the most important of his life," says Safire—delivered in Moscow on April 20, 1972, before a small audience of top Kremlin leaders, including Leonid Brezhnev.

In *The Time of Illusion,* Jonathan Schell discusses the substance of the speech and the circumstances of its revelation at some length, ascribing importance to it as a key to Kissinger's methods as a top national-security adviser. He agrees with Safire's suggestion that publication of it helps, at the very least, to clarify much about Kissinger's approach to ending the Vietnam war that might otherwise seem inexplicable. The aim of the speech specified in the text was to provide the Kremlin leaders with an objective profile of President Nixon's "attitudes, orientation, and predictability," so that they could know exactly what sort of man they would be dealing with when he arrived in person the following month for his summit meeting with Brezhnev. According to the *draft,* writes Schell, Kissinger would be presenting himself not as the President's spokesman, but rather "in the manner of a man standing back and objectively describing the President."

Needless to say, it isn't often that the agent of one power presents himself to the heads of another—professedly hostile—power as an objective intermediary! Kissinger's apparent aim in this, says Schell, was to gain "credibility with Brezhnev" for what he had come to say about President Nixon—especially about how "tough" he still was, and about how "unpredictable" he could be when crossed. How did Safire of the *Times* get hold of such a speech? And why is it the only significant document of the Kissinger "underground record" that has so far surfaced? Schell reminds us of Safire's past. Before joining the *Times* as an editorial columnist, Safire had been a top Nixon speechwriter, and, as he stresses in his book, he had enjoyed great intimacy with Kissinger during the years they served together under Richard Nixon. Sooner or later, almost every draft of any speech produced in the White House passed through Safire's hands.

In *Before the Fall,* Safire describes the hectic speechwriting activity that preceded Kissinger's trip to Moscow. The confidential April speech and Nixon's public remarks at the summit meeting had to be coordinated, and Safire gives us a glimpse into how the coordinating process worked: "When Ray Price and I asked Henry Kissinger for guidance on the tone of the remarks for the President, he replied waspishly: 'Tough. None of your goddam peacenik-y toasts. This is not like China, swearing eternal friendship. Tough.' Price, a man not ordinarily given to oral argument, snapped back: 'We were writing hawkish speeches for Nixon when you were turning out dovish statements for Rockefeller, remember?' Both Henry and I looked at Ray with surprise and new respect; the shy former editorial writer reddened. With a diplomatic touch, Henry said that the tone of the toasts should be along Ray's tough-sounding lines, with a heavy overlay of reminders about comradeship and bravery in World War II."

Safire also tells us about how hard Kissinger worked on his own speech and about the kind of expert help he sometimes sought. During final preparations, for instance, "Anatoly Dobrynin, the fast-talking engineer who was the well-connected Soviet Ambassador to Washington, spent a lot of time with Henry Kissinger in the corner office of the West Wing," Safire notes, "and then the two men left secretly for Moscow. (Kissinger later said proudly that it was the first time a Soviet Ambassador flew to Moscow in *Air Force One*.)"

Accompanied by Helmut Sonnenfeldt and other trusted aides, as well as by Dobrynin, Kissinger landed in Moscow on April 19, and the speech Satire had chosen to make public was delivered as scheduled the following day. "Making some diplomatic cuts," Satire explains in his *Harper's* article, "I will quote from the fourth and final draft of Kissinger's opening statement to the Soviet leaders. Henry confirmed to me that it is substantially what he actually said. It is a useful study of what Kissinger thought Nixon wanted Brezhnev to know before the two leaders met. I take no delight in using classified material, but the Soviets heard Kissinger's appraisal in early 1972, and it will do no harm for Americans to review it now."

At this point in the *Harper's* article we get a highly suggestive sentence—about Kissinger's profile of his White House boss—which Safire will delete from the paragraph before it reappears in his book. "In retrospect," he had originally ventured to say, the passages on Nixon in the speech "read as if Kissinger intended deliberate irony, but, at the time he hoped to enhance Nixon's reputation for fierceness, he couldn't foresee the fumbling weakness later revealed in the taped conversations with Halderman and Dean."

In this connection, Schell recalls that *Harper's* later printed a letter from Kissinger chiding his old White House confidant for having given a slightly wrong impression. Though there was no denying that the published text of the speech "accurately reflected what he had said to the Russians," Kissinger wanted to make it clear that he had really taken "quite a different line" with the Soviet leaders than Safire seemed to imply. That chiding letter may not account fully for Safire's prompt deletion of the phrases about Kissinger's perhaps deliberate irony, but it suffices to show how far we are at this point from anything even remotely resembling the start of a Pentagon-papers penetration of Kissinger's "national-security" sanctuary.

Still, the passages published by Safire deserve the kind of close scrutiny Mr. Schell has given them. The most significant are those that link Nixon's pursuit of an honorable peace in Vietnam with inauguration of Soviet-American detente. Kissinger speaks glowingly at one point of the President's broad and abiding concern "to reach everlasting agreements" with the Soviet leaders; but then he adds:

"At the same time, he can be tough and even ruthless in dealing with specific problems. You probably recognize that the President is bound to see the present situation in Vietnam not only in its local context but as a renewed effort by outside powers to intervene in our domestic political process. Moreover, *as President he is bound to be keenly sensitive to the fact that our last President was forced to vacate his office because of the effects of the Vietnam war. President Nixon will not permit three Presidents in a row to leave office under abnormal circumstances.* It may seem that what he is doing to prevent this from occurring is 'unpredictable'; it is in fact quite consistent with his fighting instincts . . . . His political biography testifies to that."

The sentences italicized above, it needs to be stressed, are italicized without comment in Safire's printed text to indicate that they represent Kissinger's original emphasis. If not deliberately ironic, they seem in retrospect to be at least ominously prescient. On the theme of Nixon's "fighting instincts," Kissinger adds: "Let me make this more specific and relate it directly to you. The President has a reputation from his past as an anti-Communist. You may think that this is a basic prejudice which sooner or later will assert itself. (Actually, I would not find such a view on your side surprising. I would have thought that you would regard it as normal that a 'capitalist' should be anti-Communist and that you would not respect him if he were not.) But as a practical matter the President . . . will not lose sight of the special role that our two countries must play if there is to be peace in the world. That, rather than anti-Communism, is the point that will again and again reassert itself . . . .

"But we must be realistic: a lasting and productive set of relationships, with perhaps hundreds of thousands of our people working with each other and perhaps billions of dollars of business activity, can only be achieved in a healthy political environment. . . . The President wants to be frank with you: he cannot make commitments, say for credits or tariff concessions, if these measures do not command wide support among our public and in the Congress. . . . Moreover, we must make sure that once commitments have been entered into they will not soon be undermined. . . . I say this not because we want you to 'pay a price' for economic and other relations with us or because we expect you to sacrifice important political and security interests for the sake of trade relations. I say it as an objective fact of political life."

For "diplomatic" reasons, apparently, Safire refrains from citing in its entirety a passage where Kissinger stresses how inextricably linked detente and a favorable image for America in Vietnam have become for Nixon in this election year. The Soviet leaders must be advised, says Kissinger, that Nixon is very upset by their support of Hanoi's persistent efforts "to win the war *and drive the President from office.*" Again the italicized emphasis is in Kissinger's draft; and Safire comments: "That dramatic way of putting it—blatantly improper for a representative of a democracy—was understandable to the Soviet leadership to whom survival in the place of power was the name of the game."

Schell too is struck by the impropriety of the italicized phrase. But he is struck even more by the fact that Kissinger all the while has obviously been separating his motives as a detente negotiator from those of his White House boss. It is Nixon who wants a landslide victory in the November election, so he can proceed comfortably as a politician with his detente cold-war reversal; it is Nixon who hints at unpredictable initiatives if the Soviets don't move to get him a settlement in Vietnam that American voters can live with and that can be guaranteed to last at least as long as he's in office. These are clearly represented as Nixon's personal motives, not as part of the intrinsic logic of detente.

"In other words," writes Schell, "according to the *draft,* Kissinger didn't *want* the Russians to help the President get re-elected by paying a price in Vietnam; it was just an objective fact of political life that if they wanted the 'billions of dollars of business activity' to go forward they would have to pay that price"—at least while so unpredictable a President remained in office.

The Carrots and The Stick

That is the substance of the speech that William Safire—who knows what went into it—characterizes as the most important of Kissinger's life.

In retrospect it is clear that, assuming they were not offered with deliberate irony, the admonitions of April, 1972, were not much heeded in Moscow. The Soviet leaders apparently gave little thought to restraining the North Vietnamese who, on March 30, 1972, had launched their massive Spring Offensive, invading South Vietnam with more than 200,000 Soviet-armed regular troops. During their Moscow meetings, Kissinger and Nixon were to agree, moreover, that the new armies brought into the South at that time could remain there, as part of a *status quo ante* settlement, after all American troops were withdrawn. That had been another "carrot," added to the carrots of grain deals, technology transfers, credits, and strategic-arms concessions, that Kissinger had been authorized to dangle before the

Soviet leaders to gain their cooperation for a final settlement of the war in the spirit of detente.

Yet what about the proverbial stick, the forceful inducement, that is supposed to backup carrot offerings? In a campaign speech of 1968, Nixon had talked about the stick that Eisenhower used to elicit communist cooperation in Korea. "How do you bring a war to a conclusion?" the former Vice President had asked, drawing on his first-hand knowledge as an insider. "I'll tell you how Korea was ended. . . . Eisenhower let the word go out–let the word go out diplomatically–to the Chinese and the North–that he would not tolerate this continued ground war of attrition. And within a matter of months they negotiated." Eisenhower's "stick" had been a threat that he would use America's most advanced weapons–and use them predictably well–if the communist leaders failed to exercise restraint and the local aggression continued.

Behind Kissinger's admonitions twenty years later, the only threat was the one that Nixon himself (according to Safire's eyewitness account) reiterated in person at the May summit meeting. "I have the reputation of being a hardline anti-Communist," he told the Kremlin leaders; to which Alexei Kosygin replied with a thin smile: "We know, we know." What Eisenhower's *official* threat of "massive retaliation" had achieved in Korea was now to be achieved by the force of Nixon's much-publicized past "unpredictability."

We all know what fate overcame that unpredictable stick after the carrots had been predictably eaten. On August 9, 1974, Kissinger's White House boss very accommodatingly took his unpredictable self out of the way of further detente negotiations by delivering his signed resignation of the Presidency into Kissinger's very own hands. And in late April, 1975, three years almost to the day after Kissinger's Kremlin speech, the last Americans still in South Vietnam were quite unceremoniously driven into the sea. That served to "settle" the war finally not otherwise than the Kremlin leaders who heard Kissinger's perhaps ironic briefing of April 1972 had intended it to be settled. They had understood the nature of the force behind Kissinger's words: Vietnam was *not* to be another Korea–that had been decided long before Nixon got his unexpected opportunity for a political comeback–even if it meant that a third American President in a row would have to leave office under abnormal circumstances.

EUPHORIA IN WARSAW

From Safire's point of view, the secret Kissinger visit and the Moscow summit meeting were intrinsically successful. If all had "gone according to plan," he writes, the result would indeed have been to "fuse together the needs of conflicting and distrusting powers" in a manner "so complicated and engaging that it would be impossible to separate the intertwined ganglia without too much mutual pain." To have been with Kissinger where ultimate decisions were made to reverse 25 years of cold-war relationships was no small thing: and Safire therefore dwells proudly on the idea for a moment.

"On the way back from Moscow," he reminisces, "we stopped in Warsaw and Henry was euphoric. After the Polish state dinner, he and I walked out of the Malinovsky Palace about 11:00 P.M., followed by his Secret Service guard a dozen paces back. . . . As we walked through the dark new-old streets saying little, Henry reflected on the events of the past couple of weeks; where the world was, where he and I were walking; and he said in what struck me as honest affection. 'Not bad for a couple of Jewish boys, huh?'" Safire then asked about his companion's old sense of being an outsider in the Nixon White House. Things hadn't changed much, Kissinger mused: "one wrong step and he was finished; all the vultures would eat him up. But he said it was all worth it, because what he and Nixon were doing really counted for something, and if they had not happened to be there at this time, who knows who would have missed the chances the President and he were not missing?" Safire then asked Kissinger what he and Nixon could conceivably do together as an encore after their Moscow detente-triumph. "Henry," writes Safire, "didn't hesitate for a minute. 'Make peace in Vietnam,' he said."

In other words: detente at the summit must come first, then settlements in the peripheral areas—rather than the other way around, which had been the cold-war approach! Whether by means of "containment" or "massive retaliation," the cold-war strategies had called for communist abandonment of local aggression before a relaxation of tensions on a global scale could be attempted. Kissinger had now reversed the priorities. He and Nixon had gone over the heads of the Hanoi communists straight to the top men in the Kremlin. They had offered plenty of carrots and had brandished Nixon's past as a quaint but still credible stick; and that would now suffice, Kissinger had apparently persuaded our President to believe, to induce the Soviets to do for us in the peripheral areas what our new approach forbade us to do for ourselves.

Such were the happy promises of that euphoric time in Warsaw. Safire reminisces further that he and Kissinger talked briefly about the books they would inevitably write. ("Yours will he better," Kissinger had said, "because you have to be only 90 percent right.") Only then does a rueful note intrude in Safire's account. "We could not know," he writes "that a combination of Russian bargaining shrewdness, weird crop conditions, and bureaucratic ineptitude would make the forthcoming grain deal [negotiated by Helmut Sonnenfeldt] appear scandalous; or that during the time we were in Moscow a small group of workers for the Committee to Re-elect the President was planting listening-devices on the telephones of Democrats in their Watergate Headquarters; or that in the coming year the Soviet press would be in the odd position of denouncing American impeach-Nixon demands as aimed against the policy of detente."

This is the point where Jonathan Schell very emphatically parts company with Safire in interpreting the promise of Kissinger's Kremlin speech. Schell too reads it as the most important of Kissinger's life. But he rejects the notion that unforeseeable Russian shrewdness, the bungling Watergate burglars, etc., intervened to spoil its promise. He insists on the contrary that all that happened to our Presidency and to our Vietnam war effort after April 1972–the entire sequence of seemingly chaotic events by which so may of us were led to believe that "both in Indo-China and at home the United States had been overtaken by a wholly accidental and therefore wholly absurd fate"–really had a built-in logic that mirrored, and indeed derived from the logic of that Kremlin speech.

In that speech, says Schell, Kissinger was "spelling out the lesson that the whole conduct of the Vietnam war was meant to teach." And basically it was the lesson of Kissinger's own limited-war doctrine, developed theoretically in the late fifties to provide, as Schell phrases it, a more humane way of "coming to grips with the question of human survival in the nuclear age." Its central idea had been that our local wars should hereafter have fail-safe ceilings beyond which we would never escalate, if such escalation might endanger the survival of mankind on this planet. The trouble with the doctrine, says the author of *The Time of Illusion,* is that it has always been difficult to sell if thoroughly explained. "One might say," he writes, "that it was in the very nature of the doctrine that it had to be presented misleadingly to the public and the world. For to explain the policy fully would be to undermine it."

When the limited-war doctrine became government policy in the early sixties, its advocates found that to move things along they had to resort increasingly to equivocations, purposive ambiguities, distortions, outright deceptions, and sometimes all of these together.

During the war's escalating phase, the necessity to mislead didn't do much perceptible damage to our political process, says Schell. A serious strain began to be felt when the cut-off point for escalation was reached under Johnson. But it was when the de-escalation phase started under Nixon, with Kissinger himself making the decisions, that our constitutional system began to feel a pulling at the seams.

At any rate, says Schell, if you want the key to all that has tormented and tortured our Republic during the Nixon years, you must look for it in the right place: "not in the character of the President or in the personalities of his aides," but in Kissinger's limited-war doctrine and the use to which he began to apply it in April 1972, with his speech to the Kremlin leaders. But we must examine Mr. Schell's line of argument against the Kissinger doctrine more closely.

13. KISSINGER'S WAR:
A REVISIONIST PERSPECTIVE

On the night before he succeeded to the Presidency of the United States, Gerald Ford, Vice President by appointment, asked the man he was about to succeed if he had "any particular advice or recommendations for him." In his memoirs, Richard M. Nixon recalls the question and his specific reply: "I said that the only man who would be absolutely indispensable to him was Henry Kissinger." Why should Kissinger's continuance in office have seemed indispensable to a virtually demented President in the depths of his personal disgrace? Jonathan Schell's view is that the key to the crisis that brought Mr. Nixon down is to be sought "not in the character of the President or in the personalities of his aides," but in the Kissinger doctrine of limited war. That doctrine, says Mr. Schell was supposed to "provide the United States with an effective means of promoting its interests and ideals at levels of violence below the brink of nuclear war; instead, it provided the notorious quagmire in Vietnam into which the United States poured its energy and power uselessly for more than a decade . . . and precipitated a wave of disrespect for a particular President which resulted in his forced resignation from office." What is at issue now is the role of Kissinger himself, as well as his doctrine, in precipitating the first resignation of an American President.

When Menachem Begin hurried to Washington earlier this year to lay his country's case for its *blitzkrieg* invasion of Lebanon before our President, our newsmedia did not fail to underscore for us the extraordinary sense of practicality, if not protocol, that prompted the Israeli Prime Minister to confer first with Henry Kissinger, then with Mr. Carter, and then again with Kissinger, before his swift return to his own country.

Kissinger is out of office now. Why shouldn't he be consulted by foreign heads of state on how to deal with our President? Moreover, the sort of case that Mr. Begin had come to make for his country falls squarely within the sphere of Kissinger's academic as well as public-service expertise. The Israeli strike into Lebanon was clearly a limited-war enterprise. The Palestinian Liberation Organization had mounted a terrorist mission on Israeli soil, operating presumably out of a Lebanese sanctuary. It had attempted to secure the release of

P.L.O. agents in Israeli jails. The mission failed. Those jails now hold more P.L.O. agents than they did before. But then why the *blitzkrieg* thrust into Lebanon? Mr. Begin was obviously the Israeli leader best qualified to make a case for such massive retaliation—"by means and at places of our own choosing," as John Foster Dulles used to say. Indeed, Israel's national security policy during its first thirty years of modern statehood has been consistently and traditionally to strike decisively first and explain later. Mr. Begin knows that tradition. He has expert knowledge of what motivates political terrorists; few heads of state anywhere know better than he what can and what cannot suffice to deter terrorist activity; and he no doubt spelled out the lesson of his expertise very forcefully in arguing his case for Israel's unwavering determination to deter aggression by depending "primarily upon a great capacity to retaliate instantly."

Kissinger has, of course, devoted his life to developing, refining, and implementing a foolproof and failsafe method for deterring aggression, especially of the kind usually engaged in by so-called "national liberation" terrorist bands and terrorist guerrilla armies. Quite unlike Mr. Begin, however, Kissinger has been from the beginning much more interested in methods of *limiting* military violence when local aggression has occurred than in securing a decisively deterrent victory over the aggressor. But, as we saw in the last issue of *State of the Nation,* when he finally got a chance to explain his limited-war theory to the Kremlin leaders in person, on April 20, 1972, he had added an ultimate refinement. In the draft of the confidential speech we examined, Kissinger seemed to be pressing the idea that the best way for civilized governments to deter local aggressors in the nuclear age is to negotiate detente over their heads with the superpowers that supply them with arms and ultimate motives for local aggression.

We may call that the mediator's approach, as contrasted with traditional partisan approaches, to the problem of local aggression in the nuclear age. And it was no doubt to consult him as a mediator, rather than as an expert on what partisan Israeli fighters must do about local terrorism, that Mr. Begin turned to Kissinger both before and after his visit with Carter on that fateful occasion.

Kissinger began to prepare himself for a mediator's role in world affairs back in the mid-1950s. In *Nuclear Weapons and Foreign Policy* (1957), he had criticized Dean Acheson and John Foster Dulles for failing to assume such a role as heads of our State Department. Under the banners of "containment" and "massive retaliation," they had pursued traditional American national-security interests in traditional ways. According to Kissinger, they ought to have recognized that nuclear weapons had introduced a fundamentally new dimension.

In the post-Hitler, post-Hiroshima world, statesmanship, we are to understand, had abruptly ceased to be what it had traditionally been. To destroy Hitler, it had been necessary to wage all-out war, even to the point of developing and using atomic weapons. But by the late nineteen-fifties, in Kissinger's view, warfare of that kind—scaled to reduce an enemy to unconditional surrender—had simply (in his words) "ceased to be a meaningful instrument of policy." Indeed today, he has consistently argued in and out of public office, the assumption of progressive statesmanship has to be that our chief potential adversaries (who were, after all, our allies in World War II) will be far more rational in their approach to nuclear-age war than Hitler could ever have been expected to be.

THEORY IN ACTION: THE MOSCOW SUMMIT OF 1972

Kissinger's theory of progressive statesmanship for the nuclear age became American policy, as we all know, in January 1969. And, as we saw in Part I of this revisionist study, it began to pass from policy into irreversible action with his confidential Kremlin speech of April 20, 1972. In that speech, speaking as a nuclear-age global mediator rather than as a partisan of traditional American national interests, Kissinger projected a new Soviet-American war-time alliance. After twenty-five years of U.S. anti-Soviet cold war policy, the old anti-Hitler allies of World War II would now inaugurate—with a Nixon-Brezhnev Summit meeting in Moscow the following month—a renewal of the old-time collaboration. Acting together, the statesmen of Moscow and Washington would bring the Vietnam war to a satisfactory close by negotiating a comprehensive peace over the heads of the local combatants.

But why would the Kremlin leaders be suddenly willing to negotiate such a peace in May 1972? Hadn't the Americans already withdrawn almost all their combat forces from Vietnam, in keeping with the time schedule of the Guam Doctrine which Kissinger had formulated for Nixon in 1969? If they hadn't been willing to negotiate before that time, while our side had 525,000 troops in the field, why should they want to negotiate now? Kissinger's answer, as we may read it for ourselves in the published draft of that "most important speech of his life," amounts to this: President Nixon, the long-time tough anti-communist politician, was now ready, after months of schooling by the ex-Harvard professor, to make the Kremlin leaders an offer they simply couldn't refuse. If they agreed, they would receive at once the full benefits of irreversible Soviet-American detente—vast credits to "purchase" U.S. technology and grain, a favorable SALT agreement, recognition of the legitimacy of their dominance in Eastern Europe, and much more. In return for all that they would of course be expected to pull the reins on Hanoi, and thereby procure for Nixon the "peace with honor" in Vietnam which nuclear-age prudence now forbade him to try to procure, directly and as a matter of policy, by military means.

In retrospect it seems absurd that Nixon could ever have believed the Soviets would do for him what Kissinger's policy of coupling withdrawal in Vietnam with pursuit of detente in Moscow required of them. Did he really think his old reputation sufficed to make the Soviets want to live up to his "peace with honor" part of the deal after they had begun to enjoy the benefits of detente? Kissinger appears to have persuaded Nixon that it would suffice—provided a few things were very deliberately done, in the course of the troop withdrawals and after, to give a convincing impression of *erratic* toughness.

Jonathan Schell, as we were beginning to indicate where we broke off earlier, stresses this essentially sick aspect of the Kissinger-Nixon strategy for achieving peace with honor in Vietnam. The concluding chapter of his *Time of Illusion* is titled "Credibility," and there he says among other things: "If the President was going to risk American credibility by withdrawing from the war . . . it would have to be accompanied by many awesome displays of unimpaired resolve—displays such as the invasion of Cambodia" when half our troops were withdrawn, "the mining of the ports of North Vietnam" when almost all our troops were out, and later, "the carpet-bombing of North Vietnam in the Christmas season of 1972" when the so-called peace accords were about to be initialed by Kissinger and Le Duc Tho in Paris.

The Nixon-Brezhnev Moscow summit meeting of May 1972 took place, it needs to be recalled, *after* our pilots had for the first time in the entire war been permitted to mine the busy harbor at Haiphong. Days before that, over 200,000 regular Soviet-armed North Vietnamese troops had poured into the South virtually unopposed by American air power; in fact, while Hanoi had been "building up" for its Spring offensive that year, the commander of U.S. air operations in Southeast Asia, General John D. Lavelle, had been summarily fired for having conducted "unauthorized" strikes against the build-up!

Thus the much-publicized mining of Haiphong, like the later carpet-bombing, was not a militarily meaningful move, but rather a Kissinger-orchestrated credibility gesture. "A withdrawal," writes Schell," was the most delicate of operations. Under no circumstances could it be allowed to appear an expression of loss of will." How could it be made to appear otherwise? By punctuating it with shows of fierceness; or, in Schell's words: "by mounting futile but tough-seeming military campaigns."

The idea that our government could have done such a thing simply to add "credibility" to our President's bargaining position in the Moscow summit meeting must boggle the ordinary mind. But the thing was in fact done. Last time we noted how elated Kissinger and his White House colleague William Safire were with themselves for having contributed something of their very own to the high promise of that summit meeting. But here is Mr. Schell's very different response to it: "For a moment, as President Nixon proclaimed that 'America's flag flies over the ancient Kremlin fortress' while Americans were dying in Southeast Asia in an attempt to counter the Kremlin's influence, the fighting in Vietnam came to look like something without precedent in military history: a war in which generals on the opposing sides combined into a joint command."

And here we come to the crux of Mr. Schell's book, to what assures it a place of permanent importance as a contribution to revisionist study of the Vietnam war. Jonathan Schell is an Eastern-establishment intellectual with impeccable liberal credentials. What he has given us is not in any strict sense an anti-Kissinger book. It is, rather, an anti-Vietnam-war, anti-Nixon, pro-newsmedia book. Throughout, one gets the impression that the author would have been pleased to be able to show that the "split policy" of coupling brutal shows of fierceness with retreat in Vietnam and negotiation of detente in Moscow was Nixon's very own idea. But he knows, and acknowledges with candor, that it simply isn't so. As he explains:

"In the framework of Kissinger's thinking, it made perfect sense to move toward the summit, and so toward peace, in the sphere of direct relations with the Soviet Union while simultaneously moving toward confrontation, and so toward intensified war, in the sphere of Vietnam policy. As far back as 1957, Kissinger had noted and deplored 'the notion that war and peace, military and political goals, were separate and opposite.' Now, under his guidance, war and peace were being pursued simultaneously. At the summit, the President would work for a relaxation of nuclear tension (what he now called a 'generation of peace'), and in the 'peripheral areas' he would continue to make demonstrations of his credibility (what he now called 'respect for the office of President of the United States')."

THE INCREDIBLE CREDIBILITY DOCTRINE

According to Schell, what Kissinger got President Nixon to do in Vietnam and Moscow during his first term was precisely what his predecessors McGeorge Bundy and Walt Rostow had earlier aspired to get Presidents Kennedy and Johnson to do, but–as *The Pentagon Papers* later revealed with relatively little success.

John F. Kennedy, one needs to recall, had often cited Kissinger by name, before the 1960 presidential election, as his academic authority for pointed criticisms of the massive-retaliation strategy; but the Harvard professor was never part of the Kennedy team that initiated our military involvement in Vietnam. During Johnson's elective term, however, Kissinger intervened personally twice to try to keep the experimental war on track: first by volunteering to get a better "exchange of signals" with Hanoi, and then to help Leslie Gelb with his anti-Johnson Pentagon Papers project. ("One of the scholars called in early to help guide the project," *Time* recalled in its June 28, 1971 issue, "was Harvard's Henry Kissinger, who is now President Nixon's national security advisor and chief White House strategist on the war.") Finally, under Nixon, after the experiment came close to being liquidated by Clark Clifford who despised the concept of such a war, Henry Kissinger took over to see it through to the end. First he exhilarated his hapless President with the "retreat to victory" scheme of the Guam doctrine, then he led him to the dizzy heights of the Moscow summit, as we have seen; and then, down from there, precipitously, to the puppet-like collapse of August 1974–"anticipating the fall some nine months later," as Schell declines to permit us to forget, "of the regimes that the United States had supported in Vietnam and Cambodia."

Schell distinguishes between Kissinger the theoretician and Kiss-inger the presidential advisor. The theoretician cannot be blamed for the practical consequences of his theorizing about the dilemma of nuclear warfare till he joins the ranks of the decision-making political actors. But thereafter he is to be judged with his decision-making peers. Whether academic strategists, corporate executives, or profes-sional politicians, the political actors who implemented the limited-war theory in Vietnam down through 1975 are in no way to be excused "from responsibility," writes Schell, "on the grounds that they did what they did for the cause of human survival." Their overriding concern may well have been to relieve mankind's fear of a nuclear Armageddon, but their actual performance was for the most part one of "sheer mendacity, fumbling, and brutality." Guided by their theorizing, our government took on "appearances not only of helplessness, irresolution, and incompetence but of duplicity and ruthlessness." Worse than that, Schell concludes, as "a catastrophe in its own right," their doctrine of limited war caused "the needless devastation of the Indo-Chinese peninsula . . . drove two Presidents into states of something like madness and led to the near-ruin of our political system."

With electrifying brevity, Schell thus sums up the essence of our Vietnam-involvement strategy: "One might say that the plan was to pay for nuclear peace with limited war." Containment and massive-retaliation had also been limited-war strategies. But they had never been advanced as failsafe substitutes for nuclear war. The Acheson design called for confronting the local aggressor on the field of aggression, initially, with just enough force to stop him in his tracks temporarily. If he then persisted in his aggression with increased violence, the force of our resistance would be escalated open-endedly till he was forced to quit. The Dulles design had been equally open-ended. But instead of engaging the enemy directly on the field of aggression, it gave us the latitude to "respond vigorously," if we may cite Dulles's words again, "at places and with means of our own choosing." In either case, however, the enemy would have our prior assurance (even as the P.L.O. has Israel's today) that, if he persisted in his aggression, our side would match his force at every level, doing finally whatever had to be done to contain him.

How does Kissinger's new strategy differ from these? In its initial phase it would be quite like the Acheson approach. The enemy would be engaged on the field of aggression, and our side would escalate its resistance to match his escalating force of aggression. But simultaneously—and this supplies the essential innovation—we would let the enemy and the world know that we were exercising nuclear-age prudence, that from the beginning we had prescribed a force-ceiling for ourselves beyond which we would never go, or even threaten to go. In other words, our resistance to local aggression would no longer be open-ended.

Was this a veiled prescription for surrender when the alternative was escalation into a general war? No, said Kissinger: for, once our force-ceiling was reached, we could remain at that level for as long as we wished. At any time thereafter, the less-well-supplied local aggressor might well tire. Then the result would be superficially the same as in Korea–but without the "reckless and shortsighted" threat that President Eisenhower fell back on in 1953.

FALSE COUNSELORS, BENIGHTED PRESIDENTS

The trouble with the new doctrine, as Mr. Schell keenly observes, is that the men who decided to implement it in Vietnam in the early sixties could never quite bring themselves around to explaining it unambiguously to anyone outside their own circle. We cited Schell's judgment on the subject elsewhere: "One might say that it was in the very nature of the doctrine that it had to be presented misleadingly to the public and the world. For to explain the policy would be to undermine it." Once we moved into Vietnam, in fact, government strategists soon found it easier to put their thoughts into action than into words. Before long, writes Schell, they and the Presidents they served together with the "public they were supposed to represent," began to "live in two different worlds and to cease to understand each other."

Did anyone ever tell President John F. Kennedy, in unambiguous terms, that the ultimate object of our Vietnam involvement was to pay for nuclear peace with limited war? Did Kennedy ever contemplate *losing* in Vietnam? The evidence of *The Pentagon Papers* runs against any such idea. He seems to have been persuaded rather that the new doctrine was simply a more prudent way of pursuing superpower goals in the nuclear age-goals worthy of a Roosevelt or Churchill–without hasty recourse to superpower means.

Superpower means had been used to attain superpower ends in the closing Japanese phase of World War II when atomic bombs were dropped on Hiroshima and Nagasaki, thereby reducing American casualties abruptly in what might otherwise have been a much prolonged war; and after the war, the assumption of the Truman-Eisenhower strategists had been that superpower ends and superpower means would thereafter be inextricably linked. But then came that wisp of glory called Camelot. Why not pursue glorious ends without recourse to needlessly militant means?

That was clearly the line initially taken with President Kennedy. America in the nuclear age would continue to do all that a superpower acting for the free world could be expected to do. It would act to make the world a better, a safer place, with liberty and justice for all. But it would do so with full appreciation of the unspeakable dangers mankind faced in the very fact of the existence of nuclear weapons. After all, the new limited-war strategy called upon Americans to fight–not surrender–for nuclear peace. That sounded right. One could hear in it something of the heroic ring of the Lincoln-esque inaugural address of January 1961. Why should Kennedy's advisors in those early days have risked saying anything more? Our troops were splendidly armed and well trained for the most part. The chances were very good that the local aggressors might come to their senses long before our resistance peaked to the prescribed cut-off point. Let sleeping dogs lie. Why worry about a perilous bridge you may never have to cross? Our Presidents can be told what they may finally have to know, in sum, when and if the last chips of the limited war doctrine are actually brought into play.

In Mr. Schell's view, the decision of our government's top national-security strategists not to tell our Presidents precisely what they had in mind for us in Vietnam marks the start of a crisis in our government which, before long, was to threaten the foundations of the Republic itself. That crisis, he says, must not be confounded with the Watergate scandal which really was only one of its surface symptoms. We've heard so much about the Watergate lying, about Plumbers units circumventing the F.B.I. and C.I.A. to plug national security "leaks," about fierce shows of hounding-down Daniel Ellsberg and prosecuting the New York Times for publishing secret documents which purportedly show how Presidents Kennedy and Johnson had secretly sought to "win" in Vietnam. Yet all of that, says Schell, is but a surface aspect of the rot of deception that had inevitably to set in, once our government, "impelled by strategic objectives that the public did not understand," let itself be involved in a new kind of war–Kissinger's kind of war–"whose necessity only presidential advisors, it seemed, were able to fully fathom."

14. CARTER AND MOYNIHAN VS. KISSINGER: FREEDOM OR PEACE?

In his U.N. speech of March 17, 1977, President Carter thus defined the three basic goals of America's cooperation with other nations: "First, to maintain peace and to reduce the arms race; Second, to build a better and more cooperative international economic system; And third, to work with potential adversaries as well as our close friends to advance the cause of human rights." Such emphasis on human rights marks a sharp break with the Kissinger approach to foreign policy. It is true that when Daniel P. Moynihan and William F. Buckley were at the U.N., they championed the cause of human rights publicly the way Mr. Carter has. But their chiefs, pursuing detente with Moscow at all costs, preferred to accept their resignations rather than support their views. The President's initiative here therefore confronts us with this question: Can foreign policy be conducted on the Moynihan-Buckley-Carter human rights premise? Or must our government, for the sake of "peace in our time," sacrifice what Carter has identified as the traditional American commitments to "freedom, self-government, human dignity, and mutual toleration"?

Public opinion polls show that most Americans, regardless of party, support President Carter's stand on human rights. It is the kind of posture our people apparently like in a President, even in the midst of "awesome" super-power negotiations to reduce the strategic arms buildup.

There has been some dutifully partisan criticism from Republicans, of course. That is hardly avoidable. Back in 1965, it will be recalled, Lyndon Johnson broke with the left wing of his own party to adopt what was in effect the Barry-Goldwater approach to the war in Vietnam. He had hoped Republican conservatives would support him in the move. Instead, they very partisanly began exploiting the Democratic split to elect a Republican in 1968. If Mr. Carter ever thoroughly alienates the same left wing between now and 1980, we may indeed get a repetition of the sort of unprincipled alliance that led to Nixon's election in '68. But we are still far from it now.

GEORGE WILL: THE DETENTE DRUNK HAS ENDED

In fact, the most sanguine praise of this Carter human-rights ini-

133

tiative has thus far come from a critic who is normally pro-Republican: *Newsweek's* Washington correspondent George Will, who used to cover the same beat for William F. Buckley's *National Review*. Will has often commented on how dangerously low our national morale has sunk since the Vietnam surrender and the Watergate presidential disgrace. From that perspective, he greets with rising hope the way President Carter has linked his stand on human rights with firmness on SALT II. This is evidence, according to Will, that "the U.S. government's detente drunk has ended," that "Carter has begun the arduous process of bringing Soviet leaders to a new sobriety about relations with the United States." Those leaders, Will concludes, are "understandably grieved" that Kissinger has been replaced by Carter as "architect of U.S. policy," for they "found Kissinger agreeably secretive, and never tiresome about human rights."

Still, haven't we had human-rights crusades in America before? And hasn't the brunt of them had to be borne almost invariably not by professed communist enemies but by old-time, anti-communist allies in Asia, Africa, South America, or the Iberian Peninsula? The record is clear. Typically such crusades start in the columns of the *New York Times* or *Washington Post*. Then they escalate to top-priority news coverage on the national TV networks. Finally Washington responds: pressures are applied, our ally bends, and more often than not its leaders fall. Yet in the end, instead of a triumph of human rights, what we are much more apt to get is simply a surrender of disgraced American clients to local communist cadres that enjoy unqualified support from Peking or Moscow. We can hardly marvel, therefore, that the few remaining anti-communist governments abroad are wary of Carter's "rhetoric" in this instance. They fear that, as in the past, real sanctions will be applied against them but not against communist or pro-communist violators of human rights.

And yet, if this Carter initiative is really nothing more than what we have had in the past, how does one explain the extraordinary opposition it is getting from our domestic supranationalist intelligentsia? Many of Carter's sharpest critics on this issue are veterans of the old newsmedia crusades that toppled Diem and Thieu and pursued the "generalissimi" of Nationalist China and Spain into their graves. According to such critics, Carter's venture into their "specialty" has not been sufficiently selective. Moscow, they point out, has perceived it as a deliberate attempt to reverse the Kissinger approach to Soviet-American detente which Kissinger had hoped to make irreversible; and what upsets them particularly is the fact that the President has quite obviously intended it to be so perceived.

Illuminating in this respect is a recent column by Jack Anderson in which he notes that, despite broad popular support, Carter's "abrasive advocacy of human rights" has been "strongly opposed by a large part of our intellectual and business community." Like the Communist Party leaders in Moscow, these establishment critics–mostly men of wealth and advanced education–have apparently preferred the Kissinger approach to detente. Their view, according to Anderson, is that in the nuclear age a President has to watch his words, especially when dealing with the communist superpowers. We have to be realists, they say; and by that they mean, says Anderson, "that we must in effect recognize diversity that each society has the right to its peculiar institutions." But that appeal to realism, so frequently heard from Kissinger, Anderson now rejects as specious. It amounts to asking us, in the name of realism, to ignore reality, to pretend not to see the very real difference "between free choice and rule by extermination" and "between individuals with inalienable rights and lumps of pulverized flesh."

What about the claim that, on a practical level, more can be done for human freedom in communist lands by Kissinger-style, under-the-counter arrangements than by public protests? According to Anderson, it is a hollow and hypocritical claim, since those who press it now have really given up on freedom. The truth is, he concludes with severity, that "to this influential minority there are values and goals that stand above freedom–so high that they would rather the President didn't even talk about it."

Freedom, in other words, has lost out in a new hierarchy of values shared by an influential minority of intellectuals and businessmen; when challenged now, freedom must simply submit in silence so that higher goals may be attained! Anderson breaks off here without telling us what those higher goals are supposed to be. Profits from grain and technology deals with the communist powers, perhaps? Or a fusion of capitalist and communist managerial expertise to organize a strike-proof, low labor-cost global economy? No–nothing so ruggedly blunt as that. When supranationalist intellectuals and transnational capitalists join forces (as they certainly have today) to promote Soviet-American detente, it is left to the intellectuals, not the capitalists, to articulate the shared principles. And what our intellectuals now claim to value above human freedom–so high that they would rather the President didn't even talk about it–is of course *peace.*

"HOW MUCH DOES FREEDOM MATTER?"

What price peace? In his last year in office, Henry Kissinger tried desperately—with cunning, secrecy, deception, and contempt even for law, as the *New York Times* acknowledged—to set us irreversibly on a course away from freedom toward peace. There is no alternative to peace in the nuclear age, he used to argue. If, to get peace, we had to stop championing human rights in public, if we had to become extremely pliant in SALT negotiations, that, according to Kissinger, had simply to be. Our overriding responsibility, as he saw it, was to spare mankind a nuclear holocaust. A flamboyant Daniel Moynihan could resign his U.N. ambassadorship if he liked, rather than be silent about human rights violations, and a rigorous Paul Nitze could resign his post as chief SALT negotiator if he thought Kissinger was ready to concede too much; but so long as Kissinger was at the helm, the ship would remain on course.

The importance of Carter's human rights stand, coupled with his firmness on SALT II is best perceived against that Kissinger-Moynihan-Nitze background. What Kissinger could get away with under Presidents Nixon and Ford, no one will be able to get away with under a President who proclaims, as emphatically as Carter has lately done, an American commitment to human freedom. America will cooperate with other nations to keep the peace and better economic conditions for all, he has said; but what it values most and will never sacrifice is its commitment to freedom.

"How Much Does Freedom Matter?" was the title of an article by Daniel Moynihan that appeared in *Atlantic Monthly* at a time (June, 1975) when its author was between jobs in the Kissinger State Department. In a past issue of *State of the Nation* (Sept., 1975) we noted with what exceptional frankness Moynihan there acknowledged that at some point between 1961 (when Kennedy took office) and 1974 (when Nixon left office) freedom had ceased to matter for the top architects of American foreign policy. Abruptly the compass-heading of our ship of state was swung around 180 degrees so as to head us directly away from freedom; and it was done, according to Moynihan (writing in a confessional mood), by a cadre of decision-makers who were never publicly authorized to make the reversal.

The American national commitment to freedom began with the War of Independence against England. And down through World War II, when Roosevelt joined Churchill and Stalin to crush Hitler, our heads of state consistently maintained for us "a posture in the world" (so Moynihan writes) "in which we chose freedom, and saw ourselves as its natural ally and defender." After World War II, what divided Hitler's chief conquerors was the issue of freedom. The policy under Truman and Eisenhower was to "contain" communist expansion, by massive retaliation if necessary, wherever or whenever it threatened the freedom of our clients or allies. Kennedy's inaugural address of January, 1961, in which he said Americans would "pay any price, bear any burden . . . to assure the survival and the success of liberty," was a reaffirmation of the traditional commitment.

But in the early 1960s we began to experience what was at first, in Moynihan's words, a "barely perceptible process of disengagement" from that traditional commitment. We were deep in the Vietnam war. The level of American troops fighting in the field was being steadily increased. Yet, behind the scenes, there was a correspondingly steady decline in determination to "actually win for freedom" in Vietnam. Then, abruptly, what had been barely perceptible became obvious. There occurred, writes Moynihan, "a sudden and definitive shift . . . like a great sailing ship coming around."

That definitive shift took place in March 1968. On March 1, Clark Clifford had replaced Robert McNamara at the Pentagon, with instructions to supply 206,000 additional troops requested by our field commanders in Vietnam. As Clifford later acknowledged in a *Foreign Affairs* article (July, 1969): "I had taken office at the beginning of the month with one overriding assignment—responding to the military request to strengthen our forces so that we might prosecute the war more forcefully." But by the end of the month, Clifford had so obviously failed to carry out his one overriding assignment that his President, in despair, gave up any further attempt to move ahead forcefully in the war or in his expectations for a second elective term.

What happened to our foreign policy after that has since been variously described, chiefly by anti-Johnson Democrats, journalists, and academicians. Moynihan's image of a "great sailing ship coming about" is certainly apt. "The boom, hauled and tugged," he writes, "moves slowly, resistingly at first, when with an abandoned sweep it hurtles across the keel line. The ship lurches, settles, and then, as if there had never been another direction, moves forward on the opposite track. Those who were tugging knew what to expect, even if they may have doubted for a moment their ultimate success. Those who ducked are still on deck. The ship moves on, oblivious of its past, an affair henceforth of logs and courts of enquiry."

The same turnabout has been described somewhat more prosaically by Townsend Hoopes in his *Limits of Intervention: An Inside Account of How the Johnson Policy of Escalation in Vietnam was Reversed* (1969, 1973). The *New York Times* gave the first edition of the Hoopes book a cover-page review (Nov. 16, 1969) by Max Frankel. The heading read boldly, "A Conspiracy of Doves in the Pentagon," and, together with a picture of the Pentagon, the first page featured a string of pictures of the participants for and against the President– Hoopes, of course, but also Bundy, Enthoven, Warnke, Nitze, Vance, and McNaughton, as well as McNamara, Clifford, and Johnson– most of whom, except the dead, are now back in the news.

Frankel's opening words were: "In the game that governments play, when the emperor has no clothes, you must begin by telling him there's a hole in his shoe. The slogans with which we have contemplated retreat are piling up beside the euphemisms by which we slid into the war. Retreat to enclaves. Stop the bombing. Negotiate. De-escalate. Abandon. Search and Destroy. Cease fire. Vietnamization. Who will say failure? Townsend Hoopes says it, in a brief and largely personal memoir of his observations as President Johnson's last Under Secretary of the Air Force. *The Limits of Intervention* is . . . a bolt of light . . . about the frantic effort in March, 1968, to persuade a new Defense Secretary, Clark Clifford, that victory in Vietnam was unattainable by any tolerable means and the subsequent conspiracy to persuade Lyndon Johnson to act as if he agreed."

But Clark Clifford's own account of what happened remains authoritative. In his "Vietnam Reappraisal" for *Foreign Affairs* he says frankly that when he first met with the Pentagon task-force he had inherited from McNamara, his instructions from the President were unambiguous. "We were not instructed to assess the need for substantial increases in men and material," he writes; "we were to devise the means by which they could be provided. My work was cut out."

Clifford knew that, some months before, the military had gone over McNamara's head to speak directly to the President. Their charge, as Hanson Baldwin has revealed, was that McNamara had consistently failed to inform the President about their official estimates of the strictly military requirements for victory in Vietnam. Given the extraordinary political restraints–that they were not to pursue the enemy into his sanctuaries or destroy his Hanoi depots and Haiphong port facilities–they had estimated back in 1964 (and Baldwin saw the estimates) that, with 500,000 to 800,000 American troops in the field, it would take perhaps ten years of dogged fighting to assure the survival and success of liberty in South Vietnam.

Having heard the military, Johnson fired McNamara and hired Clifford, a veteran architect of the Truman containment doctrine. But McNamara's ghost–the spirit that animates the so-called Pentagon papers even now–was not easily exercised. In his first week with the inherited taskforce, Clifford tried hard to work up a plan for moving 206,000 additional troops in Vietnam. But, in his words, "try though we would to stay with the assignment of devising means to meet the military's request, fundamental questions began to occur over and over."

JOHNSON'S FALL, NIXON'S RISE

In terms of Moynihan's image, there was much tugging and hauling to bring the boom around. Clifford simply couldn't have his way. The military had specified their war needs, and the President had instructed Clifford to supply them. But here were men who simply would not comply with a Defense Secretary's instructions. Did they perhaps have better plans of their own to accomplish the same end? They hesitated to say. For days the meetings were at an impasse, till Clifford backed them to the wall and they had to speak. In his *Foreign Affairs* article, Clifford then gives us this momentous sentence: "When I asked for a presentation of the military plan for attaining victory in Vietnam, I was told that there was no plan for victory in the historic American sense." The next question was: "Why not?" And then the dam broke. The political restraints long since imposed upon our military, it was acknowledged, precluded and were intended to preclude the very possibility of military victory, even if the President and his field commanders hadn't yet grasped the point!

That was the "conspiracy of doves in the Pentagon." Its fate at that moment was squarely in the hands of Clark Clifford. It was war time. Clifford might have urged his President to free the Pentagon and the war effort generally of such conspirators. Instead he let himself be persuaded that Vietnam's freedom could not be worth the price that would then have to be paid for it. So he did what Max Frankel says he did: he joined the opposition and, for a time even took the lead in trying to persuade the President to "act as if he agreed" with what was in essence a total defiance of presidential prerogatives.

A few days later, Johnson virtually confessed to the American people that he was not able to have his way in Washington. He hinted that too many people around him had loyalties to the previous administration which they had apparently not transferred to him. Perhaps as a Southerner who had gained the Presidency because of an assassin's bullet, he wasn't the man to do effectively what then needed to be done. He would therefore not seek re-election. In

Vietnam, meanwhile, he would try his best to hold the line for his successor.

That successor, unfortunately, turned out to be Richard M. Nixon. By March 1968, he had already been perceived by anti-Johnson Democrats as just the sort of man to "captain" the ship of state on its reverse course. I.F. Stone had made the point back in 1966, and Walter Lippmann had publicly agreed. Nixon had learned the lesson of his disastrous defeat in the California gubernatorial race of 1962 and had chucked aside his anti-communist militancy. In the 1966 mid-term congressional elections, pro-Johnson candidates had fared badly because anti-Johnson Democrats had openly supported Republicans against them. Recognizing an opportunity for his breed of politician, Nixon exclaimed at the time: "The peace party always wins. I know my own party. If the war is still going on in '68, there is no power on earth can keep them from trying to outbid the Democrats for the peace vote."

That was the "New" Nixon—as devoted to peace as he had previously been devoted to anticommunist militancy. I.F. Stone and Walter Lippmann hastened to assess the "uses" to which such a converted politician might be put. Anti-Johnson Democrats listened and acted. If they were ever to regain control of their party, they would have to see to it that Johnson and his supporters were thoroughly defeated in '68. Yet, to put a "respectable" Republican in the White House wouldn't do, since that might result in a prolonged Republican incumbency. Nixon, a loner, highly vulnerable as a public personality, could be counted on not to entrench Republicans. He would get in because anti-Johnson Democrats refused to support Johnson's man; and then, after he had done his job of settling the ship of state on its new course, a suitable occasion would surely present itself to be rid of him. In fact, once the Vietnam war was "safely lost," Nixon was perceived as the most obviously vulnerable man in American politics.

Till his last breath as President, Nixon remained a devotee of the "cause of peace" that had gained him the White House. When he announced his resignation on August 8, 1974, he in fact offered this pathetic apology, which virtually disqualifies him to be ranked as a true President of the United States: "When I first took the oath of office as President five and a half years ago, I made this sacred commitment: to consecrate my office, my energies and all the wisdom I can summon to the cause of peace among nations."

As we have noted elsewhere, the President's very specific oath commits him to preserve, protect, and defend our national union of which the Constitution is the organic law. Nothing in that Constitution authorizes a President to consecrate his *office* to the "cause of peace among nations." In its Preamble, six ends are specified, every one of which is to be preferred to peace, when a choice is forced upon us. To "secure the blessings of liberty to ourselves and our posterity" while we perfect our national union is certainly our most solemn charge.

KISSINGER OR MOYNIHAN?

It was with Richard Nixon, not with Lyndon Johnson, that freedom ceased to matter for the Government of the United States. In 1975, when he raised the question in his *Atlantic Monthly* article, Moynihan apparently still had hopes that, with Nixon gone, his friend Henry Kissinger might begin to reverse course and give freedom its due. Such hopes led him to accept appointment as our Ambassador to the U.N., where he intended to renew his advocacy of human rights. To continue to move away from freedom, he had warned, "could constitute an accommodation to totalitarianism without precedent in our history."

We all know what happened to Moynihan at the U.N. Pressure from Kissinger silenced him and forced him to resign. Since then he has been elected U.S. Senator from New York. In his first important Senate vote, when Paul Warnke's appointment as chief disarmament negotiator reached the floor, he rose with Senator Jackson to oppose confirmation. For that, the *Post* characterized him as the New Hawk from New York."

Perhaps before long, as Senator, Moynihan will decide to do the nation a great service by calling for a full-scale investigation of the turnabout he described in his *Atlantic Monthly* article. Many who tugged and hauled and ducked are still on deck—and they are now objecting to Carter's efforts to put us back on course, under the banner of human rights, after eight years of what George Will has called our "detente drunk." We have had enough of accommodating totalitarianism for the sake of peace. In this or any other age, freedom must matter to us, or we have ceased to be Americans.

15. FROM KANT TO KISSINGER
AND BRZEZINSKI

Here in our nation's capital, where "flights for peace" to distant places are an almost daily occurrence, it is perhaps fitting to recall that the earliest instance of shuttle diplomacy for peace on an interplanetary scale appears to have occurred during that bitterly prolonged war between the states not the American but the ancient Greek states—which we have all come to know as the Peloponnesian war.

Thucydides tells us nothing about it, unfortunately. But we learn from Aristophanes that the world's first astronaut-for-peace was an Athenian of substantial private means named Trygaeus. When the war's bad press turned his heart against it, he organized an ad hoc anti-war committee, got himself a powerful fuel-guzzling, air-polluting dung-beetle for a spaceship, and took off for the translunar dwelling-place of the gods, hoping to petition them for a speedy return of peace to war-torn Hellas.

But Zeus and the rest, knowing what poor use men usually make of peace, refused to hear Trygaeus. Hermes, a sort of press secretary, offered the divine excuses. Peace, he said, was at the bottom of a well, where Mars had dumped her for safekeeping, covered over with a pile of huge rocks. The site was nearby. If Trygaeus and his committeemen really wanted to get peace out prematurely, they'd simply have to do it on their own. This they gladly undertake to do. The sweet goddess is raised, and before long, the space-shuttle diplomacy has her back on earth for a sort of TV talk-show, where the pros and cons of war are debated and where the anti-peace people, then as now, lose.

Of course, today, top-level peace retrievers flit about in fuel-guzzling ships that are far more powerful than Trygaeus' dung-beetle. Still, when they show us the retrieved goddess, she looks as if she has indeed been at the bottom of a well. Can't we, in this technetronic age, do better than that for peace?

KANT'S IMPERATIVE FOR PEACE

The most faithful high priests of the sweet goddess in our time say that we can. Rostow says that what we need is a conceptual purge of the present for the sake of the future. If we want permanent peace, nationhood will have to be sacrificed on her altar. Then Mars will get dumped in a well, and peace—*teste David cum Sibylla*—will be enthroned to reign on earth forever, world without end.

But it seems that our modern high priests of peace prefer to trace their lineage back not so much to the shuttle-diplomacy of Trygaeus as to the stern anti-eudaemonistic ethics of Immanuel Kant who, in 1795, published a now world-famous pamphlet titled *Perpetual Peace (Zum ewigen Frieden)*. What makes that pamphlet attractive to the modern academic mind, even when employed in advising Presidents, is its skepticism on the theoretic level, coupled with a dogmatic conviction on the practical level that perpetual peace will inevitably result if people will simply do, individually, what they are supposed to do.

Kant believed that human reason could never learn the truth about things in themselves, that it would have to content itself, theoretically, with manipulating mere appearances or phenomena. But in the sphere of willing, the very fact that reason could not be affected by reality from the outside, guaranteed the absolute freedom of the will. What does reason tell itself as *will?* According to Kant, it does not so much tell, as command. In the subjective moral sphere, reason gives itself this categorical moral imperative: "Act only on that maxim of your will through which you can at the same time will that it shall become a principle of universal legislation." In his *Perpetual Peace,* Kant assumes that his readers have understood and accepted his categorical imperative. For what is implicit in that imperative is made explicit in the pamphlet, namely, that when men act morally they prepare the world for world law, world courts, and universal acceptance of the decisions of world courts.

The question that is by no means settled here is this: Does Kant's deduction of the inevitability of permanent peace from his categorical imperative suffice to qualify him as an advocate—an 18th century advocate—of world government "beyond the nation-state"? F.H. Hinsley, in his *Nationalism and the International System,* assures us that it does not. Kant often uses such expressions as the "federation of free states," "free federation," and a "federal union of nations." But, as Hinsley demonstrates, those terms are used, in their original Latin sense, "strictly to mean agreement reached and maintained by treaty," never to mean the formation of a single new state made up of the old nations. A state, Kant says, "is not a possession like the soil. It is a society of men which no one but themselves is called on to command or dispose of. . . . To incorporate it as a graft into another state is to take away its existence as a moral person and to make of it a thing." Kant concludes quite explicitly that a "state of nations contains a contradiction; many nations would in a single state constitute only one nation, which is contradictory since we are considering the rights of nations towards each other. . . . " In other words, to solve problems of international relations by getting rid of the nations would be, says Kant, like solving problems of interpersonal relations by getting rid of the persons.

Still, isn't it a matter of historical record that, as Rostow asserts, nations in their independence have been the war-makers par-excellence? That may be. But Kant the moralist is not interested in the historical record. The facts of history are objects of knowledge for pure reason, and can therefore never be known for certain. It is not by way of history but through mind itself, Kant stresses, that we move from the categorical imperative to the inevitability of perpetual peace. Simply do your moral duty, Kant reiterates, and a divine providence or humanistic fate will take care of the rest.

Carl Friedrich's Marxist Transformation

The most influential interpreter of Kant's peace doctrine in the American academy has been Carl Friedrich of Harvard. Through favored pupils and colleagues, Professor Friedrich has indirectly but powerfully influenced the sort of advice American Presidents have received on questions of war and peace since 1961, but more particularly since Henry Kissinger and Zbigniew Brzezinski have gone to Washington. Significantly, Friedrich's edition of Kant's famous pamphlet, with his long introduction, notes, and commentary, is titled *Inevitable Peace,* not *Perpetual Peace.* The introduction points out that, for all his love of peace, Kant never really developed a valid solution for the "problem of war," precisely because he never developed a valid concept of world government. Kant, says Friedrich, advanced to the concept of a federation of nation-states; but, beyond that, he steadfastly refused to advance. "Federalism," writes Friedrich, "is better than nothing, but far short of a sure means of preventing war. That means can be found in one, and only one, solution: a united government of the world." Friedrich, as we shall see, champions that solution.

Yet if Kant's advocacy of peace is essentially defective, it has nevertheless, Friedrich assures us, a high inspirational value. Kant is, after all, a great man. Moreover, to supply what is lacking in his doctrine of peace, we have only to turn to two later, far more historical-minded thinkers, who give force to ideas. "To me it seems clear," writes Friedrich, "that Marx and Engels, in a very real sense, carried out Kant's 'idea for a universal history with a cosmopolitan intent,' for they understood precisely what Kant had urged . . . indeed, it is not too far-fetched to say that Marx and Engels were the only ones to attempt this task which Kant wished to see attempted, and of which he admitted that it would call for a man with a good knowledge of history."

Marx and Engels thus supply the historical support for Kant's otherwise abstract leap from the categorical imperative to perpetual peace. But they do not supercede Kant. What is needed, according to Friedrich, is integration. "In the beginning," he writes, "I stated that I do not consider myself a Kantian. Kant is not enough. There is more to man than his mind. There is, for instance, his economic well-being." Similarly, he adds, "I do not consider myself a Marxian. Marx [too] is not enough, even when re-interpreted by Lenin, Stalin, and their more moderate critics." What would be enough is what Kant, Marx, and Engels shared, if it could be consistently and humanistically elaborated. Friedrich's concluding words on the subject read as follows:

"Kant and Marx and Engels were all shaped . . . by a universal sympathy for man. These three, and the others whom we find in their company in the never-ending quest for peace, loved man. Deep down below the bottom of their restless energetic minds there lived a faith which words cannot express. It is the faith that animates all the great world religions. It is the faith all humanism seeks to salvage when faith declines. This faith provides the only real ground for believing in inevitable peace. It is inevitable only because man cannot escape his own destiny of fulfillment as man."

FROM FRIEDRICH TO ROSTOW

I think it is fair to say that a humanistic synthesis of Kant and Marx has, in fact, been attempted—perhaps directly under Friedrich's influence—by the three most famous recent American presidential advisors for national security affairs. Walt Rostow's *Stages of Economic Growth,* for instance, is subtitled *A Non-Communist Manifesto* because, as Rostow explains, its "stages-of-growth . . . constitute an alternative to Karl Marx's theory of modern history." The Marx-Engels Communist Manifesto distinguished four stages of growth: feudalism, capitalism, socialism, and finally communism, which is to be, indeed, a global community of perpetual peace. In his *Non-Communist Manifesto,* Rostow says that the end envisioned by Marx is "a decent and legitimate hope; an aspiration; and even, a possibility." The trouble is that Marx has got the stages of growth leading up to it wrong.

To begin with, there are not four stages of growth, says Rostow, but five. The first stage is that of traditional society, with its antiquated concepts of nationhood, sovereignty, the right to wage war, etc. It survives virtually as a fossil. A second stage consists of the pre-conditions for industrial takeoff. Then comes takeoff, then the drive to industrial maturity, and finally the stage of high mass-consumption. But there is a "beyond." The Soviet Union is on the verge of high mass-consumption; but, for fear of the U.S., its leaders are holding it back. The United States, already on the verge of the "beyond," doesn't yet quite know what to make of its opportunities. One thing is certain: if the communists, with American help, can be brought fully into the stage of high mass-consumption, says Rostow, the chances of world peace on a humanistic plateau, beyond both mass-consumption and the nation-states, will be greatly advanced.

That was Rostow in Cambridge Mass., in 1960. When he came to Washington in 1961, he brought with him, as he later explained, two guiding principles in the form of quotations pasted in the back of a favorite book. One was the following from John Maynard Keynes: "Words ought to be a little wild, for they are an assault of thought upon the unthinking. But when the seats of power and authority have been attained, there should be no more poetic license. . . . When a doctrinaire proceeds to action, he must, so to speak, forget his doctrine, for those who in action remember the letter will probably lose what they are seeking."

The companion quotation was this, from Winston Churchill: "Those who are possessed of a definite body of doctrine and of deeply rooted convictions upon it will be in a much better position to deal with the shifts and surprises of daily affairs than those who are merely taking short views and indulging their natural impulses as they are evoked by what they read from day to day." Rostow, under Presidents Kennedy and Johnson, let himself be guided by these quotations. He kept his doctrine, but minced and minished his words as Keynes advised, especially after he replaced McGeorge Bundy in the White House basement. But on November 20, 1963–two days before President Kennedy's assassination–there was more than a touch of the old poetry in a Rostow speech which stood up for America against the Soviets in this fashion:

"One of the oldest claims of communism—namely, that it is a doctrine and movement which transcended the ancient claims of nationalism—has never looked less persuasive. On the contrary, despite debate and difficulty the non-Communist world is making real progress in finding ways in which dignified and proud nation-states can concert for larger common purpose. . . . Dangerous clashes of nationalism still exist in many parts of the free world and absorb a high proportion of the energies of diplomacy in the search for pacific settlement. But building on the most fundamental of the commitments of free men—namely, to search and find collective solutions in a free environment of diffuse authority—we are making real progress."

KISSINGER AND KANT AT THE U.N.

It was not Rostow, however, but his successor at the President's ear, Henry Kissinger, who brought the Kantian commitment to peace, as rectified by Carl Friedrich, to bear most directly on top level American foreign policy decision-making. At Harvard, Kissinger had been one of Friedrich's favorite pupils. Yet, in the end, to complete his graduate studies, Kissinger shifted from Friedrich to William Yandell Elliott. Reminiscing recently, Friedrich himself reported his pupil's reason for the shift. "I am interested in the practical politics of international relations," the future Secretary of State told his Kantian mentor, "and you are interested in philosophy and scholarship."

Kissinger too had made many frank statements about nationhood and sovereignty before coming to Washington. The *Necessity for Choice* (1960-1961), for instance, rises to truly Kantian heights where Kissinger chides the Western nations for inclining toward unity only when threatened by a common enemy. "The ultimate unity of the West," he protests, "depends on what we affirm, not on what we reject. We of the West, who bequeathed the concept of nationalism to others, must summon the initiative and imagination to show the way to a new international order. Nothing is more crucial than for the West to develop. policies that make for true community." In *The Troubled Partnership,* five years later (1965), Kissinger focuses on the efforts of the NATO countries to hold together while President Kennedy was cultivating detente with Moscow over their heads. With equal frankness he there concludes that "institutions based on present concepts of national sovereignty are not enough. The West requires a larger goal. . . . Clearly, it will not come quickly; many intermediate stages must be traversed before it can be reached. It is not too early, however, to prepare ourselves now for this step beyond the nation-state."

The nation-state system no doubt once had a useful historical function to perform; but now its time is past, and statesmen of the West must face up to that fact. "For a while longer," says Kissinger with the same sort of regard Marx liked to express for the past utility of capitalism:

"For a while longer the West can continue along familiar lines. The traditional machinery . . . is well designed to produce the appearance of amity. But if [we continue] to confuse form with substance, energy will increasingly have to be spent in reconciling illusion with reality. Each nation will be thrown on its own resources and will emphasize policies that magnify divisions. At each previous critical juncture the West–though with much travail–found forms adequate to its needs. It made the transition from feudalism to the nation state. Its challenge now is whether it can move from the nation state to a larger community and draw from this effort the strength for another period of innovation."

For most of his time in Washington, Kissinger had Nixon's conservative constituency to contend with. So, like Rostow, he watched his words. But when he became Secretary of State, he must have felt morally bound to shout his moral convictions about perpetual peace at least once or twice from the housetops, provided they were appropriate housetops.

Kissinger's maiden speech as Secretary of State was delivered at the U.N. His theme was the state of the world, and he stressed what he called the global problems of war, hunger, terrorism, inflation, and pollution. "Can we meet the inevitable challenge of the future," he asked, "with our system of nation states?" His answer was an emphatic *no*. In his words: "Two centuries ago the philosopher Kant predicted that universal peace would come eventually–as the creation of man's moral aspirations or as the consequence of physical necessity. What seemed utopian then looms as tomorrow's reality: soon there will be no alternative." Then, speaking as a man newly qualified (by the imminent disgrace of his boss) to make ultimate decisions on American foreign relations, he did not hesitate to say:

"The United States has made its choice. We strive for a world in which the rule of law governs. . . . We envisage a comprehensive, institutionalized peace, encompassing all nations." Against the hesitations of internationalists who still feel, as Reinhold Niebuhr sometimes felt, that conditions were not yet ripe for a world government, Kissinger warned: "The ideal of a world community may be decried as unrealistic–but great constructions have always been ideals before they became realities." And he exhorted, finally: "Let us dedicate ourselves to this noblest of all possible goals."

Later, at the annual Al Smith Memorial Foundation dinner in New York, Kissinger returned to the theme. After summarizing his recent successes in shuttle-diplomacy–peace in Vietnam, peace nearly achieved in the Middle East, strengthened peaceful relations with the Communist powers, and new partnerships for peace with old allies–the ex-Harvard professor offered this Kantian projection of inevitable peace: "But now–indeed partly because of our success–we experience the birth pangs of a new order. We face a new dimension of challenges, more pervasive and complex, with perils at once more subtle and profound. At the midway point between the end of the second World War and the end of this century, we find ourselves also midway between the nation state front which we began and the global community which we must fashion if we are ever to live in peace. . . . The fact is that all nations–East and West, aligned and non-aligned–are part of one global system and dependent on it for their peace."

BRZEZINSKI AND GARDNER

While Rostow was at Johnson's ear, Kissinger, still in the academy, used to criticize his style though not his ends. While Kissinger advised Nixon and Ford, he got the same kind of criticism from Zbigniew Brzezinski. Like his predecessors, Brzezinski too has developed a stages-of-growth theory to rectify Marx's vision of history so as to make it a more humanistic validation of Kant's expectations of peace. In several of his writings but at greatest length in his book *Between Two Ages: America's Role in the Technetronic Age,* Brzezinski makes the point that the Western peoples have advanced through three great stages and are now entering a fourth and culminating stage. The first stage was an age of religion: coupling the idea of divine providence with a "narrowness derived" as he says, "from massive ignorance, illiteracy, and a vision confined to the immediate environment."

Then came the age of nationalism. This matched Christian equality before God with national equality before the law. It thus "marked another giant step in the progressive redefinition of man's nature and place in our world." In the wake of Western nationalism has come Marxism which, says Brzezinski, "represents a further vital and creative stage in the maturing of man's universal vision." But there is more. Beyond religion, nationalism, and Marxism is the emerging technetronic age of rational humanism on a global scale.

Brzezinski's rational humanism is inevitable. Yet it can be obstructed or facilitated in its advent by human choices. The pressing question for him, as for Kissinger, is therefore this: Can our traditional American national institutions support the progressive changes that are about to come upon us?

Making the same point in his *Necessity for Choice,* Kissinger had asserted that every society, at some time, must ask itself whether it may not have "exhausted all possibilities of innovation inherent in its structure." Out of the same mold, with echoes of the same language, comes this passage in Brzezinski's book. "Tension is unavoidable," he writes, "as man strives to assimilate the new into the framework of the old. For a time the established framework resiliently integrates the new by adapting it in a more familiar shape. But at some point the old framework becomes overloaded. The new input can no longer be redefined into traditional forms, and eventually it asserts itself with compelling force. Today, though, the old framework of international politics—with their spheres of influence, military alliances between nation-states, doctrinal conflicts arising from nineteenth-century crises—is clearly no longer compatible with reality."

Once upon a time, says Brzezinski, the nation-states were the only significant players in international relations. But, today, "short of war, the game is truly played on a more informal basis, with much more mixed participation. . . . [M]ini-states are overshadowed by multi-million-dollar international corporations, transnational organizations of religious or ideological character, and the emerging international institutions. . . . The world is ceasing to be an arena in which relatively self-contained 'sovereign' and homogeneous nations interact. Transnational ties are gaining in importance, while the claims of nationalism, though still intense, are nevertheless becoming diluted." We are entering, in sum, a "new era—an era of the global political process."

How is America to face up to all of this? Brzezinski considers the high hopes of some of his colleagues to seize the bull by the horns with a declaration of *inter*dependence in 1976 to be followed by American ratification of a world constitution by 1989. "Realism, however, forces us to recognize," says Brzezinski, "that the necessary political innovation will not come from direct constitutional reform. The needed change is more likely to develop incrementally and less overtly." There will be a gradual blurring of distinctions between public and private institutions as it becomes apparent that our national institutions—once effective—can no longer meet the challenge of contemporary problems.

That is the usual charge that globalist thinkers make against the nation-state. Its institutions are no longer adequate. But is it a valid charge? Not according to Gunnar Myrdal. In the days when he was still an ardent world federalist, Professor Myrdal wrote with extraordinary candor: "In spite of world wars and depressions we have seen in each of our advanced countries a tremendous rise in productivity, security of employment, and standards of living, and also greater equality of opportunity for the individual citizens and a general equalization of incomes and wealth. In the last forty years, with all their international turmoils, these countries have witnessed a more rapid national integration than ever before in history. The ordinary citizen is apt to believe—and very largely with good reason—that the national policies by which this has been brought about are good, even if they are exactly those which are pictured as the causes of international disintegration."

In other words, it is not the incompetence but the competence of nation-states that makes them obstructions in the way of realizing the Rostow-Kissinger-Brzezinski ideal of perpetual peace. The ordinary citizen is therefore not apt to accept the proposed radical changes, if they are frankly presented to him. Richard Gardner, Brzezinski's colleague at Columbia who helped recruit Jimmy Carter for the Trilateral Commission, has faced up to this dilemma. In an article for *Foreign Affairs* titled "The Hard Road to World Order," he acknowledges that few people today "retain much confidence in the more ambitious strategies for world order that had wide backing a generation ago—'world federalism,' 'charter review,' and 'world peace through world law'." It is plain now that direct, simple solutions will not do. Advising the sort of prudence Rostow recommended, Gardner concludes:

"The hope of the foreseeable future lies, not in building up a few ambitious central institutions of universal membership and general jurisdiction as was envisaged at the end of the last war, but rather in the much more decentralized, disorderly and pragmatic process of inventing or adapting institutions of limited jurisdiction and selected memberships to deal with specific problems on a case-by-case basis . . . . In short, the 'house of world order' will have to be built from the bottom up rather than from the top down. It will look like a great 'booming, buzzing, confusion' . . . , but an end run around national sovereignty, eroding it piece by piece, will accomplish much more than the old-fashioned frontal assault."

We are indeed far removed here from the idealism of Immanuel Kant. Having lost faith in honest advocacy of their aims, the Gardners of our time have decided on misdirection, on slow erosion of the fabric of American national institutions. Friedrich had urged that Kant's idealism be coupled with the revolutionary historical realism of Karl Marx, so that statecraft might be put in the service of perpetual peace. Here we have a decision to couple Kant's idealism with public duplicity, with end runs around sovereignty, eroding it piece by piece, while serving directly under Presidents who take a solemn oath to preserve, protect, and defend the national union of which the Constitution is the organic law.

When Kissinger was about to leave office, the *New York Times* in its farewells noted how committed Kissinger was to peace and what he seemed prepared to do to realize it. An editorial of January 16, 1977, said at one point: "Kissinger's story as a statesman turns on an image of a world at the brink of nuclear disaster, with 'no alternative to peace.' . . . Individually, his policies can be shown to have produced only modest advantage and often great disadvantage and grief. But he was working from a larger script. This, at any rate, was the essential Kissinger behind the day-to-day cunning, and maneuvering, the secrecy and the deception, the contempt for bureaucracy, and even law."

Cunning, secrecy, deception, and contempt even for law and all for the sake of peace? Let us hope that President Carter's Brzezinski is not prepared to go that far. I can't say here what effect such an approach to decision-making for national security affairs is apt to have on the future development of American political pluralism, but I know what effect it is bound to have on the American academy if distinguished academicians continue to sacrifice truth for the sake of expedient end runs around traditional concepts of nationhood and constitutionally ordained and established national institutions. Before it has quite ripened, our academy will have contaminated itself at the core with a spreading rot from which there can be no easy, and certainly no painless recovery.

The Peace and Freedom of Peers

And yet, why not a United Nations Organization converted into a true world government, with a world court, and power enough to enforce treaty obligations? Or, in terms of the Kantian-Marxian synthesis proposed by Friedrich and his disciples: Why not a world state with enforceable peace, on either an American liberal model, or a

Soviet despotic model, or a humanistic combination of the two, or even some third world model designed to redistribute the goods of the world according to appetites? It is a topic for another panel. But, in the remaining time, I can say at least this:

To form a world-state for the sake of peace is to discard, of course, the very possibility of a gradual elevation of all peoples in the world to equality in freedom. The very logic of a global regime with a monopoly of coercive power—a regime without a peer to balance and challenge its omnipotence and thereby render its government responsible—precludes its cultivation of the freedom of its subjects.

The point is that a universal state capable of enforcing global peace, is, in its very concept, a *defective* state. It can prevent war while it enjoys a monopoly of coercive power; but it cannot perfect and secure its citizens, or rather, its subjects, in personal freedom because it is not itself, as a state, free in any meaningful sense. In a fully matured political community of the kind that a Walter Bagehot would call a community of government by discussion—what we have is the development of recognizable national identity or, as Kant was ready to say, personality.

Personality is essentially "awareness of one's existence as a unit in sharp distinction from others. It manifests itself on the level of the state as a relation to other states, each of which is autonomous vis-a-vis the others. Such autonomy in self-awareness is the most fundamental freedom which a people possesses as well as its highest dignity." The modern Jews, who have attained great heights in the arts, culture, and statecraft of the many nations in which they have been citizens, have felt the importance, nevertheless, of rallying together to give their well-being the crowning fulfillment of political autonomy in the state of Israel.

It was a Roman state claiming global jurisdiction for the purpose of keeping the peace that forcibly scattered the Jews almost two thousand years ago. That was one way of keeping peace in the Middle East. It is a peace, of course, without freedom that can thus be kept. But, in the end, even the global dominance of a United Nations Organization with teeth (which is to say, an absolute monopoly of power to enforce peace and therefore anything else it "pleases") must reveal itself to be illusory. Dominance without a peer is, by definition, uncheckable and therefore tyrannical dominance. It does no good to say that its government will be staffed by representation and is to consist of only good people. Either it has a monopoly of power, or it cannot keep the peace. And monopoly of power is inherently despotic at best.

Free men do not try to make world states to regulate their freedom. The best state for free men (and women) is the smallest state that suffices to make possible leisure enough for some to develop, for the good of all, their highest potencies. The Greeks knew the truth of this. Even the Romans started a city-state. Later, they came indeed to love peace enough to make themselves the world's jailers–only to sink into a despair that de-Hellenized and de-Romanized them, so that they were conquered piecemeal by freedom-loving barbarians. There is a mean–a virtuous middle status–between the Greek city-state extreme (which does not suffice to secure freedom) and the Roman world-state extreme (which transcends freedom with its jailer's monopoly of power); and that mean is the nation-state system, where one state capable of expanding in power is checked by other states capable of expansion, but in accord, instead, to secure their severalty.

Briefly: Freemen make states to regulate their freedom; free states in turn regulate their freedom not by making "still another state," irresponsibly large, but by making history. History's court is indeed a world court in the profoundest sense. Above history, transcending all ambitious statecraft, are the time-arresting moments of artistic beauty, religious grace, and philosophic truth. History rules the nations, but the art, religion, and philosophy in which national genius fully expresses itself in the course of history exercise an ultimate spiritual sovereignty on earth that bows, as the ancients knew, only to heaven.

Coercive government is a necessary evil. It is to be preserved because necessary. It is to be kept limited, checked, balanced, because evil. The checks on government most supportive of individual freedom are those that are applied internally through a separation of powers, and externally through preservation of a system of comparably free states. Such a system was once limited to Europe. The United States, 200 years ago, led the way in breaking the European monopoly. Now, the system is on the verge of becoming global. The superpowers, with their globalist ideologies, must learn to restrain their appetites for enforceable peace. They must not be permitted to sink into the imperialist jailer's error out of ignorance. They must be made to face consciously the choice between the despotism of a monopoly of coercive power and the freedom of a preserved severalty of independent states. The superpower that takes the lead in supporting the nation-state system will prove to be civilization's great benefactor for the foreseeable future.

Nothing ought to be of greater urgency for the emergent nations than to press the superpowers to revitalize the nation-state system, in thought as well as deed. Some of the emergent nations are far from being "recognizably" sovereign. Often their "national liberation" belligerency itself is a foreign import—however loud the cries for national independence maybe. But the nation-state *system* is something else. It can, and will, in due course, admit to full membership every people sufficiently conscious of the value of freedom to be able to claim for itself, and maintain, a truly separate and equal station, as a recognized peer, among the powers of the earth.

16. CONCLUSION:
THE FIXED FIGHT

In *The White House Years,* Henry Kissinger from time to time interrupts his self-confident narrative to offer us portraits of American generals who found themselves incapable, in the end, of coping with the new kind of war they had been asked to fight in Vietnam. As the theorist *par excellence* of that kind of war, Kissinger writes of their difficulties with a rich mixture of sympathy and reproof. Of General Westmoreland, whom he familiarly refers to as "Westy," he says, for instance:

"Like so many of his colleagues he had launched himself into Vietnam with self-confident optimism only to withdraw in bewilderment and frustration. Saddled with restrictions for which there was no precedent in manuals, confronted with an enemy following a strategy not taught at our command colleges, he soon fell into a trap that has been the bane of American commanders since the Civil War: substitution of logistics for strategy. . . . The Vietnam terrain, the nature of guerrilla warfare, the existence of sanctuaries, all combined to make it impossible for Westmoreland to wear down his adversary as he sought. Instead, the North Vietnamese hiding in the population and able to choose their moment for attack wore us down. And then the 1968 Tet offensive, though a massive North Vietnamese military defeat, turned into a psychological triumph by starting us on the road to withdrawal. (In fairness it must be stressed that Westmoreland labored under political restrictions that barred any of the major maneuvers that might have proved decisive—sealing off the Ho Chi Minh Trail in 1967, for example.)"

That is typical of Kissinger's Disraelian approach to his theme. The manuals and the command colleges had not prepared "Westy" as he ought to have been prepared—and would have been, had he studied Kissinger's books or attended his limited-war strategy seminars at Harvard. Particularly Disraelian is the parenthetical acknowledgement that *political* restrictions had barred the general's use of *any* of the major maneuvers that might have proved decisive. Yet, as any reader of Kissinger's books recognizes at once, they were restrictions of precisely the kind prescribed by Kissinger to keep limited wars limited.

156

But there is worse. Kissinger suggests that the massive North Vietnamese defeat in the Tet offensive of 1968 had almost automatically been turned into a psychological triumph for Hanoi "by starting us on the road to withdrawal." That was not, as we have seen, Westmoreland's view of the situation. He ascribed that withdrawal (which turned the entire handling of the Vietnam war into a "shameful national blunder") to policy-decisions taken by Nixon and Kissinger early in 1969–decisions which, as he put it, committed the United States "to a withdrawal strategy, and omitted any demand for a *quid pro quo* from Hanoi."

Indeed, elsewhere in his memoirs Kissinger boasts of the fact that, before his arrival on the scene in 1969, there had been no plans for American troop withdrawals. Despite what may have been Clark Clifford's personal views, the Johnson Administration had never made an official move in that direction: and Kissinger is pleased to cite Clifford's own words of September 29, 1968–"the level of combat is such that we are building up our troops, not cutting them down"–words the Defense Secretary reiterated as late as December 10, 1968. It was left to "us," Kissinger says, to take the "bold initiative." And then, with a characteristically ambiguous Disraelian turn, he adds: "In our innocence we thought that withdrawals of American troops might help us win public support so that the troops which remained and our enhanced staying power might give Hanoi an incentive to negotiate seriously."

Westmoreland's successor in 1968, General Creighton Abrams, is given a harsher, much more sharply critical portrayal. His great time of trial, according to Kissinger, came upon him in early 1972, just prior to and during the massive "Spring Offensive" launched by Hanoi for the purpose of placing over 200,000 regular North Vietnamese troops in the South, in time for the "Truce" then being negotiated by Kissinger and Le Duc Tho. By early January 1972, after repeatedly confirmed reports of a grand scale enemy invasion-build-up in the North, General Abrams very responsibly "requested authority to disrupt the enemy's preparations by air attacks north of the DMZ." Henry Kissinger received the request, and in his memoirs he notes that Abrams "concluded with a reminder that [given the extent of the unilateral American force withdrawals to that point] this would be the decisive battle and that he as field commander needed the maximum flexibility in advance."

That had hardly been an unreasonable request, from a traditional military standpoint. In the celebrated Israeli Six-Day War of 1967, the Israeli victory had in fact been assured by the pre-emptive air strikes that disrupted the Egyptian invasion buildup before a single Egyptian fighting unit had reached the Israeli borders. But, needless to say, the Israeli armed forces had never been placed under the restraints of the Kissinger limited-war doctrine. That doctrine specified an altogether different response under the circumstances. Kissinger, as he tells us, hastily convened his national security "Senior Review Group on January 24 to consider General Abrams' request." None of the Group's members, we are told, was "eager to renew the attacks on the North" which had caused so much campus-tension at home during the Johnson years. And so the Group's recommendation to President Nixon, passed on to him with a Kissinger memo, was that he should "let Abrams have part of his cake but not the bombing of the North."

Abrams was authorized to step up his bombing activity *below* the DMZ, where it could not affect the invasion buildup. It was during this period of Kissinger's *containment* of Abrams that (as we mentioned earlier) four-star General John D. Lavelle came to be stripped of his command of all American air power in Southeast Asia, and demoted two ranks, for his "unauthorized" strikes (against anti-aircraft batteries, primarily) north of the DMZ. When he was later brought for a hearing before a congressional investigating committee, General Lavelle defended his action in these terms:

"With the increased aggressiveness of the North Vietnamese and the large number of North Vietnamese regular army units that had taken up positions to move across the DMZ . . . I made interpretations that were probably beyond the literal intention of the rules. I did this since our crews were operating in an environment of optimum enemy defense. . . . As the Commander on the spot concerned with the safety of the crews, at the same time trying to stop the buildup that was going on, I felt these were justifiable actions. . . . If I had it to do over, I would do it again."

General Lavelle had been dismissed before the North Vietnamese Spring Offensive of 1972 was actually launched. Abrams was thus effectively denied even an illicit opportunity for pre-emptive air strikes that might have caused at least *some* disruption. But that was not all. There was worse in store for him. Kissinger, assuming an air of academic objectivity, explains: "Meanwhile, we were confronted with the contradictory necessities of the domestic situation. . . . On January 13, 1972, even while North Vietnamese forces were massing, we thought it necessary to announce a withdrawal of another 70,000 American troops by May 1. In less than three years we had withdrawn 480,000 of the 545,000 troops that we had found in Vietnam when we entered office. . . . Neither Nixon nor I thought we could risk the most sensible decision, which would have been to halt withdrawals when a major offensive was imminent."

Thus, just as General Westmoreland, before 1968, had been under political restraints that "barred any major maneuvers that might have proved decisive," so General Abrams, facing Hanoi's massive invasion of the South in 1972, was similarly restricted, but with something else added—the American unilateral troop withdrawals which, by May 1, 1972, were scheduled to bring the troop level to below zero (545,000 minus 480,000, minus 70,000!). The invasion of the South began (as expected by the military, but not by "Middle America" on the homefront) on March 30, 1972. Immediately the Kissinger national security establishment which had, up to that point, forbidden all effective opposition switched gears. For, according to the subtleties of the Kissinger doctrine, displays of "heroic" resistance were required, after planned retreats, to placate the feelings of "Middle America"—in this case, President Nixon's silent-majority constituency.

On April 4, Kissinger called together his Washington Special Actions Group (WSAG), made up, as he says, "of middle-level representatives of State, Defense, CIA, and the Joint Chiefs of Staff, and me as Chairman." He told its members "that the President was determined to defeat the offensive." Later in the day, as he says, he asked every agency within the national security establishment "to give absolute priority to defeating the offensive." But during the course of the following day, it rapidly dawned upon him that it would prove "difficult to translate this determination to the battle-field." There were many reasons for that, he acknowledged; but basically, as he explained to the members of the WSAG, it was a question of spirit. "Our impression is," he told his Washington colleagues, "that our commanders have had it drilled into their heads that we want a minimum of activity and that they will receive rewards for getting out fast. They are not aggressive enough."

General Creighton Abrams, particularly, we are next informed, was not aggressive enough. As Commander in the field, it was up to him to do what President Nixon wanted, which was to defeat the offensive (after having been deprived of the means); and, in Kissinger's view, he simply fell short of the mark, he failed the supreme test. Mixing a semblance of sympathy with self-exonerating reproofs, Kissinger puts it this way:

"For four years General Abrams had performed, with dignity, one of the most thankless jobs ever assigned to an American general.

. . . Starting in the middle of 1969, he was asked to dismantle his command at an ever-accelerating rate while maintaining the security of South Vietnam. . . . He succeeded to a remarkable degree. By the time Hanoi struck in 1972, more of the countryside than ever before was under Saigon's control. . . . Still, deep down, General Abrams knew that he was engaged in a holding action in a battle for which even a small strategic reserve of American ground forces would almost surely have been decisive. For three years his command had been turned into a withdrawal headquarters. . . . Washington had been hurrying him out of Vietnam; now it suddenly urged him to prevail with his shrunken assets."

One *almost* gets the impression there that Kissinger would have wished, on April 5, 1972, to undo what he had done to prevent the proposed attacks by Abrams (and of course Lavelle) on the North, and to undo also the decision to prepare the remaining American troops in Vietnam for withdrawal. Abrams (Kissinger has just told us) had known he was in a holding action in a battle "for which even a small strategic reserve of American ground forces would almost surely have been decisive." But that small reserve had not been allowed him! Why not? Because the Kissinger theory of limited war called for superpower self-restraint under the circumstances.

Kissinger had spelled out that answer for us back in 1957. "The end result of relying on purely military considerations," he had written, "is certain to be all-out war. . . . Since the military can never be certain how many forces the opponent will in fact commit to the struggle, and since they feel obliged to guard against every contingency, they will devise plans for limited war which insensibly approach the level of all-out conflict. . . . The political leadership must, for this reason, assume the responsibility for defining the framework within which the military are to develop their plans and capabilities. To demand of the military that they set their own limits is to set in motion a vicious circle." And again: "Limited war presents the military with particular difficulties. [It] can be kept limited only if . . . at some point one of the protagonists prefers a limited defeat to an additional investment of resources, or if both sides are willing to settle for a stalemate in preference to an assumption of increased risk."

Refining the doctrine in 1960, where he particularly stressed that the *necessity for choice* could not be left to the military, Kissinger had added: "The most likely outcome of a conflict fought in this manner is a stalemate. . . . It is preferable not to peace, but to surrender or all-out war." And here Kissinger supplied the startling clarification we have already discussed. "Since surrender will not be our national policy," he wrote, "it is important to get our choices straight. Limited war is palatable only when compared with other even starker alternatives. . . . It is, to be sure, a subtle and complex task, and it presupposes a rare blend of psychological, political, and military skill. Yet facts cannot be evaded by refusing to admit their existence. . . . A nation which cannot be trusted [to accept limited defeat or a stalemate] when strong will hardly be able to deal with the much more difficult task of living in dignity when impotent."

Can anyone imagine Henry Kissinger, or one of his like-minded predecessors in the Kennedy and Johnson administrations, trying to explain that doctrine with any "hope of success" to a Lieutenant Calley or a General Westmoreland or a President Johnson? A "subtle and complex task" indeed! Jonathan Schell, as we saw, tried with all the sympathy in the world to give the doctrine its due, but in the end the weight of it, he acknowledged, overwhelmed his conscience. "One might say that the plan was to pay for nuclear peace with limited war," he felt forced to conclude, "and that it was in the very nature of the doctrine that it had to be presented misleadingly to the public and the world. For to explain the policy fully would be to undermine it."

The question is: How does a government that takes its security advice from a Henry Kissinger go about inducing citizens to fight and die in a war which has been pre-arranged ("it takes two to keep a limited war limited") so that its most likely outcome will be a stalemate? It would amount to telling the soldier in the field of a time to come when, for his own spiritual good and the material survival of the rest of the world, he may simply have to "throw" the fight to his third- or tenth-rate opponent and content himself, on a lower level, with a "Purple Heart," perhaps, or a posthumously awarded Congressional Medal of Honor.

The fact is that our limited-war strategists haven't yet really risked telling that to even a single one of our fighting men. Certainly by March 1, 1968, neither President Johnson, nor the Joint Chiefs of Staff, nor the newly-appointed Defense Secretary Clark Clifford, had been told any such thing. Otherwise Clifford could hardly have been charged at that time with "responding to the military request to strengthen our forces so that we might prosecute the war more forcefully." And what are we to make of Henry Kissinger's relaying a presidential order to General Abrams to "defeat the offensive" of the invading North Vietnamese armies after the general had been deliberately deprived of the means of doing so?

In the parlance of gamblers, what went on instead amounted to "fixing" a fight, not by bribing or criminally threatening the stronger contender, as it is usually done, but by cajoling or subverting him into fighting the wrong kind of fight. The result then is that, the more he follows instructions, the worse things go for him. It was surely some such experience that exasperated Lieutenant Calley and, of course, General John D. Lavelle, too, on a higher level. The poor subverted fighter walks into punches, he swings wildly, his strength and training seem to count for nothing; until finally he comes out of the ring beaten and demoralized, but still unwilling to believe that his "managers" could all the while have been betting on a stalemate, if not on his outright defeat.

Was that not precisely the plight of all our officers and men in Vietnam, from the buck privates straight up to General Abrams himself, in the spring of 1972? The Kissinger limited-war doctrine had taken its prescribed toll. No judgments in the field had been left to the military. Abrams could almost surely have defeated the offensive with "even a small reserve of American ground forces," as Kissinger acknowledged; but the General and his fighting men had been denied that reserve, even as they had been denied the militarily indispensable support of pre-emptive air attacks on the enemy invasion-buildup. And yet, writing as if he had not himself manipulated the conduct of the war to bring about precisely such results, Kissinger here indulges himself in this utterly vicious Disraelian assessment of Abrams' "competence":

"It is intended as no derogation of a superb military leader to say that General Abrams could not adjust rapidly to this new situation. . . . Torn between his convictions and his obedience to civilian authority, he increasingly took refuge in routine. His refusal to change normal operating procedures even for the Laos operation contributed to its failure to achieve decisive results. (The basic fault, however, was to attempt decisive results with insufficient forces, for which all senior officials, including myself, must bear the responsibility.) And in 1972 he saw the North Vietnamese offensive in strictly local terms. . . . His responses were testy, occasionally pedantic, disquisitions on the prerogatives of the field commander. This finally drove me at one point to tell Moorer [Thomas Moorer, Chairman of the Joint Chiefs of Staff] in exasperation that the Commander-in-Chief had some prerogatives as well."

Typically Disraelian, once again, is the parenthetical acknowledgement that Kissinger himself, together with "all senior officials," to be sure, "must bear the responsibility" for having ordered the military in Vietnam to "attempt decisive results with insufficient forces." Concealed there is the hard fact that Kissinger's limited-war doctrine demanded precisely that. If a limited war is to be fought and lost by a superpower without precipitating a "Middle America" backlash (or worse) at home, then getting the military to fight with insufficient resources—which is to say, heroically, but in vain—becomes a necessity.

Kissinger complains of the "pedantic" disquisitions he got from General Abrams, who sought—like General Lavelle—to save his men under unprecedented circumstances of political restraint. His use of the word *pedantic* reminds us of what Hannah Arendt called the banality of evil. At Nuremberg, as we noted, the Nazi war leaders were charged with many crimes; but scheming with the enemy to fix the war's outcome, the way criminal gamblers fix prizefights, was not one of them. They ordered their troops to fight to win, the way our World War II soldiers fought to win, and the way our Lieutenant Calleys and General Lavelles tried with desperate dedication to do in Vietnam. The civilian policy-planners who staged our bloody Vietnam adventure certainly don't qualify as war criminals in the Nuremberg sense; what they did to America through its fighting men is something *sui generis*. As we said at the outset, perhaps in years to come, after the feared recriminations have come and gone, historians will conjure up an appropriate name for it. Kissinger rather boldly acknowledged that his approach to war in the nuclear age represented a decisive break with traditional American concepts of national security. He spoke with scorn of what he called "the trappings of sovereignty" and urged that "institutions based on present concepts of national sovereignty" be abandoned as containing within themselves a threat to mankind's survival in the nuclear age.

Such views are by no means out of place in the American academy. But applied as principles in the actual conduct of national security affairs they can indeed have consequences that make them, in Professor Coral Bell's phrase, an impeachment matter. Was the war in Vietnam deliberately prolonged, after January 1969, to secure an ending for it consistent with Kissinger's limited-war doctrine? The toll in lives and limbs and minds in Vietnam was very great. General Abrams protested against it with "pedantic" disquisitions on the responsibilities of field commanders. We know the forms that the protests of the Lieutenant Calleys and General Lavelles took. General Westmoreland, who was not much inclined to voice his complaints, has called at length for an official inquiry at least as persistent in its quest for the truth as the Watergate inquiries that forced President Nixon to resign. Speaking of the conduct of our Vietnam war, particularly after January 1969, Westmoreland has said: "It is not in our national interest to sweep the mess under the rug."

The mess, we have tried to show, had its theoretic foundations laid for it back in 1957; what it had become by 1975, our "Middle America" saw for itself on its TV screens. Revisionist historians of the future have here a large investigative assignment laid out for them.

PART THREE

MORE ON KISSINGER

17. VIETNAM: MASK OF PEACE

President Nixon is, by political instinct, a fox not a lion. With his speech of November 3, on the eve of the American municipal and regional elections, he revealed once again his determination to rely on political cunning, rather than on statesman-like *virtù* to get him through the Vietnam crisis.

In scheduling a major foreign policy address for Election Eve, Nixon was, of course, following Lyndon B. Johnson's precedent of a year ago, when, in a last-minute effort to shift the electoral balance in favor of Hubert Humphrey, the outgoing President announced a total halt of American bombing in North Vietnam. Johnson's move was clearly understood at the time to have been a political bribe. And it almost worked. Many anti-nationalist intellectuals who had vehemently opposed Johnson after February 1965, were induced to speak out for Humphrey, and the balance began to shift noticeably. But when the votes were counted, the net result was that the tremendous bribe—which amounted to a complete capitulation by Johnson to his ideological enemies—had been paid in vain. The anti-nationalists had their bombing halt and owed nothing for it to the in-coming Nixon Administration. They could freely press new demands on the new President, vilify him as they had vilified Johnson and Humphrey, shut down universities, and hammer incessantly in the news media on the "immorality" of the American war effort in Vietnam, till he could be forced to confront them in a final showdown.

The question now is: How will Nixon face his anti-nationalist critics? Will he like Johnson, let himself be prevailed upon to offer substantive bribes to quiet them or even to purchase their support? Or will he forget about elections and re-elections, so as to confirm himself in his solemn oath of office, which binds him to "preserve, protect and defend" the sovereign national union?

It is impossible to answer such questions, as yet. Nixon was an enigma for his enemies before his election to the Presidency—and now he has become an enigma for his supporters as well. Which of them, for instance, would presume to interpret with certainty the meaning of his November 3 speech, purporting to reveal the basic principles of the new "Nixon Doctrine"? The war in Vietnam is to

---

Adapted from a version published in *Il Borghese,* November, 1969

be ended, Nixon says in that speech, not by fighting on to victory, as the United States has usually done in past wars; nor even by fighting till the enemy is forced to negotiate a mutually acceptable cease-fire, as in the Korean war; but by the altogether novel plan of simply withdrawing all American combat ground forces in accordance with a definite, though flexible, "secret timetable," regardless of "what happens on the negotiating front" in Paris.

Frowning with confidence, Nixon has assured the American people, via TV, that, when all American fighting troops are out of Vietnam, the world will see—if the plan works—that the United States has not lost a war, but rather that it has won "America's peace." And it will see also—again if the plan works—that America's wartime ally has not been betrayed to the fury of a common enemy—for, by the time all American troops are withdrawn, the South Vietnamese government will, it is hoped, be adequately prepared to defend the freedom-loving Vietnamese against the communist tyranny.

Much has been said of the President's appeal to the *silent majority* of patriotic Americans to support him against the *vocal minority* of war-protesters who have been urging him to purchase peace at any price. But it should be noted that the speech also contains a direct appeal to the war-protesters themselves, to whom the President says most flatteringly: "I respect your idealism. I share your concern for peace. I want peace as much as you do . . . to save . . . the lives of brave men in Vietnam, and also . . . so that your energy and dedication, which is now too often directed into bitter hatred against those responsible for the war, can be turned to the great challenges of peace." He is prepared, he says, to give these young war-protesters the peace they demand, if only they will restrain themselves from attempting to humiliate him while he is trying to do so.

Hardly less direct, though less flattering, is Nixon's appeal for similar forbearance on the part of the North Vietnamese government. And this takes us to the crux of the speech. "I want to be sure," says Mr. Nixon, "that there is no misunderstanding on the part of the enemy with regard to our withdrawal program. We have noted the reduced level of infiltration, the reduction of our casualties, and are basing our withdrawal decision partially on those factors. If the level of infiltration or our casualties increase while we are trying to scale down the fighting, it will be the result of a conscious decision by the enemy. Hanoi could make no greater mistake than to assume that an increase in violence will be to its advantage. If I conclude that increased enemy action jeopardizes our remaining forces in Vietnam, I shall not hesitate to take strong and effective measures."

Nixon is saying, in effect, that once all American troops are safely out, he means to leave the South Vietnamese government to fend militarily for itself, and in the not-too-distant future. That is what the North Vietnamese communists and the anti-nationalist war-protesters in America want; and Nixon is prepared to accommodate them, if only they will show sufficient forbearance to *let him get away with it,* without upsetting the "silent majority." If they insist, instead, on humiliating him, then his plan will surely fail. And, in that event, we may conclude, the foxes who now dominate in the American political arena will be forced to give way to the lions, and there will be an end to tolerance of the political maneuverings of alienated, anti-nationalist minorities.

A close reading of President Nixon's speech will reveal, I think, that he is prepared to pursue—though not without provision for a hasty retreat to securer ground—the course outlined for American foreign policy by his chief advisor for national security affairs, Henry A. Kissinger. As we have often noted, Kissinger is an anti-nationalist ideologue. His thesis, briefly stated, is that the era of nation-states is past, and that it is now the duty of statesmen everywhere in the world to work toward the organization of supra-national communities, as the leaders of the communist states have long been doing, and as the NATO powers may soon be forced to do, if they are to hold together effectively in the face of the communist threat.

It deserves to be noted that, as far back as April 1963, Nixon had expressed himself on the subject of NATO in similar terms. Addressing the American Society of Newspaper Editors in Washington, D.C., a few months after his humiliating experience in the California election of 1962, Mr. Nixon revealed that he knew what the communications oligarchy wants to hear from a defeated right-winger who hopes to make a political comeback. "The United States," said Nixon, "must take the lead now in expanding NATO from a purely military alliance to a political confederation, the primary object of which will be to develop a unified and total defense strategy for the United States and for our European allies. . . . The hour of decision in this critical issue has arrived. A political, as well as a military, confederation of free nations is an essential element in the strategy for victory over the dictatorship of the communist world."

Today, of course, Mr. Nixon no longer talks of victory over the communist world. Under the expert tutelage of Professor Kissinger, he has no doubt come to see that a NATO political confederation for security against communism can be, at best, but one of several intermediate stages to be traversed before the "ideal destination" is reached. In Kissinger's guarded words: "The West requires a larger goal. . . . Many intermediate stages must be traversed before it can be reached. It is not too early, however, to prepare ourselves for this step beyond the nation-state. . . . The challenge facing the West now is whether it can move from the nation-state to a larger community and draw from that effort the strength for another period of innovation." (*The Troubled Partnership,* pp. 248-9)

But how are the patriotic citizens of the Western nations—the counterparts everywhere of Nixon's *silent majority*—to be prepared for the transition to membership in a supra-national community? Kissinger has provided an answer in his doctrine of "limited war." If the silent majorities in all lands can be habituated to "not winning" in a series of limited wars, if they can be induced to believe that, in the nuclear age, the only *thinkable* kind of war is the limited war, in which statesmanship consists of always seeking a substitute for victory, they will soon cease to take pride in their traditional nationhood and be much better disposed than they are now to accept the idea that national loyalties are destined to give way to broader loyalties. This is the lesson to be learned from limited wars, and national leaders who undertake such wars ought to have precisely that lesson in mind. Once again, in Kissinger's guarded words: "Limited war must be conceived always as an opportunity to prevent a final showdown. We must enter it prepared to negotiate and settle for something less than our traditional notion of victory." (*The Necessity for Choice,* p. 64, Anchor Book ed.)

Ever since the inauguration of John F. Kennedy in 1961, the United States has been pursuing just such a course in its conduct of the struggle in Vietnam. Mr. Nixon is, therefore, deceiving the American people when he suggests that what he is now proposing represents a basic change in policy. Lyndon Johnson tried to make a basic change, but failed. The "conspiracy of doves in the Pentagon"—to cite the *New York Times* caption for Max Frankel's review of Townsend Hoopes *The Limits of Intervention*—succeeded in its "frantic effort in March, 1968, to persuade a new Defense Secretary, Clark Clifford, that victory in Vietnam was unattainable by any tolerable means and the subsequent conspiracy to persuade Lyndon Johnson to act as if he agreed." Nixon is not proposing a new policy, therefore, but simply a return to the old course originally projected by Kissinger's predecessors, McGeorge Bundy and Walt Rostow, during the Kennedy years. And yet, with the shrewdness of a fox, the American President somehow manages to remain *in utrumque paratus*. If his plan for peace in Vietnam results in a *humiliating* defeat which the silent majority of Americans is unwilling to endure, he has already indicated that he means to place full blame on the "vocal minority," which has consistently urged him to pursue a policy of unilateral withdrawal. With oracular brevity, he has underscored the prospect of nationwide recriminations looming ahead; "I have chosen a plan for peace. I believe it will succeed. If it *does* succeed, what the critics say now won't matter. If it *does not* succeed, anything I say then won't matter. . . . Because let us understand: North Vietnam cannot defeat or humiliate the United States. Only Americans can do that."

The most enlightened response to the November 3 speech to date, has come from Bonn, Germany. In the *Frankfurter Allgemeine* we read: "No statesman can basically change within 10 months a strategic situation which has developed in 10 years of military activity. . . . *Vietnamization is a pretext for the abandonment of Southeast Asia.* . . . America's friends should realize that the political situation of their ally is assuming *the proportions of a Greek tragedy."*

18. THE ATROCITIES OF MARCH 1968

March 1968 may prove to have been the most fateful month in the history of America's brief tour of duty as the world's first ranking power.

All the world now knows that on the 16th day of that month the so-called massacre of My Lai occurred. Not since the years of the great propaganda wars against Germany has the world witnessed a comparable hue and cry about "atrocities" and "war criminals." With unanimity, the anti-nationalists of the news media have seized upon the alleged eyewitness accounts and lurid pictures as proof of their charge that Americans have been fighting an "immoral" war in Vietnam—a war they cannot win and would nave no moral right to win, if they could.

If the United States can manage to survive as a sovereign nation, despite the collusion of its intelligentsia with its professed enemies, the record of history will show that a truly great atrocity was indeed committed in March, 1968—though not in Vietnam and not by American soldiers, but rather, in Washington, D.C., and by the anti-nationalist ideologues who have dominated American foreign policy and defense-planning since the inauguration of President Kennedy.

To see the My Lai incident in true perspective, one must recall that on March 1, 1968, President Johnson had replaced Kennedy's Defense Secretary, Robert McNamara, with his own man, Clark Clifford, to whom he had given a specific order to reverse McNamara's "no-win" war strategy. American commanders in Vietnam, utterly dismayed by the policy designs of Walt Rostow and McNamara, had finally persuaded Johnson that, with 200,000 additional troops, they could immobilize the Viet Cong and end the war successfully despite the political restrictions that kept them from bombing Hanoi, mining the harbor at Haiphong, or pursuing the enemy beyond the borders of South Vietnam; and the new Defense Secretary was ordered to supply those troops.

Viewed in the light of Johnson's specific order to Clifford, the military significance of the American order to "wipe out" My Lai becomes clear. The village was a communist stronghold, out of which the Viet Cong's 48th Local Force Battalion, ablest of the com-

---

Adapted from a version published in *Il Borghese,* November, 1969

munist fighters, had frequently operated. Many of its straw huts were walled with brick on the inside. The ground beneath was a labyrinth of military tunnels. Yet when the Americans broke through, they found no Viet Cong on hand to defend their South Vietnamese civilian collaborators. Why not? Because, if the Viet Cong were to stand firm everywhere to defend all the villages they exploit and control through their terror tactics, they would soon be deprived of what has been their chief military advantage in the Vietnam fighting.

All who know the situation acknowledge that what makes the Viet Cong nearly invincible is their freedom to pick and choose when to fight and when not to fight. Anti-nation defense strategists characterize the tactics as a form of "unconventional warfare." They like the term because it appears to strengthen their claim that there is no military tradition competent to deal effectively with the "novelty" of the problems, and that professional military commanders must therefore be guided by "creative" civilian experts in the national quest for meaningful solutions. Nixon's chief civilian defense expert, Henry Kissinger, has correctly assessed the Viet Cong advantage. "Guerrillas," he has written, "need only join battle where they enjoy local superiority, but the defenders must be strong everywhere in anticipation of the unexpected. No longer is the ability to occupy territory decisive, for the real target has become the morale of the population and the system of the civil administration. If these can be undermined through protracted struggle and terrorism, the insurgents will prevail no matter how many battles the defending forces have won. But then Kissinger proceeds to emphasize the alleged "novelty" of the Vietnamese war, asserting that "what makes the situation particularly complex is that there is no purely military solution to guerrilla war." What is required, he insists, is a political-military approach based on creating "a stable enlightened government" which must be constructed "while the guerrilla war is going on"—a task that is certainly beyond the competence of military commanders and for which even the "creative" civilian experts have not yet developed a plan that is certain to work.

That, in brief, is the essence of the limited no-win war policy consistently advanced by the Rostows, McNamaras, and Kissingers —a policy which, as Kissinger boasts, "raises more questions than it can supply answers."

American military commanders have consistently rejected this limited war analysis. They have held that the Viet Cong tactics are quite conventional and that the proper military response is at least as old as the campaign of Fabius Maximus against Hannibal in the

Second Punic War. The Romans of Hannibal's time knew that they could deprive him of the advantages of guerrilla warfare only by carrying the fighting beyond his positions, into Carthaginian Africa—which would be the equivalent of an American-South Vietnamese invasion of North Vietnam; or, if that were not feasible, by forcing Hannibal to choose between defending his Italian civilian collaborators in hundreds of scattered towns or losing control over them. Until the Romans were able and willing to carry the war to Hannibal's home base, they were limited to the second alternative. And how they succeeded in it is certainly relevant to any serious consideration of the American predicament in Vietnam.

In his descent from the Alps, Hannibal occasionally invested a town along his way, not so much for the booty of able-bodied men and goods he could carry off, but in order to inspire "terror in towns further on." Indeed, as Polybius relates, Hannibal "traversed the country without resistance, for, in storming towns, he usually ordered the slaying of all adults who stood in his way—an order he was pleased to give because of his intense hatred of the Romans." And yet, just as the Viet Cong claim to be fighting to liberate the South Vietnamese from the American imperialist yoke, so Hannibal used to say to the townspeople he terrorized that he "was not there to fight against Italians but in behalf of Italians against Rome."

Only after long years of marauding up and down the peninsula was Hannibal finally forced to protect rather than merely terrorize and exploit the townspeople who collaborated with him. It was the policy of Fabius Maximus that forced him to do so. Plutarch, who was no military strategist, mistakes the new situation as advantageous for Hannibal observing that "he who held no town, no market or sea port, whose troops lived by pillaging, who was ever roving, as it were, with a huge troop of banditti, now became master of some of the best provinces and towns." But Hannibal knew better. To his closest companions he then "confided for the first time, that he had always thought it difficult, but that he now held it impossible, with the forces he then had, to master Italy."

The main burden of the "Fabian" military strategy was to nullify Hannibal's terroristic control over civilian collaborators. It was as if an American commander had said to the South Vietnamese villagers of My Lai: "If you collaborate with the Viet Cong for any reason, but particularly if you sympathize with their cause and believe they are going to win, then you must beg them not to abandon you—you unfortunate civilians who are too old or too young or too weak to accompany them on their marches. Beg them to leave fighting men behind in your village, and in all villages like yours, so that we will find them here when we attack. Otherwise you must consider it their inhumanity, not ours, that leaves you exposed to our fighting power."

These are hard sayings. But after 40,000 American soldiers have died and hundreds of thousands have been wounded in Vietnam, we must not hesitate to say them. In March 1968, Johnson had ordered implementation of a policy designed to immobilize the Viet Cong. Clifford's "one overriding immediate assignment" on the first of March was, as he has said, "to strengthen our forces in Vietnam so that we might prosecute the war more forcefully." What happened instead was that the new Defense Secretary let himself be talked out of obeying the President's direct order by a team of advisors whose responsibility it should have been to aid him in obeying. Clifford has with much candor revealed how, in the course of that fateful month, he learned for the first time that the defense establishment organized under President Kennedy–headed by McNamara, Bundy, and Walt Rostow–had no plan for military victory in Vietnam, that it was thoroughly committed ideologically to the "no-win" limited war concept, and that it was evidently prepared to frustrate the President himself in the event of a final showdown.

Clifford's "conversion" took place perhaps on the very day U.S. troops broke into My Lai. Without informing Johnson of the full extent of his conversion, he joined his advisors in what has since been hailed by the *New York Times* as the "Conspiracy of Doves in the Pentagon." As a direct consequence of Clifford's capitulation, Johnson suddenly found himself isolated in Washington–literally up against the wall–without any high level support for his escalation of the war in Vietnam. Then came the sorry spectacle of March 30, 1968, when the Commander-in-Chief of our armed forces went before the nation to abdicate his responsibilities in a gesture of abject despair. The campaign to "dump" a President of the United States had been a success. The North Vietnamese could not defeat and humiliate America. Only Americans could do that.

As we noted elsewhere, some of Clifford's "defense aides" of March, 1968 have now begun to boast of their involvement in that "conspiracy of Pentagon doves." Former Under Secretary of the Air Force, Townsend Hoopes, who was part of it has written what he calls "an inside account of how the Johnson policy of escalation in Vietnam was reversed," in which he dwells on the "frantic effort in March, 1968 to persuade Clark Clifford that victory in Vietnam was unattainable by any tolerable means and the subsequent conspiracy to persuade Johnson to act as if he agreed." According to Hoopes,

until his replacement by Clifford, McNamara had been at the heart
of the "idealistic" conspiracy to prevent an American victory in
Vietnam. Hoopes praises McNamara for having gone before the
Stennis Committee on August 25, 1967, to minimize "without White
House clearance," the effectiveness of our strategic bombing of
North Vietnam; which—as John Roche has observed—amounts to
praising him for having "double-crossed" the President.

Johnson fired McNamara. But he was only one of many. The rest
of the team of anti-nationalist counselors he had put together with
the collaboration of Bundy and Rostow remained behind to "educate" his successor and frustrate the President—to say nothing of our
commanders and fighting men in Vietnam.

There you have the real atrocity of March, 1968. Its chief victims
are all the American soldiers who would not have died, or who at
least would not have been sacrificed in vain, had Clark Clifford succeeded in supplying the additional troops requested by our military
in Vietnam. One day, when all the hypocritical moralizing about My
Lai is quieted, there will be heard a cry for vengeance from the
depth of our national conscience. Vice President Agnew has already
indicated for us how the majority of Americans is apt to respond to
such a cry. Where Nixon really stands remains to be seen. Our fear
is that, so long as Kissinger continues to advise him, he must remain
entangled, as he is now, in the conspiracy of anti-nationalists which
he has as yet failed to repudiate.

19. CAMOUFLAGED SURRENDER IN VIETNAM: NIXON MUST DISMISS KISSINGER OR KISSINGER MUST VOLUNTARILY RESIGN

The Kissinger-Nixon foreign policy has failed in all its major trials. Its worst failures have been in the UN vote which ousted a signatory of the original charter; in the India-Pakistan war, where we "supported" Pakistan just so we could get used to losing; and in the so-called Vietnamization of our cowardly retreat in Southeast Asia.

If Richard Nixon were a true statesman, rather than a politician bent on re-election, his failures would long ago have led him to break up the Nixon-Kissinger team. Kissinger is the President's chief advisor. The failures must either be charged to his bad advice—in which case he ought to be dismissed for having counseled poorly; or they must be due to Nixon's failure to heed good advice—in which case Kissinger ought to feel obliged to resign. Those are the statesman-like alternatives. That Kissinger remains in office despite such abject failures is proof that the professed foreign-policy goals of the Nixon administration are by no means its true goals.

Why does Nixon cling to Kissinger? The answer may well be that, in his commitment to a pseudo-Quaker peace and re-election, our President finds Kissinger's talents for ambiguity particularly serviceable. Tragically for America, Nixon is wedded to the notion that he, personally, can only win by being a loser. It is the lesson of his political "comeback" after the California gubernatorial election of 1962. Be dogged in defeat; lose again and again, but keep at it; sooner or later your doggedness will catch the opposition napping.

That's the formula of Nixon's opportunism. The anti-nationalists of the Eastern Establishment were quick to recognize it. After they "dumped" Johnson for having tried to win in Vietnam, those cabalists seized at once on Nixon's ambition and his loser's style as a tool for realizing their will. In their eyes, Kissinger is now an internationalist miracle worker. He is their modern Daniel who has ventured into the lion's den—among the Buckleys and Goldwaters—not to be devoured by them, but to shut their mouths so that America might henceforth be governed by the duplicity of political foxes rather than lions.

John Kenneth Galbraith, James Reston, Max Lerner, Walter Lippmann—all openly despise Nixon. But how full of praise they are for Kissinger! How solicitous they are for his safety, lest the lions' mouths be opened once again, before the cabala's mission is accomplished!

Think of the miraculous daring of Kissinger's Red China mission. That mission led to William Buckley's suspension of support of Nixon. Yet, even while Galbraith was honoring him for it with a public dinner at Harvard, Kissinger managed to retain Buckley's trust. After the Peking visit, Kissinger again very daringly maneuvered to exonerate himself with Buckley by "confiding" that, despite appearances, the visit had been for him a terrible nightmare. Sharp-eyed Max Lerner has marked Buckley's persistent loyalty. Contrasting my criticism of Kissinger with Buckley's steadfast reluctance to criticize, Lerner wrote recently:

> *Buckley says only that the China trip turned out a nightmare for Kissinger, which suggests that he knows Kissinger well enough and knows history well enough not to make Kissinger the subject of a stab-in-the-back myth, as some of the far Right would have it. But the attempt will be made, and it is part of the price that America will have to pay for trying to reverse a quarter-century of history in a week.*

Kissinger's handling of the Red China visit was a spectacular triumph for the internationalist cabala. But his handling of the India-Pakistan crisis was no less deft. India and Pakistan have long been governed by pro-Russian and pro-Red China regimes. America thus had no business taking sides in their conflict. Yet, through convenient leaks to Jack Anderson, it was "revealed" that Nixon "favored" the anti-American government of Pakistan over the anti-American government of India. And so our country was linked to the "losing side." Now it appears that India and Pakistan will "unite" in a joint condemnation of the United States—India on the grounds that we opposed her, Pakistan on the grounds that we abandoned her in the critical hour.

And what about the Vietnamization doctrine that veils our cowardly retreat in Vietnam? The editors of *National Review*, who used to support it, now correctly assess it as a cruel hoax, particularly in its latest phase, which consists in a futile bombing of North Vietnamese supply routes, instead of the supplies themselves. James Burnham has written [April 28, 1972]: "Nixon's Vietnamization is inherently self-contradictory . . . because it seeks to keep the enemy from reaching his goal without defeating him." Unless the enemy is *defeated,* Burnham explains, South Vietnam must sooner or later fall. Conceivably, he concludes,

> *South Vietnamese troops plus U.S. airpower and naval guns will stop
> and push back the North Vietnamese advance. But the underlying issue
> will not be affected. For Richard Nixon, South Vietnam's survival as
> an independent non-communist state has a lower priority than Ameri-
> can withdrawal and his own re-election. It is therefore probable that
> South Vietnam will not so survive, just as, in an analogous structure of
> priorities, Free China did not survive as a U.N. member.*

In the May 12 issue of *National Review*, an editorial carries Burn-ham's criticism a step forward. There it is argued that Nixon's escalated bombing of North Vietnam and his naval bombardments "are justified only if his policy in the end succeeds; if it is to fail, they are wrong, militarily, politically and morally." Then comes the gravest charge ever pressed against Nixon by the Buckley conservatives: "If the Vietnam war is going to end in any case with a Communist takeover, either directly or through the more likely route of a coalition government, then it is time to bring the fighting to a quick close. . . . Nixon must not forget that the Vietnamese and his own countrymen are the chips he is playing with."

Are we headed for a coalition government as a camouflaged surrender? David Livingston, the leftist union leader who deals intimately with Hanoi leaders as well as with Kissinger, has quoted Kissinger on nationwide TV as having said that after ten years of relentless fighting, it would be "unreasonable" to expect the communists to accept anything less than a coalition government.

But we don't need anyone else's word for it. Kissinger had said precisely that in his book *American Foreign Policy,* published early in 1969. Discussing a negotiated settlement, he there wrote: "To be sure, Hanoi cannot be asked to leave the NFL [Vietcong] to the mercy of Saigon." He therefore proposed "international supervision" of a coalition peace which grants not just the South Vietnamese but the whole "people of Vietnam what they have struggled so bravely to achieve: an opportunity to work out their own destiny in their own way."

That is a cunning, purposively ambiguous restatement of the anti-American charge that the U.S. really never had any business "intervening" in a Vietnamese domestic conflict. Anticipating arguments recently advanced by Senator Jacob Javits in the Senate Foreign Policy Committee hearings on Vietnam, Kissinger concluded from his supra-nationalist perspective: "As for the United States, if it gains a reasonable time for political consolidation, it will have done the maximum possible for an ally—short of permanent occupation."

That abominable line of reasoning suggests that the American people should willingly have suffered 46,000 deaths and 300,000 other casualties in Vietnam merely to help an ally. All that we value in the West obliges us to reject such a notion. Either our soldiers have died to stop a communist advance that ultimately threatens our national survival, or they have died in vain. Academic architects of the "No-win" war strategy may cling to the belief that fighting without victory is worth the casualties if it can teach Americans the virtue of "losing for peace" in the nuclear age. But one day the cries of our dead soldiers are bound to come back to us out of the grave to condemn the whole business of limited wars–of wars "we can afford to lose"–as a great act of treason for which retribution will have to be exacted.

In any case, while there is still time, Kissinger must be stopped. And William Buckley is the man who can best stop him. Several years ago, Buckley said to me that Kissinger was either a great patriot or the worst hypocrite in the history of the world. Even now, filled with gloom over what he sees happening at home and abroad, Buckley still argues loyally that *things would be worse in the White House* if Kissinger weren't there. But the time has come to end all that. After the disastrous consequences of the Kissinger-Nixon doctrine in the UN, in India, and Vietnam, the alternatives are plain. Either Kissinger has given good, patriotic advice which Nixon has failed to implement–in which case Kissinger ought to resign; or he has been giving bad advice–in which case Nixon must dismiss him.

Claiming the rights of friendship with both Kissinger and Nixon, Buckley ought to press for one or the other alternative. Except for his hold on Nixon, Kissinger would of course be only a relatively harmless professor, with whom Buckley, if he liked, could well afford to match wits at frequent intervals.

20. A RED-CHINA PUPPET SHOW:
NIXON KOWTOWS,
KISSINGER PULLS THE STRINGS

Kissinger, Chou En-lai, and Mao Tse-tung understand one another. We have Chou's word for it. Having reached substantive agreement among themselves in their secret talks of last July and October, they have now acted in concert to take a compromised President of the United States to the cleaners. Mr. Nixon has been induced to play Chamberlain in Peking. With the inscrutable Kissinger ever at his ear, he has offered to purchase "peace in our time" by submitting unconditionally to the five non-negotiable "principles of peaceful co-existence" in which the Chinese communists have summed up *all* their major demands on the United States.

Since the end of World War II, millions of Americans have fought in Asia, and tens of thousands of them have died, to prevent total domination of the continent by communist imperialism. Now, for superficial reasons drummed into his head by Kissinger, Nixon has decided to repudiate that tremendous sacrifice. He has joined our enemies in holding that the American-Red Chinese conflict in Korea was a mistake, that the United States should never have "Americanized" the fighting in Vietnam, and that Taiwan is henceforth to be regarded as an integral part of Mao's China, despite the fact that there is now a fully accredited Nationalist Chinese embassy operating in Washington.

Nothing is more false than Nixon's pretense that his Asian "week that changed the world" has somehow left our relations with Nationalist China intact. That lie first surfaced in Kissinger's Shanghai press conference on the meaning of the joint *communiqué* of February 27, 1972. Nixon's Secret Agent was asked at that time: "Why did not the United States Government affirm its treaty commitment to Taiwan, as the President and you have done on numerous occasions?" To which, with his usual air of cosmopolitan intrigue and *chutzpah*, Kissinger replied:

> *Let me deal with that particular aspect once . . . and not have to answer it in the innumerable elliptical forms in which it will be presented. The particular issue is, of course, an extraordinarily difficult one to discuss on the territory of a country with which we do not maintain formal diplomatic relations and for which this particular issue is a matter of profound principle.*

> *Let me, therefore, state it once . . . and not repeat it: . . . the treaty*
> *will be maintained. But I would appreciate it if that would be all that*
> *I would be asked to say about it under these circumstances.*

Kissinger's reluctance to speak frankly on Red Chinese soil, is of course, double-edged (in keeping with his current double agent's role). Tricky Dick, the reply suggests, may be concealing an ace up his sleeve, which he will play when the horse-trading gets really tough and he needs to exact important concessions from *either* Mao or Chiang.

But the duplicity of it is too much even for liberal Max Frankel, chief news analyst of the *Times,* to endure. Frankel fears that Kissinger may have gone too far too fast. The Red-China puppet show may have overtaxed the credulity of the American people. The Cook's tour of Great Halls and Great Walls, even the toasts and table-hopping, may have been endurable. But what worries Frankel most is the aftermath of Kissinger-Nixon explanations. "In the afterglow," he warns, "the pretenses of politics and the pretensions to allies and the obsession with the negotiated semantics of the communique are already threatening to overwhelm the event." As for the "big lie" about U.S.-Taiwan relations, the head of the *Times* Washington Bureau concluded:

> *The real record of this journey is not the communique. The picture that*
> *ought to linger is the one of President Nixon, seated between Premier*
> *Chou En-lai and Mrs. Mao Tse-tung, in the Great Hall of the People,*
> *watching women soldiers in ballet shoes shooting target practice at a*
> *caricature of Chiang Kai-shek. The President said the next day that he*
> *loved the dancing and music, and he called it a play with a powerful*
> *message.*

Kissinger has thus maneuvered an American President into appeasing Red China. His next task is to lead Mr. Nixon to Moscow for more of the same, so that he can pretend to be "balancing powers" when he is, in fact, balancing surrenders. In Shanghai, Kissinger was asked point blank about Nixon's obvious acceptance of the communist terms for "peace" in Asia. As reported in the *Times,* the question read: "Henry, is this the first time that a President of the United States has formally picked up the language of the five principles of peaceful co-existence?" In his reply, Kissinger dismissed with impatience the notion that, in the pursuit of peace, it mattered a fig who gives or takes what. He cannot say for sure, he begins, whether this was the first time an American President had literally adopted as his own the communist Chinese peace terms. But that, he insists, is irrelevant.

> *The question is not who put forward the proposals. The question is: Does it contain principles that we can live by? Since we have said we are prepared to apply these principles in the next part on the nonuse of force, and since both sides have stated this, it does not really make a crucial difference who put the proposals forward first.*
>
> *The basic objective of this trip was to set in motion a train of events and an evolution in policy . . . in which a great deal depends on the assessment by each side of the reliability of the other in being able to pursue this for the amount of time necessary to see it prevail.*

Those final words need to be puzzled over a bit, or we may miss the message Kissinger means to convey to his internationalist colleagues. Whether this American sellout can "succeed"—he is saying—depends on the reliability of the Nixon Administration to pursue it long enough to make the course irreversible. The Red Chinese and the Goldwaters, Thurmonds, Towers, and Reagans must be appeased simultaneously. It is a dangerous stunt. As Frankel warns, one bad turn, even a single misdirected word, may bring the whole edifice of anti-nationalist intrigue tumbling down. It is not inconceivable, for instance, that the Buckley conservatives—led by Senator Jim and editor Bill—might suddenly lose all patience and *(mirabile dictu)* join forces with the George Wallaces and Curtis LeMays, in a three-pronged populist-military-intellectual drive of last resort, to clear the cabala of anti-nationalist deceivers out of our government once and for all.

We must never permit ourselves to forget the tragic experience of Clark Clifford with that cabala back in March 1968. As new Defense Secretary, he had been ordered by President Johnson to supply the military with all they required for victory in Vietnam. But he found that his task force of top presidential defense advisors flatly refused to assist him in carrying out that order. He then asked whether they had better plans of their own for attaining victory. Their response was the shock that broke Clifford's will. In his own words: "When I asked for a presentation of the military plan for obtaining victory in Vietnam, I was told that there was no plan for victory in the historic American sense."

That surfacing of a "conspiracy of doves in the Pentagon" ought to have caused an upheaval in American politics. But poor Clark Clifford simply didn't have the heart for it. The number of ivy-league and pseudo-ivy league cabalists that would have had to be purged was simply too large. Johnson was therefore advised to leave the purging to his successor who, it was anticipated, would be Richard Nixon.

But with Nixon, alas, came the inscrutable global appeaser Henry Kissinger. Kissinger is unique in the Nixon Administration. In one of his boastful *tête-à-têtes* with Gloria Steinem, he himself acknowledged that "in a Democratic administration there would be 20 like him, but that in the Nixon era there is only him." On the same theme, I wrote many months ago:

> *Kissinger is but one man. For the great majority of Americans, he hardly exists. Yet he has the President's ear. And a man in that position, long skilled in pleading the internationalist cause, with decades of experience as study director and spokesman for the Council on Foreign Relations, could very well manage to set the nation on a course from which there might be, at some point, no turning back.*

Those words were written in March 1970. It is now March 1972. Kissinger has set us on a course of surrender in Asia. His next move is to deliver our benighted President–crammed full of election-campaign platitudes–to Moscow for a European surrender. Have we no recourse against it? Can we not rally together a mass of patriots, drawn out of all parties, to raise the hue and cry which it is our duty to raise when the felon has been caught in the act and attempts to flee? Like the highway thieves who strip disabled cars, the Bundys, Rostows, and Kissingers have been at work since 1961 stripping our country of its sovereign nationhood.

If we act with passionate resolve, the rascals can yet be purged. Americans on the right must forget all their longstanding differences till the thing is done. But if, instead, we let Kissinger pursue his present course "for the amount of time necessary to see it prevail," then we had better call on the God of our Fathers to cover us with mountains for our shame.

21. "HOWEVER VAGUE, HOWEVER ELUSIVE, HOWEVER INDIRECT": KISSINGER'S PLEA FOR A FACE-SAVING FORMULA

We had unnatural weather in New York City on January 22, 1973, just as the major TV networks went on the air with the evening news. There were claps of thunder, lightning flashes, and a cloudburst of torrential rains. And it was fitting.

The news was that Henry Kissinger had flown off to Paris to sign America's veiled Vietnam surrender. Then there was a communist film clip showing two American B-52 pilots recently taken prisoner in North Vietnam. All the world could see at a glance that they were dishonored, expendable, and abandoned subjects of a defeated power. And then finally came the flash that Lyndon Baines Johnson had died.

That was quite a day. President Johnson had been "dumped" from office in 1968 for having proposed to end the Vietnam war by winning it. Liberal internationalists dumped our President; but most Republican conservatives as well as moderates looked on with approval, anticipating that it would enable them to enjoy some share of the spoils of Washington with a victorious Richard M. Nixon.

Henry Kissinger's trip to sign the Vietnam surrender is the completion of that "dump Johnson" movement; and the pathetic picture of our POWs paraded as losers is a foretaste of the humiliation we must all sooner or later suffer together. We stood by passively while a *coup d'etat* took place in Washington in 1968. We know we deserve the humiliation. . . .

Kissinger was in trouble in mid-December. To many Washington observers it appeared as if his four-year career as Mr. Nixon's alter ego might have ended abruptly with his anguished news conference of December 16, 1972. He seemed then to be on the verge of becoming what diplomats and historians of diplomacy sometimes refer to, technically, as a "human problem."

That news conference had obviously been a presidential command performance. Mr. Kissinger had long ago promised his White House boss an "honorable discharge" from the Vietnam war before re-election day this year. As we all saw on TV, he had brought home a "draft agreement" in late October that was supposed to have done the trick. But on close inspection, it looked to Mr. Nixon's eyes too obviously like an open surrender of South Vietnam to the communists for him to risk acceptance without Saigon's approval. And so Saigon had to be consulted, then Hanoi once more, then Washington, and then Saigon again—till the whole thing seemed to have collapsed completely.

It was an embarrassing moment for Kissinger. But he brazened through it. Unblushingly determined to see this no-win war to a no-win end, he faced the TV cameras alone to explain his "temporary" failure. With a heavier foreign accent than usual (the TV commentators noted the fact), he blamed it all on those "damnable demands for verbal clarifications" that came out of Saigon first, then out of Washington, and finally out of Hanoi.

How malicious word-play had scuttled his best-laid plans for an honorable peace in Vietnam became the theme of Henry Kissinger's December news conference. And its climax was surely his anguished plea to Hanoi for permission to introduce a last-minute, face-saving figure of speech: "Some reference in the agreement—however vague, however elusive, however indirect—which did not, which would make clear that the two parts of Vietnam would live in peace with each other and that neither side would impose its solution on the other side."

"However vague, however elusive, however indirect." Surely we have there Kissinger's emergence as a human problem. At issue is the single most important item on the President's agenda for an honorable peace—the political integrity of South Vietnam—and Mr. Kissinger shamelessly petitions the enemy, with self-discrediting words, for a face-saving formula!

Real "peace with honor" lies at the antipodes of where Mr. Kissinger's busy mind has been for the past four years. President Eisenhower got himself an honorable peace in Korea. But he did it by the ancient means, long known to honorable societies the world over, of making the persistent enemy "an offer he can't refuse." As Commander in Chief of our military, Mr. Eisenhower simply warned the North Koreans and the Red Chinese that if they didn't stop their attacks across the Korean DMZ at once, he would use America's most advanced weapons to pacify them, regardless of world repercussions.

What did Mr. Nixon—Vice President at the time—think of Eisenhower's strategy for peace in Korea? We know what Henry Kissinger thought of it. For several years at the Council on Foreign Relations he worked with the top critics of Eisenhower's policy. Publication of his *Nuclear Weapons and Foreign Policy* in 1957 established him as the nation's chief ideological opponent of massive retaliation and chief advocate of a substitute, less dangerously provocative, national defense strategy. His career as a civilian war strategist has since then been built on a commitment to define some foolproof, fail-safe way of preventing American presidents from ever again using threats of massive retaliation to end a "limited war."

A war limited in Kissinger's new sense is one in which our side must give the enemy unambiguous assurances that we will not in any event seek to destroy him militarily. Those assurances to the enemy will stand, at the same time, as pledges to ourselves not to let any deed of the enemy provoke us into generalizing the war.

More precisely, in Mr. Kissinger's sense, a limited war is one that a major power like the United States knows it "can afford to lose," if the only alternative to accepting defeat is recourse to threats which would generalize the war. Generalization of a limited war is to be avoided at all costs, of course, because by definition a general war is one that a major power like the United States "cannot afford to lose," and therefore fraught with "wholly unacceptable" risks of escalation to the level of a nuclear holocaust.

Kissinger's predecessors, McGeorge Bundy and Walt Rostow, shared his view of limited war. Except during President Johnson's brief period of recalcitrance in 1968, they managed to keep our military involvement in Vietnam quite deliberately limited. Since January 1969, Mr. Kissinger's feigned hawkishness has complicated matters. To distract attention from the strategic significance of our retreats to less menacing positions in Vietnam, he has tried to punctuate them with a series of face-saving military flourishes: a Cambodian invasion when half our troops had been withdrawn, a Haiphong blockade when all were withdrawn, and now a flurry of massive bombings while our President is being pressed to sign the surrender on the dotted line.

But there is a limit to cover-ups in a pull-out as vast as ours in Vietnam. Mr. Kissinger's December news conference was the end of the line. There he begged for a final cover-up—however vague, however elusive, however indirect—which might placate the conservative mass of Americans at least long enough to see him, if not his White House boss, safely out of office. The question now is: Can he talk Mr. Nixon into actually taking the final step which will set him down in history as the first American President to lose a war voluntarily, if not by cowardly design?

General Maxwell Taylor, who obediently implemented the limited war strategy under Presidents Kennedy and Johnson, has already advised Mr. Nixon publicly not to take that final step. In a recent *Times* Op-Ed column he has argued—unanswerably, I think—that peace with honor has long since ceased to be possible in Vietnam. What then are the alternatives?

Perhaps we haven't the will, perhaps it is no longer worth this nation's while, to make the enemy an offer he can't refuse. If so, the next best course, says General Taylor, is to end our commitment without a "formal agreement involving Hanoi and the Viet Cong." We could then still salvage a small measure of honor by continued use of our air and naval power to postpone indefinitely a complete communist take-over of South Vietnam.

Mr. Nixon has a hard choice ahead of him. For the reasons General Taylor gives, he cannot honorably continue to pursue the limited-war course Mr. Kissinger has laid out for him. That course can lead only to a public pillory, at best. Since his December news conference, it has been Mr. Kissinger's private ordeal to stand exposed alone in that pillory. But now the crunch is on to see whether Mr. Nixon will passively join him there or manfully reverse a mistaken national security policy.

22. *NATIONAL REVIEW'S* WHITE HOUSE CONTACT: THE KISSINGER-BUCKLEY ODYSSEY

The story of how Henry Kissinger rose from refugee beginnings in the Bronx to become not merely the first Jewish-American Secretary of State, but also the first Cabinet leader to prompt and receive a presidential resignation, is bound to be told over and over again, with varying emphasis. So far, the most authoritative versions have stressed the instrumentality of four principal benefactors: Fritz Kraemer, who first awakened Kissinger's political ambitions; William Y. Elliott, who facilitated his career at Harvard; and Nelson Rockefeller, who led him into the inner circles of the Eastern Establishment. In his latest book, William F. Buckley insists that his name must be added to the list, that it was in fact he who introduced Kissinger to Nixon in 1968 and made possible Kissinger's appointment as chief advisor for national security affairs—from which all the rest followed.

William Buckley's *United Nations Journal: A Delegate's Odyssey* is not primarily about Henry Kissinger; but, as Neal B. Freeman notes in the Sept. 27, 1974 issue of *National Review*, Kissinger "drops into the narrative frequently which visitations are described with great sympathy. There is a special relationship between the two men which Buckley's account illuminates." *National Review*'s Associate Publisher, James P. McFadden, is more specific in recommending the book to subscribers: "Buckley reveals the never-before published details of his friendship with Henry Kissinger (it was Buckley who introduced Kissinger to the White House!), plus Buckley provides an absorbing description of Kissinger in action during the Arab-Israeli War."

The book is full of "fascinating anecdotes," says Mr. McFadden. According to Mr. Freeman, it "might be described as a child's treasury of diplomatic incidents." And *Publishers Weekly*'s assessment, circulated with advance copies, reads in part: "Buckley from the old bottle, but how time has mellowed his vintage. Here . . . sitting as a U.S. delegate to the UN General Assembly in the fall of 1973, Buckley seems wholly in his element—a relatively impotent participant in world affairs, hence chiefly an ironic observer, setting down his perceptive notes on official pomposity, hypocrisy and absurdity. The man is droll, and his rhetorical barbs seem to have taken on the rotund playfulness of a man happily at play in the field of the Word—because he can do no other. The result is one of his best books in a long time, full of plums . . . and a sure-handed illumination of the way some 100-plus sovereign nations perform a ritual quadrille around Buckley's credo, the Universal Declaration of Human Rights —which appears in the appendix."

Buckley informs us early in the book that he and Kissinger have been friends since the mid-fifties. Buckley had just founded *National Review* and was moving to the center of the drive that would get Barry Goldwater the GOP nomination in 1964. He could hardly have been described then as an impotent, ironic observer "happily at play in the field of the Word—because he can do no other." Kissinger took the initiative for their first meeting. "He was at Harvard," writes Buckley, "and serving also as editor of *Confluence,* an academic quarterly. Brent Bozell and I had recently published a book on the McCarthy controversy, several chapters of which intensively studied the whole loyalty-security problem into which McCarthy had waded. Kissinger asked me to write an essay for his journal; I did; and it never appeared. A year later he asked me to go to Harvard to lecture to his international seminar. I did, once or twice. . . . Often when he came to New York, we would visit, usually at lunch. He was then closely associated with Nelson Rockefeller."

The Buckley-Kissinger friendship was thus over ten years old when, in the spring of 1968, Kissinger suddenly gave it a new turn by asking Buckley to a meeting with Nelson Rockefeller. Buckley had written a column criticizing the New York governor—unfairly, in Kissinger's judgment—and they both wanted a chance to set the record straight. As Buckley recalls the meeting, after some preliminary small talk about George Wallace (who had just appeared on Buckley's *Firing Line*), Rockefeller undertook, "at rather exaggerated length," writes Buckley, "to recount to me his role at the founding of the United Nations." The governor stressed that he had personally intervened, in the nick of time, to prevent a threatened communist take-over of the "mechanisms of the fledgling organization." The account was interesting, Buckley notes, yet one "had the feeling that it had been delivered before. Especially, one had the feeling that Kissinger had heard it before, though his attention was exemplary."

That meeting proved, in retrospect, to have been only a feeler for what was to be attempted a few months later at the 1968 Republican Convention. Acting for Rockefeller, Kissinger asked Buckley to serve as a mediator with the Goldwater wing of the GOP in the event Rockefeller was nominated. "My responsibility, Kissinger urged, was to demonstrate to American conservatives that the country would be better off with Rockefeller as President, than with a Democratic President." Buckley urged in response that the question was entirely academic, since Rockefeller couldn't conceivably win the nomination unless Goldwater himself intervened in his favor, which he had no intention to do.

Rockefeller wasn't nominated—but Kissinger's point had been made. If ever there was a need, or occasion, to bring the GOP right-wing into line in support of Rockefeller-type ends, Buckley (in Kissinger's judgment) was the man to ask.

The need surfaced for Kissinger soon after Nixon's nomination. "He asked to lunch with me," writes Buckley. "He had a few ideas he thought would be interesting to Nixon, in framing his foreign policy speeches. But these ideas he must advance discreetly, as he would not wish to appear, having just now left the dismantled Rockefeller staff, to be job-seeking."

Thus courted, Buckley's response was all *noblesse oblige*. He called Frank Shakespeare at the Nixon headquarters and recited Kissinger's qualifications. Shakespeare, in turn, "went to Len Garment and John Mitchell, neither of whom had heard Kissinger's name before. They were impressed by his credentials, and said they would introduce him to Nixon, except that Nixon was out of town campaigning. Kissinger's drafts were cordially received."

Knowing what we now know about the Len Garments and John Mitchells of the Nixon staff, we must wonder what Buckley can mean in telling us that they were "impressed" by Kissinger's credentials. After even a cursory review of Kissinger's background, what must have impressed them most was that a top Harvard advisor of Nelson Rockefeller could have managed to get so strong a recommendation from conservative Buckley. There was no follow-up on that initiative, however, before election day; and so Kissinger (as Buckley reports it) simply had to make another try after election day.

It was late November, Buckley "was lecturing in Los Angeles, and staying with friends in Pasadena"—which, by normal standards, would make him relatively inaccessible. Yet "Kissinger reached me by phone." He simply had to have a personal meeting with President-elect Nixon to save him from a Clark Clifford scheme to embarrass him with an impossible situation in Vietnam. This time Buckley's intervention is decisive: "I telephoned New York, a personal meeting was set up between Kissinger and the President-elect, and a week or so later my phone rang. 'You will never be able to say again that you have no contact inside the White House.'"

That's the never-before revealed Buckley story of how Kissinger made it to the White House. Superficially it contradicts all other versions of Kissinger's rise, in which he is invariably represented as Rockefeller's very personal contribution to the Nixon administration, groomed for precisely the job he was offered, and sent down there with a $50,000 personal gift to tide him over. And yet Buckley's account from his special vantage point, is manifestly accurate. The hard political fact is that, however willing Nixon may have been to "receive" Kissinger straight from Rockefeller, a detour to bring him in by way of Buckley had obvious advantages. Buckley had been asked to act as mediator between left- and right-wing Republicans in the event of a Rockefeller nomination. He could now perform the same kind of service on another level. Having been introduced to the Frank Shakespeares, Len Garments, and John Mitchells as a Buckley favorite, Kissinger could now join Nixon with invaluable conservative as well as liberal credentials. Thus, from an ambitious courtier's point of view, the professor's long courtship of William Buckley had finally paid off handsomely. While pocketing Rockefeller's gift of $50,000, he could well afford to tell Buckley: "You will never be able to say again that you have no contact in the White House."

On the record, it appears that Kissinger pursued Buckley in order to give himself conservative credentials. But the story by no means ends there. Buckley recalls his first meeting with Kissinger *in office*. Careful to stress on whose initiative the meeting took place, Buckley writes: "It was the spring of 1969, a Friday. Could I go down to see him? I told him it would have to be on Sunday, or not again for ten days as I was off on a lecture tour. 'I will send a jet for you,' he said. We discussed the details, and I told him I would take the ten o'clock shuttle back to New York. 'No,' he said, 'the jet will take you back.' He paused then over the telephone. 'This,' he said, 'is going to ruin academic life.' My escort officer, aboard the little White House jet, was an amiable, young-looking colonel—Alexander Haig."

Kissinger's young-looking emissary probably led Buckley straight down into the White House basement, and the three were perhaps linked together there for an historically pregnant moment: ex-professor Kissinger, destined to become Secretary of State and President of the United States, in effect, for Foreign Affairs; ex-colonel Haig, soon to become, by leaps and bounds, first a two-star, then a four-star general, and finally supreme commander of the NATO forces; and *National Review* editor Buckley, earmarked for. . . . But what in the world could fittingly be in store for the man who made it all possible by introducing Kissinger to the White House in the first place? That question takes us to the heart of Buckley's *United Nations Journal.*

Late in 1973, on the very day that Kissinger was confirmed as Secretary of State (and after Haig had temporarily laid aside four stars to become White House Chief of Staff), Buckley too was confirmed in a State Department post. Kissinger's appointment came directly from Nixon; Haig's had no doubt been personally arranged for him by Kissinger; Buckley's assignment, by contrast, came through a relatively unknown intermediary, John Scali, Permanent U.S. Representative to the UN. One morning in mid-June 1973, over breakfast in his UN suite in New York, Ambassador Scali had abruptly asked Buckley whether he'd consider serving as a delegate to the 28th General Assembly of the UN: "What he had in mind for me, he elaborated, was to be U.S. Representative on the Human Rights Committee. 'You'd occupy the same chair Eleanor Roosevelt occupied,' he smiled, 'and Daniel Patrick Moynihan two years ago'."

Before deciding yes or no, Buckley asked whether the offer had been cleared with Nixon, and whether Senator Fulbright would let his Committee approve the appointment. Nixon hadn't been consulted, but Scali had "cleared it with General Haig who was 'terribly enthusiastic.'" As for Senate confirmation: "Don't worry about Fulbright," said Scali.

Buckley took the offer. His motive? A case, he says, of "pure, undiluted Walter Mittyism." General Haig, we have heard, was terribly enthusiastic. Fulbright was agreeable. What about Kissinger? On this critical point–whether Kissinger had a hand in getting him to sit in Eleanor Roosevelt's UN seat–Buckley, in retrospect, is cautious. He had breakfasted with Kissinger "at his office in the White House a week or two before he was named Secretary of State," but hadn't mentioned his own forthcoming State Department appointment. "I reasoned that if he knew about it already and desired to discuss it, he would do so; if he did not know about it, it might embarrass him that he didn't know about it, so better not to bring it up."

At the time of confirmation, it had been Kissinger's expressed wish (and therefore also President Nixon's) that his first pronouncement as Secretary of State should be an address to the UN. Why not have William Buckley's conservative auspices for that, even as they had been available for his entry into the White House? Delegate Buckley would be only one of many in attendance at his boss's UN inaugural. Still, they would make their entrances together. "He, and we," writes Buckley, "would debut at the opening session of the General Assembly. He would speak, we would listen."

Buckley listened to Kissinger's UN inaugural address. But he did not, like our Professor Richard C. Clark (who analyzed it in a *State of the Nation* newsletter a year ago), take it seriously. "UN speeches," writes Buckley, "are not written to be analyzed." Where Kissinger insists, with dogmatic supranationalism, that justice and truth transcend national frontiers, Buckley comments: "That is sheer diplomatic cant." And in the peroration, where Kissinger spells out his anti-nationalist purposes, Buckley finds nothing worth taking literally, and much to be dismissed, rather, as meaning the very opposite of what it purports to say.

Our Professor Clark, on the contrary, pointed out in his analysis that Kissinger's words are not so much diplomatic cant as a studied statement of the prevailing anti-nationalist doctrine of our establishment academy. At the beginning of his UN speech, Kissinger had in fact said: "Two centuries ago the philosopher Kant predicted that universal peace would come eventually—either as the creation of man's moral aspirations or as the consequence of physical necessity. What seemed utopian then looms as tomorrow's reality: soon there will be no alternative."

Addressing himself to the "problems" of war, hunger, terrorism, inflation, and pollution, Kissinger had asked: "Can we meet the inevitable challenge of the future with our system of nation-states?" His answer is an emphatic, unqualified No. "Challenges of this magnitude cannot be solved by a world, fragmented into self-contained nation-states."

"The United States," says its foreign-born Secretary of State with extraordinary presumption, running against the essence of American constitutional doctrine, "has made its choice. We strive for a world in which the rule of law governs. . . . We envisage a comprehensive, institutionalized peace, encompassing all nations." Against the hesitations of internationalists who still feel, as Reinhold Niebuhr sometimes felt, that conditions are not yet ripe for world government, Kissinger warns: "The ideal of a world community may be decried as unrealistic—but great constructions have always been ideals before they can become realities"; and he exhorts finally: "Let us dedicate ourselves to this noblest of all possible goals."

Among all of Kissinger's influential friends, Buckley is perhaps alone in interpreting such words as diplomatic cant. The chief advocate in the American academy of Kant's doctrine of *Inevitable Peace,* culminating in world government, is Harvard Professor C. J. Friedrich, who was Kissinger's favorite mentor, even though he chose finally to complete his graduate work with William Yandell Elliott instead. In making the switch to Elliott, Kissinger's explanation, as Professor Friedrich recalls it, ran as follows: "I am interested in the practical politics of international relations, and you are interested in philosophy and scholarship."

Professor Elliott, whom we have called a Harvard Patriot, has given some hints in published interviews of how Kissinger went about courting his academic favor. It is reminiscent of the initiatives with Buckley. Elliott obtained all sorts of scholarships for Kissinger, put him in charge of the Harvard International Seminar (financed by the CIA), introduced him to top people at the Council on Foreign Relations, and eventually helped him to get a tenured position at Harvard. Elliott wasn't a Kantian supranationalist. But Kissinger knew how to adapt to circumstances. As Marvin and Bernard Kalb say in their recent volume about their high-placed friend: "Kissinger has always been a political chameleon, able to take on the coloration of his environment. Hawks and doves alike thought they had found a kindred spirit in Henry."

When Kissinger's appointment as top national security advisor was first announced back in December 1968 (to *hosannas* not only from Walter Lippman, Arthur Schlesinger, and the *New York Times*, but also from William Buckley and *National Review*), Kissinger's chameleon qualities served him in good stead. "A superficial reading of some of his works," wrote a *Time* cover-story reporter, "makes him seem like a hawk, but intelligent doves regard him as Richard Nixon's most astute appointment." Since then, its advantages in the service of supranationalist diplomacy have been stressed again and again by the Lerners, Krafts, and Lippmans; with undisguised self-gratification they dwell on Kissinger's extraordinary capacity to, in effect, "wink knowingly at a Buckley while giving Arthur Schlesinger a confidential squeeze on the arm."

We are saying that, like Professor Elliott, Buckley has been used and abused by the courtier's flattery of Henry Kissinger. It is possible that Fritz Kraemer, who originally steered Kissinger into politics, and even the great gift-giving Nelson Rockefeller, perhaps, were similarly used. In a review of the Kalb book, Ronald Steel has thus aptly outlined the pattern of Kissinger's career as a courtier: "It was through a combination of flattery and apparent sincerity that he was able to move from Kraemer to Elliott to Rockefeller to Nixon. At the critical moment he gave Nixon a gentle shove toward resignation and attached himself to Gerald Ford."

Must we hereafter insert William Buckley's name in that list? In his latest book he is at pains, as we have noticed, to indicate at every turn the sort of initiative Kissinger took with him. Perhaps he wants the record to show that he has, in retrospect, at least a vague sense (a gentleman hesitates to have anything more in such matters) of having been used by the Inscrutable Henry, who will continue, it seems, to flit around the world making anti-nationalist "deals for peace" till he thinks our historic course has been made irreversible or until a national-populist uprising (perhaps in the form of a bluecollar general strike) shocks us back to sanity.

Buckley's latest public word about his "special relationship" with Henry Kissinger places them both at this year's Al Smith Memorial Foundation dinner of October 16, at the Waldorf, where Kissinger was a principal speaker. On his way into the Waldorf, Buckley was handed a booklet titled *Henry Kissinger: Soviet Agent.* During the early part of the dinner, Buckley looked through the pamphlet's "documentation" and then sent it down to Kissinger, who sat a few places away, "in the direction," as Buckley phrased it, "of the great." "Henry?," Buckley had asked in a covernote, "is this true?" Kissinger's reply, passed back to Buckley, was to the effect that such questions are best answered only before Senate Foreign Relations Committees.

It was wit, once again, from the best old Buckley bottle, as also from the now familiar repertoire of Kissinger's purposive ambiguities. But in his Al Smith Dinner appearance, Kissinger quickly passed from witty exchanges with Buckley to concentrate on his ideologue's concern for "peace in our time" with the communist powers, to be purchased at all costs, including the sacrifice of our sovereign nationhood.

Kissinger began by reviewing his successes: peace in Vietnam, peace nearly achieved in the Middle East, "strengthened" relations with the communist powers, and "new" partnerships with our allies. Then came his Kantian projection of inevitable peace: "But now—indeed partly because of our success—we experience the birthpangs of a new order. We face a new dimension of challenges, more pervasive and complex, with perils at once more subtle and profound. At the midway point between the end of the Second World War and the end of this century, we find ourselves also midway between the nation-state from which we began and the global community which we must fashion if we are ever to live in peace. . . . The fact is that all nations—East and West, aligned and non-aligned—are part of one global system and dependent on it for their peace."

To explain what is essentially wrong with an American political commitment to "inevitable peace" is a difficult task. World community is an imperialist goal. Sooner or later there must be contention to determine who precisely will have the last word in decision-making for the effective enforcement of world peace. Cowardly talk, in the guise of global diplomacy, can avert that moment of decision only as long as it is backed up by massive bribes, freely giving the enemy what he would otherwise have to fight for. But when the bribes stop, there must be complete surrender or a desperate last-minute determination to stand and fight, under the most adverse circumstances.

We may soon be faced with precisely that desperate alternative. And we may then perhaps gain a painfully clear insight into what Kissinger meant back in 1960 when he was calling upon us to commit ourselves to peace at all costs, even while heavily armed. "A nation which cannot be trusted when strong," he then wrote, "will hardly be able to deal with the much more difficult task of living in dignity when impotent." (*The Necessity for Choice,* Anchor edition, p. 101)

Is our country never to be freed from the incubus of Inevitable Peace that our Friedrichs, Bundys, Rostows, and Kissingers have laid upon us? The Buckley conservatives now seem more than half ready to break with President Ford over detente and disarmament, as well as over the usual domestic policies; there is even talk of a coalition of traditional conservatism and blue-collar, lunch-box nationalist populism to get this country back on course. But it is all meaningless so long as Kissinger's "Realpolitik for World Government" is spared. America isn't worth saving if it is to be saved only temporarily, for "inevitable" sacrifice to the Kantian or communist imperialist "ideals" of a global community—to be built on the ruins of our sovereign nationhood.

Buckley has given us hints of an intention to free himself from the Kissinger incubus. At least that is how we interpret his carefully worded revelations of Kissinger's persistent initiatives, which have brought Buckley, in twenty years, from writing an unpublished article for *Confluence* to sitting in Eleanor Roosevelt's seat at the UN. To lift that incubus is a great and arduous task; *magnum opus et arduum,* as St. Augustine expressed it when he raised his pen against the pagan champions of an "inevitable" imperialist peace in his day. But—*Deus adiutor noster est*—God is our helper.

23. *WILL AMERICA SURRENDER?*

Will America Surrender is the title of a powerful book—a national-ist-American book—by Slobodan M. Draskovich, just published by The Devin-Adair Company, One Park Avenue, Old Greenwich, Conn. 06870.

In his forward, General Thomas A. Lane salutes Dr. Draskovich for bravely speaking his mind in defense of the sovereign nation-hood of his adoptive country. Our sovereign union has many and diverse enemies these days. The international communists work night and day for its dissolution and destruction. Henry Kissinger acknowledged this in complimenting his new-found North Vietnamese friend Le Duc Tho who, said Kissinger, will not give up war as an instrument of policy till the entire world is communized.

Kissinger himself, like his predecessors McGeorge Bundy and Walt Rostow, is convinced that the era of sovereign nation-states is drawing to a close. The danger of nuclear war, he holds, requires that we give up being what we declared ourselves to be in 1776 to become "something else": an economic-oriented civil society that can gradually "converge" with Peking and Moscow in a world order where they get what they want as communists (which is world hegemony for communism) and we get what our Harvard-MIT internationalists would like us to want (which is peace at all costs).

But our communists and liberal internationalists are by no means alone in pressing us to despair of preserving our national sovereignty in the nuclear age. Since Richard Nixon's election to the Presidency in 1968, many one-time conservative stalwarts have joined the chorus. Liberal defeatism has been around in America for a long time. Now, because of the sense of guilt our Goldwaters, Reagans, Thurmonds, and Buckleys feel for having acquiesced without principle in the Nixon detente policies, we are plagued with conservative defeatism as well.

It is for its heartfelt and learned polemic against conservative defeatism that Dr. Draskovich's book is most valuable. While the American conservative movement was healthy, there was little danger that our people as a whole could be plunged into despair by the stratagems of the Bundys, Rostows, and Kissingers. But now the dikes are down. Almost every issue of *National Review* these days, for instance, carries an abject editorial-apology for Nixon policies which must make its author blush to write it. In the company of such editorials, even the toughest of the old lot, James Burnham, is inclined to despair (as in fact he does in a recent article on American patriotism).

Why shouldn't the old Republican conservatives despair? They backed Nixon; and worse, they pushed Kissinger on him, and haven't yet worked up the courage to admit they were wrong. Instead, as Draskovich suggests, they bury their heads in the sands of defeatism, while Nixon's "thugs" play dirty politics as if that were the sum and substance of conservatism today. Old anti-communist CIA hands are bribed only to be framed at Watergate, while old YAF hands get stuck in the mud of O.E.O. Those are the dirty bones thrown contemptuously to the right while Mr. Nixon backs up full speed in pursuit of a leftist peace through veiled surrender.

Dr. Draskovich correctly traces back to Whittaker Chambers (the ex-communist who so greatly influenced William F. Buckley Jr.) the cancerous despair that is now spreading everywhere on the surface of the conservative movement. He reminds us that Chambers' last book, *Cold Friday*, was originally titled *The Losing Side*, in keeping with its author's repeated assertion that, in abandoning communism, he had left the side destined to win.

Draskovich condemns as particularly fatal for American conservatism the hopelessness of these words of Whittaker Chambers: "The total situation is hopeless, past repair, organically irremediable. Almost the only position of spiritual dignity left to us, therefore, is a kind of stoic silence, made bearable by the amusement of seeing, hearing and knowing the full historical irony that its victims are blind and deaf to, and disciplined by the act of withholding comment on what we know."

Such self-indulgent irony is, of course, the vice that self-righteous "beautiful souls" (whether of the left or the right) drag along, hugged to their bosoms, wherever they go. Warning us against its contagion, Draskovich, writes: "The vital spark of will that America needs can only fly from faith, not from despair, be it liberal or conservative. It is precisely because of the failure of the conservatives in the realm of will that their policies (1952-1960 under President Eisenhower, and recently under President Nixon) have become indistinguishable from the liberal policies of President Kennedy and President Johnson, 1960-1968. The issue which is today at stake transcends the conflict between liberalism and conservatism. It is a belief in the nation itself which alone can produce the spark of will to preserve it."

Later in the same chapter Draskovich concludes: "Either Americans believe in America and can muster the will to make it victorious, or–if they do not–they will lose. If the *Communist Manifesto,* and all other communist writings, plus the criminal record of communist rule since 1917, can inspire the communists to more dedication and fervor in their struggle for world domination than the Declaration of Independence and the achievements of the U.S. can inspire Americans to stand for America and liberty–then communism will win. That is the question which Americans must answer. Actually, there is no other question, since they are all contained in that one."

Is the Nixon administration pledged to secure the integrity of our national union at all cost (as the presidential oath of office requires), or is it pursuing a policy of gradual surrender for the sake of peace? In these days that try men's souls, where can we, as conservatives, look for a forthright answer to that question? Certainly in this respect, the editorial pages of *National Review* fail us. James Burnham from time to time still speaks with refreshing frankness; yet he too, embarrassed by the ironic editorials (as we have noted), usually ends even his most realistic national security analysis in a mood of Chambers-like despair.

Dr. Draskovich's approach is very different. He is not one of that sorry band of playground conservatives who, taken in by the alleged "dangers" of McGovernism, imagine that anyone to the right of McGovern must *ipso facto* qualify as a conservative force in American politics. We have seen with what eagerness William Buckley has accepted Rostow as a hardliner, despite his long labors as a leftist to destroy America's will to defend itself.

McGovern is against all wars, including no-win wars like the one we have fought and lost in Vietnam. Rostow favors no-win wars, provided we lose them. Does that make Rostow a "hardliner"? Dr. Draskovich knows better. His chapter on "The Concept of Surrender" carries two significant captions, one from Rostow's *The United States in the World Arena,* published just before J. F. Kennedy called Rostow to Washington in 1960, the other from a Nixon campaign speech of 1968.

I have often cited Rostow's words, but they warrant repetition, lest we be tempted to forget: "It is a legitimate American national objective to see removed from all nations–including the United States–the right to use substantial military force to pursue their own interests. . . . It is, therefore, an American interest to see an end to nationhood as it has been historically defined."

The words cited from Mr. Nixon's speech of February 21, 1968, read: "The goal of the Soviets remains victory, while ours remains peace." In those days, Nixon could still take a hard line in foreign policy, for he had not as yet been induced by Nelson Rockefeller and the editors of *National Review* to appoint Henry Kissinger to succeed Walt Rostow.

Conservative acquiescence in the appointment of Kissinger to make foreign policy for the Nixon administration is the most tragic thing that has happened to our union since the Civil War. Had he served in his present post under a Rockefeller, or Kennedy, or Humphrey administration, Kissinger would have been as bad as Rostow; but at least we would have had a united conservative front to oppose him. William F. Buckley himself would long since have denounced the man as chief architect of the no-win war doctrine that has been our ruin in Vietnam, even as I have been denouncing him on that and other grounds since December 1968, when his appointment was first announced. To this day, Kissinger remains virtually immune from serious criticism from "respectable" Republican conservatives. It is therefore with gratitude and high approval that I recommend Dr. Draskovich's treatment of the subject in his chapter entitled "United States Foreign Policy for the 1970s: A New Strategy for Peace. A Blueprint for U.S. Global Withdrawal."

Again Dr. Draskovich supplies two telling captions, both from Mr. Nixon. One is dated October 10, 1963, and reads: "If the danger of war has been decreased, the danger of defeat without war has been substantially increased. We cannot meet [such danger] by a static policy of defense. Our goal must not be simply to keep freedom from shrinking but to make it grow too. Our goal must be a free Cuba, a free Eastern Europe, a free Russia, a free China."

Had he lost to Hubert Humphrey in 1968, Mr. Nixon would probably still be saying such things, and the Buckleys and Goldwaters who supported him then would be saying them much more forcefully. Now, instead, guided by Kissinger (and with at least the tacit approval of most Republican conservatives), Nixon is saying: "Today any nuclear attack–no matter how small, whether accidental, unauthorized or by design; by a superpower or by a country with only primitive nuclear delivery capability–would be a catastrophe for the U.S., no matter how devastating our ability to retaliate."

What precisely does that mean? Dr. Draskovich does not equivocate in his assessment: "This uniquely defeatist consideration, which makes the United States nuclearly the most hopeless and doomed country in the world, necessarily leads to only one possible conclusion: adapt to the world, such as it is. And Professor Kissinger draws it: the U.S. must 'harmonize doctrine and capability'." Kissinger identifies our "security" with our lives as individuals and then, after asserting that we must relegate to the past the "mutual hostility that flowed from deep-seated differences of ideology," he declares: "For us as well as our adversaries in the nuclear age, the perils of using force are simply not in reasonable proportion to most of the objectives sought in many cases."

Dr. Draskovich stresses the many indications in the Kissinger-Nixon "New Strategy for Peace" that our government's intention is to take unilateral action to avert a nuclear war *at all costs,* hoping that "others" will follow our lead. For instance, "By the examples we set, we hope to lead the way toward the day when other nations will adopt the same principles." "We hope that other great powers will act in a similar spirit and not seek hegemony." "We hope that the coming year will bring evidence that the Soviets have decided to seek a durable peace rather than continue along the roads of the past."

Subjecting the "New Strategy" to close analysis, the author notes that it is by no means new, that it actually differs from "the old Rusk-Rostow policy" only in its "repeated assertion that the 'new' policy is new."

What is Kissinger's prescription for meeting that threat of nuclear attack, even from a small power, which he says "would be a catastrophe for the U.S., no matter how devastating our ability to retaliate"? It is to negotiate *at all costs*. What is his prescription for meeting the threat of revolutionary insurrection, such as we faced in Cuba and Vietnam, and such as we may eventually have to face in western countries, not excluding our own? Here are the words of the New Strategy: "the best means of dealing with insurgencies is to pre-empt them through economic development and social reform." Kissinger explains that the "threatened" government simply has to adopt the revolutionary program as its own policy, to be enforced by governmental power. The government must renounce counter-revolutionary force and accept peaceful pre-emption of revolutionary goals as the only "constructive alternative to revolution."

In his brilliant summation of the consequences of this defeatist Kissinger strategy, Draskovich writes: "If we must avoid war at any price, since *any* kind of nuclear war would be a catastrophe for the United States, and if peace at all costs is also the 'alternative to revolution,'–it means that we have no option left at all. The powerful tides of change, the concern for economic change and social justice, the forces of revolution, are working irresistibly in favor of communism. Communism, then, *is* the wave of the future!

> *If so, the communists, who are politically literate, may interpret the Kissinger Blueprint not as a plan for peace which would safeguard both communist interests and those of the free countries, but as a plan for doing in a 'civilized' and businesslike manner, without war, revolution and nuclear conflict, that which will come to pass anyway.*
>
> *So the 'new' Kissinger policy is a throwback to the tragic days of Yalta and F. D. Roosevelt's surrender of half of Europe to Stalin, an endorsement and resuscitation of the policies of appeasement and coexistence. . . . If its main ideas were to be applied for a decade, there would probably be no 1980s for America.*
>
> *That is why the Kissinger Blueprint must be rejected. For no expert has the right to reduce the policies of the greatest country in the world to the non-choice between surrender and 'we hope,' and give the advice of despair to the President of the United States. . . .*
>
> *For all its shortcomings, the Kissinger Blueprint for world peace has one incontrovertible merit: it proves beyond the shadow of a doubt that the United States vitally needs a really new foreign policy. (pp. 330-333)*

In his last chapter, Dr. Draskovich warns us that, on the road to surrender, our government will gradually find itself deserted by everyone. Our manifest weakness will drive everyone else in the world to make some kind of deal with the communist powers while deals are still possible. Anybody can confiscate American investments abroad, with the certainty that if the American investors try to do something to prevent the theft, the Kissinger people in Washington will reject the idea as incompatible with their policy of peace at all costs. Even our ambassadors can be killed, as well as humiliated, with impunity. American citizens and American goods, no less than American soldiers, now go abroad at their own peril—just like our paper dollars, which have neither gold nor political muscle to back them up. The hyenas and wolves of the world, to say nothing of the hungry bears, haven't yet decided to tear into us, fat and weak, yet rich as we are, only because they are not yet ready to believe what they see about the suicidal tendency of our ruling classes, poisoned to the core by their long flirtation with the idea that they are qualified to rule the world with their smart talk and the tax-exempt proceeds of multinational corporations.

There is much that is painful to read in *Will America Surrender?* But we find no despair in the book. After having considered why so many conservatives as well as liberals despair and think things impossible, Dr. Draskovich turns finally to speak concerning hope. The great mass of Americans, he insists, remains intensely patriotic. They are disoriented, perhaps, by the persistent bias of the media and the silence of the old conservatives. But the patriotism is there. What is needed to ignite it is a spark of patriotic leadership.

That spark cannot come, obviously, from libertarians concerned only for their precious "free economy" regardless of our national political security. Today, libertarians of the right, backed by the multinational corporations, are simply old-time liberal internationalists with meaner dispositions and more money. Capitalism has joined the deserters of our ship of state, knowing that a government that lets its soldiers be abused will not protect the investments of its capitalist citizens.

America's only hope today lies in its average productive worker who looks patriotically to a populist leader. "What we need," says Draskovich boldly, "are angry Americans who have had enough of surrender, of constantly appeasing our mortal enemy, of trying not to displease our most vicious detractors, . . . Americans who are not willing to tolerate the constant, insistent mind-conditioning about how bad, corrupt, unjust, unfair, unfree, oppressive, racist America is, and how it must spend all its time apologizing to the world." Dr. Draskovich thus joins Walter Bagehot, who warned: "History is strewn with the wrecks of nations which have gained a little progressiveness at the cost of a great deal of manliness, and have thus prepared themselves for destruction as soon as the movements of the world gave a chance for it."

APPENDIX

(From the Congressional Record, August 4, 1971)

Congressional Record

United States
of **America**

PROCEEDINGS AND DEBATES OF THE 92^d CONGRESS, SECOND SESSION

(Proceedings of the House, August 4, 1971)

NATIONAL DEFENSE

The SPEAKER pro tempore. Under a previous order of the House, the gentleman from New York (Mr. STRATTON) is recognized for 60 minutes.

Mr. STRATTON. Mr. Speaker, I want to express my congratulations to the gentleman from South Carolina (Mr. SPENCE), my colleague on the Armed Services Committee, for taking the initiative in setting up this time today—these 2 hours of special orders he and I have taken—so that together Members of Congress on a bipartisan basis could take some time to point out some of the more disturbing aspects of the current military situation that is facing the United States.

I do not intend to take all of my time, but I believe it is important we should spend some time pointing up some of the problems we face, recognizing that there is a different story to be told from just the criticisms of the military we hear so frequently.

Mr. Speaker, for the past year or more we have been beset by a mounting anti-military movement, not only in portions of the country and in the public press but here in Congress as well, with special emphasis in the Senate but to a growing extent also in the House. This has been marked by repeated efforts to cut back our military forces, to block the development of new weapons, to discontinue our system of military recruitment, and a general bias, usually expressed in highly emotional terms, against the so-called military-industrial complex. . . . .

The point I want to make briefly here this afternoon is that while we have focused so much of our energies and our attention on eliminating unnecessary military activity, we are in real danger of having gone too far. We are in real danger of having started a process that has already cut our forces below what is adequate to meet our defense needs, and may even have already tipped the balance of world military power against ourselves. . . . .

Mr. BLACKBURN. Mr. Speaker, will the gentleman yield?

Mr. STRATTON. I am glad to yield to the gentleman from Georgia.

Mr. BLACKBURN. Mr. Speaker, I want to join my colleagues who are speaking this evening, as well as the gentleman from New York (Mr. STRATTON) and the gentleman from South Carolina (Mr. SPENCE), whom I congratulate for taking the initiative in this great and vital area of our national securty.

In all the discussions today about our strategic position, many have pointed to the lamentable decline and fading of our superiority in strategic weaponry. Others have pointed out that the current SALT talks may lead to dangerous technological and political imbalances which may leave us without the means to defend ourselves against Soviet attack.

However there is another danger, a danger of which many are seemingly unaware. Some people seem to think that it is of no practical difference whether we have nuclear superiority or not. They think that a treaty—a mere scrap of paper—can provide us with the necessary security against enemy attack.

Mr. Speaker, I wish to address myself to the real meaning of strategic superiority, and that meaning goes to the very essence of our nationhood. We forget that the ability to defend ourselves successfully is the very basis of our sovereignty.

Smaller nations can depend upon their stronger allies to remain free. But when you are the most powerful nation in the free world, there is no one to whom you can turn. If we become strategically inferior to the Soviet Union, we have lost our nationhood; we have lost our sovereignty. In short, we have lost the freedom to make our own decisions uncoerced by the rest of the world.

Moreover, there is a more subtle danger. We can also lose our sovereignty through negotiations. There is always the temptation that supranational arrangements may take the place of our Constitution as the supreme law of the land. When such negotiations could conceivably place us in a position of strategic inferiority, then it is plain that our sovereignty could be swallowed up in the trap of negotiations.

Mr. Speaker, I was greatly concerned about this question when I recently read a paper on the subject by Prof. Henry Paolucci, of St. John's University, Professor Paolucci is no ivory-tower academician. He is a distinguished scholar in his own right, and a recognized political thinker. But more important, he has been in the realm of practical politics.

Professor Paolucci warns against the atmosphere of secrecy which has surrounded the SALT talks, and points out that the Soviet Union and the United States do not enter the talks upon the same basis. Dr. Paolucci says:

Although the Soviet Union is not constituted as a nation-state—although it legally and ideologically rejects the notion of occupying a 'separate and equal station' among the powers of the earth—it has consistently exercised the prerogatives of sovereignty in its relations with the United States.

In other words, the Soviet Union has as one of its goals the elimination of the concept of the nation-state. Dr. Paolucci says:

From its inception, the Soviet Union has regarded itself as a powerful means for the realization of a stateless, classless world community, to be built upon the ruins of the traditional nation-state system. It has acted like a sovereign nation-state, but it has never accepted the nation-state system.

With such an unequal situation prevailing at the negotiation tables, Professor Paolucci believes that the Soviets will take advantage of the different goals to tempt the United States to purchase a "secure peace" by a sacrifice of the prerogatives of sovereign nationhood. Under such an agreement, the Soviets would sacrifice nothing, because they do not believe in the nation-state system anyway.

The danger comes when the architects of the American negotiating posture draw up their guidelines for the negotiating effort. Professor Paolucci points out that President Nixon's chief adviser, Henry Kissinger, is only one in a long line of Presidential advisers who have urged an end to our Constitution and the sovereignty it enshrines. Like Walt Whitman Rostow and McGeorge Bundy, says Professor Paolucci:

Henry Kissinger, too, expresed as recently as 1965 the conviction that the time was at hand for a surrender of nationhood because "institutions based on present concepts of national sovereignty are not enough." The ultimate goal of a supranationalist world community, he wrote, "will not come quickly; many intermediate stages must be traversed before it can be reached. It is not too early, however, to prepare ourselves for this step beyond the nation-state."

All of this brings us to the question then, of what is actually transpiring at the SALT talks. Are we gradually being sucked into a system that will supplant our national sovereignty with a supranational arrangement. Is this what Rostow meant by "an end of our nationhood as it has been historically defined?"

Mr. Speaker, Professor Paolucci's paper is well reasoned, and of immense benefit to all those studying this question, and would like to include it in the RECORD at the conclusion of my remarks:

THE "TOP SECRET" STRATEGIC ARMS LIMITATIONS TALKS AND OUR NATIONAL SOVEREIGNTY

If Henry Kissinger and the President he advises were committed to guarding the sovereign independence of this nation at all costs, nothing could be more conducive to the stabilizing of international relations at this time than strategic arms limitations talks with the Soviet Union.

On the other hand, if Henry Kissinger and the President he advises are committed to eliminating the possibility of a general war *at all costs,* then nothing could be more dangerous, nothing could be more disloyal than to veil in absolute secrecy, as the SALT meetings are indeed veiled, the negotiations whereby our sovereign independence of almost 200 years' standing may be bargained away.

Although the Soviet Union is not constituted as a nation state—although it legally and ideologically rejects the notion of occupying a "separate and equal station" among the powers of the earth—it has consistently exercised the prerogatives of sovereignty in its relations with the United

States. It was not in the least tempted to make a sacrifice of its sovereign independence to purchase peace even when the United States enjoyed an absolute monopoly of atomic weapons. Certainly it is not prepared to do so now. Our atomic monopoly was reduced to a preponderance before it faded into parity. And now parity has been reduced to sufficiency, which, by definition, cannot suffice to do what preponderance or parity could do. Sufficiency is a move downward.

Meanwhile the Soviets have passed from total deficiency through sufficiency (in our current sense) to parity; and they are now rapidly on the way, with only the vaguest propaganda-hint of any possible self-restraint, toward absolute preponderance. Thus, in this nuclear arms "race," the United States and the U.S.S.R. have been for a moment on the same level—but only in the sense that an elevator going down may be for a moment on a level with an elevator going up.

What are the Soviets disposed to sacrifice in the SALT negotiations to spare mankind the risks of a nuclear holocaust? We can be certain of this: they will not sacrifice their sovereign independence with all the prerogatives of their major power status.

Can the same be said of the government of the United States in this time of acute domestic turmoil and intellectual alienation? Is our political independence, our sovereign nationhood, on the bargaining table? Is it to be a sacrifice of last resort, if peace cannot be purchased otherwise?

From its inception, the Soviet Union has regarded itself as a powerful means for the realization of a stateless, classless world community, to be built upon the ruins of the traditional nation-state system. It has acted like a sovereign nation state; but it has never accepted the nation-state system; it has never defined its independence as the assumption of a "separate and equal station" among the powers of the earth. American independence is, and has been from the beginning, the independence of membership in a system of independent states. Soviet independence, on the contrary, presupposes the "fading away" of its sovereign political characteristics once the non-communist nation-state governments have been destroyed.

One way the government of the United States could purchase a "secure peace" with the Soviets would be by a sacrifice of the prerogatives of sovereign nationhood. Is it conceivable that Henry Kissinger and the President he advises might, for reasons best known to the great brain-trust of civilian war strategists who had advised our Presidents since 1961, contemplating such a sacrifice? Today, because of the shift of focus in our war-peace debate—a shift brought to unexplored frontiers by the Pentagon Papers affair—Walt Rostow can now be represented as some sort of hard-line traditionalist, whereas, when he came to Washington in 1961, he was clearly a revolutionary in his concept of "security" in the nuclear age. He had argued in *The United States in the World Arena* (New York, 1960, p. 549)):

"It is a legitimate American national objective to see removed from all nations—including the United States—the right to use substantial military force to pursue their own interests. Since this residual right is the root of national sovereignty and the basis for the existence of an international arena of power, it is therefore, an American interest to see an end to nationhood as it has been historically defined."

Despite its academic articulation, that is a highly revolutionary doctrine. The legitimacy claimed for it is certainly not an American constitutional legitimacy. It proposes to sacrifice the sovereign national union of which the Constitution is the organic law. If it indeed comes to pass, as many of our professed enemies hope, that there is an end of our nationhood, our Constitution will constitute nothing.

McGeorge Bundy shared Rostow's view of the matter. And Henry Kissinger, too, expressed as recently as 1965 the conviction that the time was at hand for a surrender of nationhood because "institutions based on present concepts of national sovereignty are not enough. "The ultimate goal of a supernationalist world community, he wrote, "will not come quickly; many intermediate stages must be traversed before it can be reached. It is not too early, however, to prepare ourselves now for his step beyond the nation-state."

Bundy, Rostow, and Kissinger have put their theory into practice in their increasingly powerful service as chief presidential advisors for national security affairs under Presidents Kennedy, Johnson and Nixon. The Ellsbergs have been impatient for results. But the Rostow-Kissinger counsel has been: Be patient in your hearts, however much you protest on the campuses and in the streets, and raise a hullabaloo with stolen "top secret" papers. Americans must learn how to lose while armed with nuclear weapons before they can be induced to give up (in Rostow's words) "the right to use substantial military force to pursue their own interests."

Is the time now ripe for negotiation to put an end to our nationhood, for taking the step beyond the nation-state? If it is done in secrecy, while the Times and its powerful allies are celebrating an end to secrecy, it will have to be registered in the annals of history as the greatest betrayal of public trust ever perpetrated in a civilized nation.

That is the great danger of the secret SALT negotiations. The "temptations" not to lose the Vietnam war experienced by Presidents Kennedy and Johnson have been extravagantly publicized. Now we ought to have comparable publicity on "temptations" of Henry Kissinger, and the "devoted pacifist" he advises, to put an end to our nationhood as it has been historically defined.

Just after leaving office in 1968, Robert S. McNamara wrote (*The Essence of Security,* p. 53):

"If the United States is to deter a nuclear attack on itself or its allies, it must possess an actual and credible assured-destruction capability . . . capable of damaging the aggressor to the point that his society would be simply no longer viable in twentieth century terms. That is what deterrence of nuclear aggression means. It means the certainty of suicide to the aggressor, not merely to his military forces, but to his society as a whole."

That was what deterrence of nuclear aggression meant in U.S. policy up until the end of President Johnson's term. But, with the entry of Mr. Nixon and Mr. Kissinger into White House offices in January 1969, there was a basic change. In the "State of the World" message of 1970, Nixon referred explicitly to the inherited policy of assured destruction, remarking that, "once in office, I concluded that this strategic doctrine should be carefully reviewed." He went on to say that, as part of that review, Kissinger and his staff would explore the following question: "Should a President, in the event of a nuclear attack, be left with the single option of ordering the mass destruction of enemy civilians, in the face of the certainty that it would be followed by the mass slaughter of Americans?" That question was answered in the 1971 message, where we read:

"I must not be—and my successors must not be—limited to the indiscriminate mass destruction of enemy civilians as the sole possible response to challenges. This is especially so when the response involves the likelihood of triggering nuclear attacks on our own population."

Thus, the policy of McNamara, which was a drastic reduction of deterrence in the quantitative sense, as compared with the Eisenhower-Nixon-Dulles policy of Massive Retaliation, is here reduced to non-existence. What McNamara defined as the *essence* of nuclear deterrence—"the certainty of suicide to the aggressor, not merely to his military forces, but to his society as a whole"—has been abandoned by the Nixon-Kissinger administration.

If the Soviets are assured, through secret SALT negotiations, that our posture of nuclear deterrence is indeed what the Nixon-Kissinger messages say it is, then that "American interest," of which Rostow wrote, "to see an end to our nationhood as it has been historically defined" will have been realized.

If we have not the will to do what McNamara defined as the essence of deterrence then we have no deterrence. We invite the ultimate form of nuclear blackmail.

Needless to say, if the secret papers on this subject are published, and, by some act of military boldness, our armed forces prevent an American surrender to blackmail, there are bound to be recriminations.

HENRY PAOLUCCI received his B.S. from The City College of New York. After serving in Europe as a navigator in the United States Air Force during World War II, he returned to New York and received his M.A. and Ph.D. degrees from Columbia University. He was a Fulbright scholar at the University of Rome and spent a year as Eleanora Duse Traveling Fellow from Columbia at the University of Florence. While still a student at Columbia, he was invited by the university administration to take on Dino Bigongiari's course on "Dante and Medieval Culture" while Professor Bigongiari was on leave.

Later, he taught English at Iona College and gave several courses in Greek and Roman history at City College and Brooklyn College (CUNY). In 1969 he accepted an offer to teach in the Department of Government and Politics at St. John's University (where he remained until his retirement, as Professor Emeritus, in 1991).

In 1964 he was asked by the Conservative Party of New York State to run on their line for the United States Senate, against Robert F. Kennedy and the incumbent, Kenneth Keating. The *New York Times* featured him as "The Scholarly Candidate" and followed his campaign with interest. Election results showed that Professor Paolucci's articulate campaign had raised the Party's standing dramatically.

His many books and articles reflect the wide spectrum of his interests and his talent for assimilating, and illuminating for others, the world of learning.

ABOUT... **WHO IS KISSINGER?**

"With his *State of the Nation*, [Professor Paolucci] is clearly our most perceptive critic of American Government."

GENERAL THOMAS A. LANE

"I enjoy so much the *State of the Nation* and find its insights and information among the most outstanding I have ever seen."

EDITH KERMIT ROOSEVELT, Washington Bureau,
Manchester Union Leader

". . . intelligence of the very first rank, . . . totally commited to America and to truth, . . . possessed of a facility in the spoken and written word which is unsurpassable."

JOHN F. KILEY (Author, Journalist, Poet)

"I doubt whether many . . . have heard of Henry Paolucci, a lively political professor and former Conservative Party candidate, who storms fitfully against Kissinger on the op-ed page of the New York Times, most recently for having 'tutored' Richard Nixon into becoming an Alger Hiss in his basic foreign policies. . . . [Paolucci's] 'Kissinger: Patriot or Hypocrite,' . . . foresees the time when America is 'overwhelmed by its professed enemies,' and when the historians—'whether they write court histories in Russian or Chinese, Hebrew or Arabic'—will have to agree that the 'cunning architect of our national suicide' was the man who made it possible for Nixon to 'sell this nation down the river. . . .' I don't like it. The responsibility for American policies rests with Nixon, not Kissinger. . . . "

MAX LERNER (Columnist, *New York Post* [1972])

"Its perspective is unique in that it is a political examination of current events employing a broad historical background. Whatever primary issues are raised, they are discussed beginning with their inception, their present stage of development, and end with conclusions about their probable long-term effect. Dr. Paolucci's treatment of his subject makes the issues at hand seem, at once, vital and historical. Underlying his prose is the narration of a struggle which occupied our fathers, and will our sons . . . . Whenever I receive a copy of *State of the Nation*, as I have today, I remind myself that I must write a letter expressing my appreciation."

GEORGE MACLARTY (May 31, 1980)

HENRY PAOLUCCI received his B.S. from The City College of New York. After serving in Europe as a navigator in the United States Air Force during World War II, he returned to New York and received his M.A. and Ph.D. degrees from Columbia University. He was a Fulbright scholar at the University of Rome and spent a year as Eleanora Duse Traveling Fellow from Columbia at the University of Florence. While still a student at Columbia, he was invited by the university administration to take on Dino Bigongiari's course on "Dante and Medieval Culture" while Professor Bigongiari was on leave.

Later, he taught English at Iona College and gave several courses in Greek and Roman history at City College and Brooklyn College (CUNY). In 1969 he accepted an offer to teach in the Department of Government and Politics at St. John's University (where he remained until his retirement, as Professor Emeritus, in 1991).

In 1964 he was asked by the Conservative Party of New York State to run on their line for the United States Senate, against Robert F. Kennedy and the incumbent, Kenneth Keating. The *New York Times* featured him as "The Scholarly Candidate" and followed his campaign with interest. Election results showed that Professor Paolucci's articulate campaign had raised the Party's standing dramatically.

His many books and articles reflect the wide spectrum of his interests and his talent for assimilating, and illuminating for others, the world of learning.